THE URBAN CHALLENGE

Graham Drake and Carl Lee

The Authors

Graham Drake is a lecturer in the School of Environment and Development at Sheffield Hallam University.

Carl Lee is a lecturer in Geography and Environmental Science at The Sheffield College.

Acknowledgements

The publishers would like to thank the following for giving permission to reproduce copyright photographs in this book: Life File: Figure 2.6, Figure 6.2a, Figure 6.2b, Figure 6.2c, Figure 21.1; Corbis: Figure 5.3, Figure 20.9; Eye Ubiquitous: Figure 7.9; The Trafford Centre: Figure 8.4; James Davis Photography: Figure 11.2. All other photographs supplied by the author.

Every effort has been made to contact the holders of copyright material used in this book, but if any have been overlooked, the publishers will be pleased to make the necessary alterations at the first opportunity.

Orders: please contact Bookpoint Ltd, 78 Milton Park, Abingdon, Oxon OX14 4TD. Telephone: (44) 01235 827720, Fax: (44) 01235 400454. Lines are open from 9.00–6.00, Monday to Saturday, with a 24 hour message answering service. Email address: orders@bookpoint.co.uk

British Library Cataloguing in Publication Data
A catalogue record for this title is available from The British Library

ISBN 0 340 73734 4

First published 2000
Impression number   10 9 8 7 6 5 4 3 2 1
Year   2005 2004 2003 2002 2001 2000

Cover photo from Life File
Typeset by Fakenham Photosetting Limited, Fakenham, Norfolk NR21 8NN
Printed in Dubai for Hodder & Stoughton Educational, a division of Hodder Headline Plc, 338 Euston Road, London NW1 3BH by Oriental press.

Contents

1 An Urban World: Global Urbanisation Trends   1

Part 1: Cities in More Economically Developed Countries

2 Urban Competition: Hierarchies and League Tables   4

3 Do the Models Fit?: Models of Urban Morphology and Change   9

4 Dynamic Cities: Population Movement Within Cities   18

5 Unfair Cities: Urban Inequality   23

6 Urban Revolution: Change in Central and Eastern European Cities   30

7 Estates of the Excluded: Social Housing Estates and Ghettos   34

8 Reviving the Inner City: Policy in British Cities   41

9 Challenging Deprivation: the Single Regeneration Budget   47

10 Inner City Pioneers: Gentrification and Reurbanisation   52

11 Sprawling Cities: Suburbanisation and Edge Cities   56

12 Threatened Centres: Changing Patterns of Retailing and the Future of City Centres   64

13 Post-Industrial Cities: Finding a New Economic Role for Cities   70

14 Repackaging the City: City Marketing and the Importance of Image   76

15 Fighting Gridlock: Urban Transport Management   81

16 Planning for the Future: Urban Sustainability   87

Part 2: Cities in Less Economically Developed Countries

17 Growing Cities: Urban Expansion and its Causes   90

18 Urban Stress: the Consequences of Rapid Expansion   97

19 Cities of Extremes: Inequality in the City   101

20 Slums and Squatter Settlements: Housing the Urban Poor   108

21 Planning the City: Providing New Urban Infrastructure   115

22 Globalising Cities: The Impact of Economic Change   121

23 Surviving the Future: Sustainable Approaches to City Management   125

24 A Summary Model for Bangalore   129

25 MEDC Cities and LEDC Cities Compared   133

Index   135

1

AN URBAN WORLD: GLOBAL URBANISATION TRENDS

Key Ideas

- Urbanisation is the process in which the proportion of the population living in urban areas increases.
- The more economically developed countries (MEDCs) generally have a higher percentage of their population living in urban areas than the less economically developed countries (LEDCs).
- The number of mega-cities and million cities is growing. The proportion of the world's largest cities situated in the more economically developed countries is falling.
- The proportion of people living in cities in some of the most economically developed countries is falling.

An urban world?

Urbanisation is the process in which the proportion of the population living in urban areas increases. This has been primarily a result of rural–urban migration. About 50% of the world's population is urban. We live in an increasingly urban world, but the degree of urbanisation in different countries varies greatly. According to United Nations estimates for the year 2000, 75% of Europe's population and 77% of North America's population is urban but for African and Asia the figures are only 37% and 38%.

Figures 1.1, 1.2 and 1.3 illustrate an important relationship between economic development and urbanisation. Those regions of the world with highly developed industrial economies are more urbanised than those regions which are less

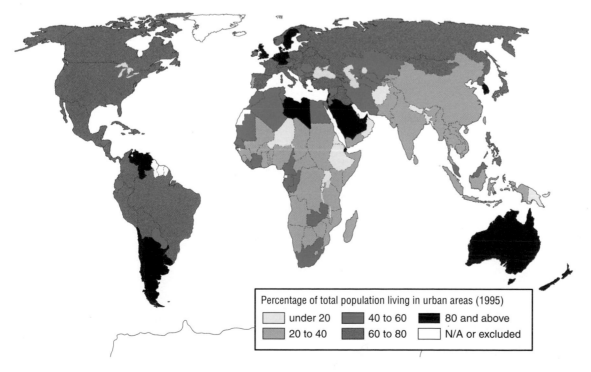

FIGURE 1.1 Percentage of the total population living in urban areas

Percentage of total population living in urban areas (1995)

- under 20
- 20 to 40
- 40 to 60
- 60 to 80
- 80 and above
- N/A or excluded

FIGURE 1.2 Estimates and projections of the percentage of the world's population living in urban areas

	1975	2000	2025
WORLD	38%	48%	61%
Africa	25%	37%	54%
Asia	25%	38%	55%
Europe	67%	75%	83%
Latin America	61%	77%	65%
North America	74%	77%	85%
Oceania	72%	70%	75%

American population is urban and yet Latin America is regarded as being part of the less economically developed world. Although this is perhaps a surprising figure it can be explained partly by the fact that Latin America is a relatively industrialised region of the less developed world.

The growth of the cities

Cities are growing as a consequence of two main processes:
- **inward migration** (i.e. urbanisation)
- **natural population increase** (i.e. birth rates exceed death rates).

In 1975, 38% of the world's population was urban compared to 48% in 2000. However, given that the total population is also growing, this hides the real extent of the population growth in urban areas. In 1975, about 1.5 billion people lived in cities. This figure has doubled to about 3 billion in 2000. This represents a growth rate of about 2.6% per annum, but this figure varies considerably from region to region and city to city. The figures also suggest that the rate of this growth has been slower in the 1980s and 1990s than it was in the 1960s and 1970s.

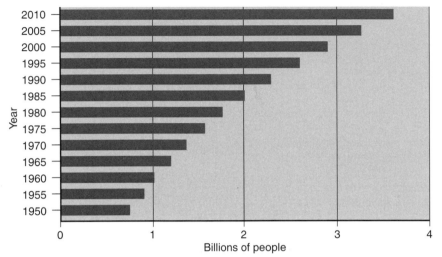

FIGURE 1.3 Total urban population 1950–2010

Million cities and mega-cities

By 1990 there were estimated to be 280 cities with more than a million people (the **million cities**) and 12 with a population of more than 10 million (the **mega-cities**). The estimated number of mega-cities for 2000 is 21. As the proportion of the world's population living in urban areas has grown, so has the number of very large cities. The majority of these million and mega-cities are now found in the less economically developed countries.

industrialised. Secondary and tertiary industries (i.e. manufacturing and services) dominate the economies of North America and Europe and this type of economic activity concentrates in urban areas. In large parts of Africa and Asia the dominant economic activity is agriculture and so the majority of the population is rural. However, it is important to point out that 77% of the Latin

FIGURE 1.4 The mega-cities (cities of over 10 million people)

City	Country	Population (2000 projection)	Predicted Annual Growth rate (1995–2005)
Tokyo	Japan	27.9 million	0.6%
Bombay	India	18.1 million	3.4%
Sao Paulo	Brazil	17.8 million	1.5%
Shanghai	China	17.2 million	2.5%
New York	USA	16.6 million	0.4%
Mexico City	Mexico	16.4 million	1.0%
Beijing	China	14.2 million	2.6%
Jakarta	Indonesia	14.1 million	3.8%
Lagos	Nigeria	13.5 million	5.1%
Los Angeles	USA	13.1 million	0.9%
Calcutta	India	12.7 million	1.8%
Tianjin	China	12.4 million	2.7%
Seoul	South Korea	12.3 million	0.9%
Karachi	Pakistan	12.1 million	4.0%
Delhi	India	11.7 million	3.2%
Buenos Aires	Argentina	11.4 million	0.7%
Manila	Philippines	10.8 million	2.9%
Cairo	Egypt	10.7 million	2.1%
Osaka	Japan	10.6 million	0.2%
Dacca	Bangladesh	10.2 million	5.0%
Rio de Janeiro	Brazil	10.2 million	0.7%

FIGURE 1.5 The mega-cities in 2000

How reliable are urban population statistics?

There are two main reasons why it is difficult to obtain reliable figures for the number of people living in cities:

1 In many countries there is no reliable official census.
2 There is no consistency between countries on how urban areas are defined.

The second point can be illustrated by using one example. Tokyo can be defined in four different ways:

Definition	Population	Area
Tokyo city	8.2 million	600 sq. km.
Tokyo prefecture	11.9 million	2,000 sq. km.
Greater Tokyo Metropolitan Area	31.6 million	14,000 sq. km.
National Capital Region	36.8 million	37,000 sq. km.

No one figure for Tokyo is any more correct than the others. So, there is a choice about which population figure to use and this makes an accurate comparison with other cities difficult.

Counterurbanisation

While city growth continues through most of the world, a relatively small number of advanced industrialised countries, such as France, Italy and Britain, which have very high proportions of their populations living in urban areas, have been seeing a loss of population from their larger cities since the 1970s. For example, there is evidence that Britain's larger urban areas are experiencing a total net population loss of about 90,000 people a year. This process is called **counterurbanisation**. Such figures have to be treated with caution for the reasons outlined above, but they do show that in some of the most economically developed countries urbanisation is no longer a significant process.

However, there is evidence that counterurbanisation was slowing down by the 1990s and it is not yet clear whether counterurbanisation is a long-term trend or not.

STUDENT ACTIVITY 1.1

Study all the information in the tables, graphs, maps and text in this chapter and write a report on the current global trends and patterns in urbanisation.

2
URBAN COMPETITION: HIERARCHIES AND LEAGUE TABLES

Key Ideas

■ All cities perform a range of functions. These functions serve the surrounding region as well as the city itself.
■ Each city can be placed in a hierarchy of urban areas with a small number of very large or important cities at the top of the hierarchy and a larger number of smaller or less important cities lower down the hierarchy.
■ City hierarchies can be based on the size of the population living in each city or on the range and importance of the functions performed by each city.

■ A small number of cities are at the top of the global urban hierarchy. These are the 'world cities' and are the most important and influential cities in the world.
■ Cities are increasingly competing with each other to attract investment. This competition is increasingly at an international level.
■ City decision-makers are increasingly aware of a 'league table of attractiveness', with those cities higher up the league table being more attractive to investors. Each city is attempting to move higher up this league table.

FIGURE 2.1 A city and the surrounding region: a city's sphere of influence

The functions of urban areas

The limit of the city's sphere of influence is sometimes refered to as the range. The range is the maximum distance a person is prepared to travel in order to use a service or function in the city.

Sphere of influence served by the city (the city's hinterland)

City

Surrounding towns and villages

People living outside the sphere of influence use the functions or services of neighbouring cities.

Urban functions can be defined as the facilities provided by an urban area. Cities have a wide range of functions including:
■ housing
■ secondary economic activity (manufacturing industry)
■ tertiary economic activity (services including shopping, entertainment, leisure and transport)
■ cultural activity (such as music, fashion, theatre, film and art)
■ administration and political power (they are usually the administrative centres of local or national government)
■ education (they usually have at least one university)
■ financial activity (such as banking and insurance).

Most of these functions serve the population of the city *and* the population of the surrounding region. (The surrounding region is sometimes referred to as the city's **sphere of influence** or **hinterland**.) For this reason cities can be described as important **central places**. A central place is a settlement which provides facilities for the population living in the surrounding region.

Of course, each of these functions can also be found in smaller settlements but:

■ only cities have the *whole range* of functions in one settlement

■ the services or functions cities provide are of a *higher order* than in smaller settlements. In other words, a city's functions are more specialised or provided on a larger scale.

■ Cities serve a larger surrounding region since people are prepared to travel further for high order functions.

For example, a city can offer a wider range of more specialised cultural activities than a town and can also provide larger cultural venues. So a typical city is likely to have at least one very large music venue which is able to accommodate thousands of people but also a large number of specialised music venues for a wide range of types of music and types of audience.

This large range of high order functions is possible because of its large sphere of influence. There is a large enough population within the city and the surrounding region to make high order functions economically viable. The larger the city is the more high order functions it is likely to have. To return to the example of music venues, London can provide a far larger number of very large venues and a far greater range of specialist venues than any other city in Britain.

City hierarchies

Within a country such as the UK there is a hierarchy of settlements with the least important settlements at the bottom and the most important at the top. At the bottom of the hierarchy there are thousands of small villages with a small number of lower order functions serving a small sphere of influence.

At the top of the hierarchy is the largest city with a large number of higher order functions serving a large sphere of influence.

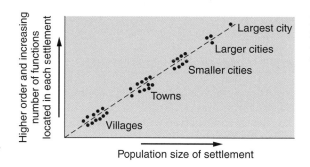

FIGURE 2.2 The relationship between size and function in a settlement hierarchy

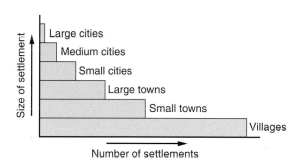

FIGURE 2.3 A settlement hierarchy

A hierarchy of British cities?

Figure 2.4 ranks all of the cities in Britain with a population of 200,000 or more according to their population and this list could be used to analyse the British urban hierarchy. However, the figures refer to the population of the city council administrative areas and not necessarily the whole of the urban

City	Population	Name and population of conurbation where appropriate
Greater London	6,680,000	
Birmingham	960,000	part of West Midlands conurbation: 2,450,000
Leeds	680,000	part of West Yorkshire conurbation: 1,940,000
Glasgow	660,000	part of Clydeside conurbation: 1,460,000
Sheffield	530,000	
Liverpool	480,000	part of Merseyside conurbation: 1,350,000
Bradford	460,000	
Manchester	430,000	part of Greater Manchester conurbation: 2,400,000
Edinburgh	420,000	
Bristol	380,000	
Cardiff	280,000	
Leicester	270,000	
Nottingham	260,000	
Newcastle upon Tyne	260,000	part of Tyne & Wear conurbation: 1,060,000
Hull	250,000	
Plymouth	240,000	
Wolverhampton	240,000	part of West Midlands conurbation: 2,450,000
Stoke-on-Trent	240,000	
Derby	220,000	
Aberdeen	200,000	
Southampton	200,000	

FIGURE 2.4 British cities with a population of 200,000 or more

FIGURE 2.5 An example
of how the relative
importance of cities can
be assessed using a
selection of functions

	University level education	TV media centre	Regional shopping centre	Resident symphony orchestra	Major international airport	Major centre for international tourism	Location of national government
London	X	X	X	X	X	X	X
Birmingham	X	X	X	X	X		
Leeds	X	X	X	X			
Derby	X						

area. Manchester for example, with a population of 430,000, forms a small part of the Greater Manchester **conurbation** with a population of 2.4 million. It might be more realistic to use population figures for the whole of each conurbation or **agglomeration**.

The alternative method of analysing city hierarchies is to investigate the type of functions in each city. Figure 2.5 shows one simple method of ranking cities according to function. You could extend the list of functions and apply the list to a different group of cities.

The global hierarchy and world cities

In an era of rapid communications and growing international mobility it might make more sense to think in terms of international rather than national urban hierarchies. Geographers have drawn up a variety of global hierarchies based on function. At the top of these hierarchies are the **world cities**. These are not necessarily the largest cities in terms of population but they are the most influential cities because they are concentrations of global financial and commercial power. They have large numbers of international bank headquarters, transnational corporation head offices and important stock exchanges. They are also a focus for international business travel and international telecommunications. World cities have been called 'command centres of the global economy'.

Geographers generally agree that the three leading world cities are New York, London and Tokyo. Many people also include Paris as one of the most important cities. There is less agreement about which other cities can claim the title 'World City'. Figure 2.7 shows how cities compare using four indicators of economic importance.

FIGURE 2.6 New York: the heart of a world city

FIGURE 2.7 A league table of world cities (to appear in this table a city has to be ranked at least third under one of the indicators)

City	Ranking based on the number of head offices of the world's largest 100 banks	Ranking based on value of the stock exchange	Ranking based on the number of head offices of the world's largest corporations	Ranking based on international passenger traffic volume passing through the city's airport
Tokyo	1	2	1	6
London	5	3	3	1
New York	4	1	2	5
Paris	2	4	7	2
Frankfurt	3	5	13	3

Globalisation and competition between cities

Within the UK and within Europe cities are increasingly competing with each other to attract scarce investment and jobs. High levels of unemployment and the need for new firms to replace the jobs lost in manufacturing industry have meant that city decision-makers have had to work hard to attract investment from within their own country and from abroad. They have also had to work hard to encourage firms to *stay* in their city rather than to move elsewhere. In recent years a number of unofficial 'league tables' have been published which rank cities according to how attractive they are to the following groups:

- investors interested in locating new firms or branch plants
- visitors and tourists who may wish to visit the city and spend money in shops, hotels, restaurants and other leisure services
- the city's own population; so that skilled, educated and affluent people remain in the city to provide a pool of skilled labour or spend money in the local economy.

City decision-makers take a lot of notice of such league tables and the good or bad publicity they bring, and they put considerable effort into trying to move higher up such tables.

CASE STUDY

A league table of British cities based on quality of life

The 'Quality of Life Research Group' at Strathclyde University have carried out research into which cities in Britain offer their residents the best quality of life. One result of their research is a 'league table' of British cities.

Many firms are interested in this kind of research. Firms which are **footloose** (i.e. not tied to a specific location) but need highly educated and motivated staff will be particularly interested. For example, firms in fields such as computer programming and software design often need to compete with each other to obtain sufficient highly skilled workers. These workers can 'pick and choose' their employer and are more likely to choose to work for a firm in a more desirable location.

City decision-makers are also interested in this type of research. Cities are working hard to attract new firms and investment to help regenerate their local economies. They are more likely to be successful if they offer a quality of life which attracts both skilled workers and footloose firms.

The Quality of Life Research Group initially needed to know what aspects of quality of life people think are important, so they completed a national opinion survey. Each person was asked to rate a variety of aspects of urban quality of life by giving each aspect a score of between 5 for 'very important' and 0 for 'no importance'. The result is shown in Figure 2.8.

The research group then used a variety of statistical indicators to assess the quality of life in each city on the basis of the 16 criteria listed. The criteria higher up the table in Figure 2.8 were given more weight than those lower down. An average for each indicator was calculated so that cities above average in a particular indicator received a positive score and those below average received a negative score. The 16 scores were then added together to give a total quality of life score. Cities scoring well in all criteria achieved a high positive score while those scoring badly had a high negative score. The resulting ranking is shown in Figure 2.9.

Rank	Aspect	% of people surveyed indicating 'very important'
1	Violent crime rate	72
2	Local health care provision	70
3	Levels of non-violent crime	66
4	Cost of living	59
5	Education provision	57
6	Pollution levels	56
7	Employment prospects	50
8	Housing costs	49
9	Wage levels	45
10	Shopping facilities	44
11	Unemployment level	41
12	Travel to work times	36
13	Scenic quality of area	33
14	Climate	25
15	Sports facilities	24
16	Leisure opportunities	21

FIGURE 2.8 What aspects of quality of life do people think are important?

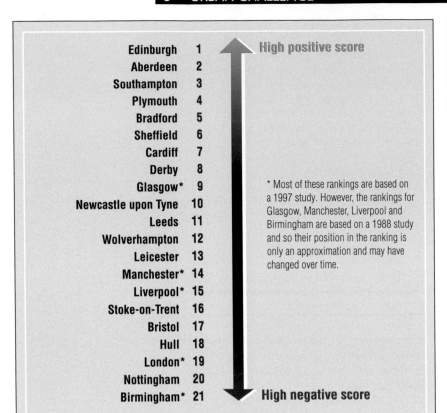

Edinburgh	1
Aberdeen	2
Southampton	3
Plymouth	4
Bradford	5
Sheffield	6
Cardiff	7
Derby	8
Glasgow*	9
Newcastle upon Tyne	10
Leeds	11
Wolverhampton	12
Leicester	13
Manchester*	14
Liverpool*	15
Stoke-on-Trent	16
Bristol	17
Hull	18
London*	19
Nottingham	20
Birmingham*	21

High positive score

High negative score

* Most of these rankings are based on a 1997 study. However, the rankings for Glasgow, Manchester, Liverpool and Birmingham are based on a 1988 study and so their position in the ranking is only an approximation and may have changed over time.

Based on R. Rogerson (1997) *Quality of Life in Britain*, Dept. of Geography, University of Strathclyde, and R. Rogerson, A Findley, A. Morris (1998) *The Best Cities to Live In*, in Town and Country Planning, October 1998.

FIGURE 2.9 British cities with a population of 200,000 or more ranked according to one assessment of their quality of life

THE WINNER

GLASGOW

No one will bad-mouth it. Choose any topic, dig for criticism and the answer from Glasgow's streets are unanimous – this is a place that young people love to live in.

Andrew, a 20-year-old student at Strathclyde University, says: "I've lived in 19 cities in my life and Glasgow is my second favourite after Hong Kong."

Glasgow looks great; like Manhattan with a touch of Barcelona, a city laid out for Hollywood car chases with continental architecture. "You can't get lost without a great deal of effort," says Andrew. "It's the way the city is laid out. I feel part of it." Not so grand that it intimidates, the city is a playground for young people.

Charles Rennie Mackintosh's Art Deco style dominates the city and young Glaswegians will tell you how much they admire his work, while in the docklands area, Sir Norman Foster's silver conference centre rises like an enormous metal tent with wings.

Rory Weller, *i-D*'s clubs correspondent in Glasgow, says the 6am club licences granted during the 1990 City of Culture year kick-started the city into believing in itself. Glasgow has produced celebrated techno producers Slam, hip label Soma (which launched Daft Punk) and outlaw sound system Desert Storm.

Glasgow is fast gaining a reputation for sartorial excellence.

Hanna Logan, a TV fashion researcher, nominates it as Britain's best-dressed city. "It's a lower-key sophistication than London," she says. "You feel as if you're in a continental city."

Mel, 21, a shop assistant, has recently moved to Glasgow from London. He is waiting for friends in the Rogano Oyster Bar. "It's wildly spontaneous because it's relatively small. You can say to people, 'Let's meet in half an hour'. The intimacy of socialising is great."

Getting around the city is easy for car-less young Glaswegians. There are plenty of buses and the Strathclyde rail network is the largest in the UK outside London. Black cabs are easily hailed and taxi drivers notoriously friendly.

Glasgow's cuisine owes much to the city's Asian population. In Canton Express, Chinese food is delivered within minutes. Hungry clubbers can find satisfaction at round-the-clock cafe Insomnia, whose motto is: "We never close. Not for a minute. Not even for Christmas."

Young Glaswegians can also find plenty of fuel for civic pride in football. Rangers and Celtic are Scotland's top two teams, and are attracting international players of the calibre of Paul Gascoigne and Marco Negri to Glasgow.

Source: *Big Issue*

FIGURE 2.10

3
DO THE MODELS FIT?: MODELS OF URBAN MORPHOLOGY AND CHANGE

Key Ideas

■ Urban models are simplifications of a city designed to help us to understand real cities.
■ The three most well known urban models are the concentric, sector and multiple nuclei models. These 'classical models' are in many respects inappropriate for cities at the beginning of the twenty-first century. A number of more recent models are useful when looking at contemporary cities.

■ Models can be used to describe *existing* patterns of land use (or city morphology) but they can also help to explain *changes* in land use or morphology.
■ Cities are shaped as a result of decisions made by a variety of groups in the public and private sectors.

What is an urban model?

An urban model is a simplification of a real city. Urban models aim to:

■ help us to understand more about real cities by showing us patterns or processes which in real life may be very complex and difficult to identify
■ be applicable to a large number of cities rather than one particular city – they are based on the idea that there are similarities between cities.

The models we are concerned with in much of this chapter are **models of urban morphology**. The term 'morphology' means 'internal structure'. They are also called **models of urban land use** since they attempt to describe or explain patterns in that land use.

The classical models

Three urban models are particularly well known and these are sometimes called the 'classical models'. They were devised by American geographers and sociologists working in the 1920s, 1930s and 1940s who were interested in trying to understand more about what was happening at that time in the rapidly growing cities of the USA.

The concentric model

The concentric model was devised by E.W. Burgess in the 1920s. It is linked to a concept called **human ecology** developed by a number of urban sociologists working in Chicago at the time. Human ecology was based on the idea that individuals compete with each other for the most favourable locations within a city. This competition is founded on the market for buildings and land: those who can afford the highest prices will get the most favourable locations. The poor will have no choice but to accept the worst locations.

FIGURE 3.1 Burgess' Concentric Zone Model

A	Central business district	The city centre is dominated by shops and other commercial functions. Due to its accessibility the land is very expensive and only businesses can afford the rents.
B	Zone in transition	This is a mixture of poor quality housing, industry and derelict land. It is an area experiencing change or *transition* as old buildings are demolished and new functions move in.
C	Zone of working class housing	Cheap housing for people on low incomes.
D	Residential zone	More expensive housing built for people on higher incomes.
E	Commuter zone	The most expensive housing. This is located in the villages and countryside around the city and attracts those who want a more rural environment and who can afford the high cost of the journey into the city each day for work.

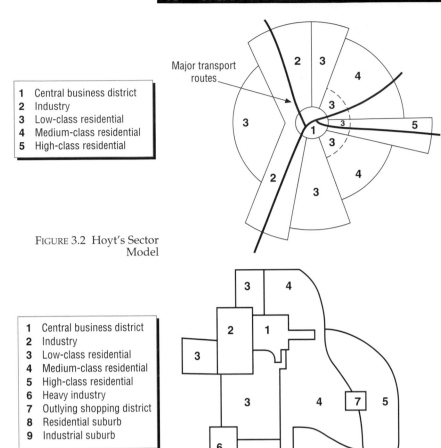

1   Central business district
2   Industry
3   Low-class residential
4   Medium-class residential
5   High-class residential

Major transport routes

FIGURE 3.2 Hoyt's Sector Model

1   Central business district
2   Industry
3   Low-class residential
4   Medium-class residential
5   High-class residential
6   Heavy industry
7   Outlying shopping district
8   Residential suburb
9   Industrial suburb

FIGURE 3.3 Harris and Ullman's Multiple Nuclei Model

The sector model

This model was drawn up by Hoyt in the 1930s. He studied over 100 different cities in the USA and came to the conclusion that while the cities showed characteristics of the concentric model and human ecology there was evidence that **sectors** or 'wedges' dominated the morphology of cities. He argued that wealthier groups preferred to live in the suburbs but still wanted to be able to travel quickly into the city centre. They used their wealth to acquire land close to fast links to the city centre (such as railway lines) but well away from industry.

The multiple nuclei model

This was devised by Harris and Ullman in 1945. The concentric and sector models both assume that a city has a single centre and that the different zones develop around that centre. Harris and Ullman argued that a city may develop around a number of different centres or **nuclei**. Some of these centres may be commercial (such as shopping centres), some residential and some industrial. These nuclei might emerge because some activities tend to cluster together (shops, for example) while others repel each other (for example, high cost housing will locate well away from industry).

Are the classical models appropriate to twenty-first-century cities?

The concentric zone model does have some major drawbacks. It was devised in the context of 1920s Chicago. Chicago has been described as the 'shock city' of the American industrial revolution. In the late nineteenth and early twentieth centuries it experienced particularly rapid immigration and growth and, therefore, was not typical even of 1920s America.

In the late 1990s, cities in more economically developed countries are experiencing very different circumstances to 1920s Chicago. They are not experiencing high population growth and a number of other important factors affecting urban areas have emerged over the last 50 years. Mass car ownership, for example, has had a major impact on land use patterns. Urban sprawl and the growth of 'edge cities' in the USA are creating new forms of urban morphology (see Figure 11.4).

Also, the model takes no account of other important factors which have given cities in other countries their particular characteristics. For example, government involvement in providing housing for low income groups is ignored. 1920s Chicago had nothing like the large areas of council housing which have formed such an important part of British cities for much of the twentieth century.

This leads to the separation or **segregation** of different types of people according to their ability to pay. As the spending power of different groups changes or as the relative attractiveness of different locations changes, so the pattern of land use in the city will also change.

Burgess studied the city of Chicago closely using the ideas of human ecology and on the basis of his findings he drew up the concentric model. He argued that Chicago was divided into a number of **concentric zones** with the lowest quality neighbourhoods close to the city centre and the highest quality neighbourhoods on the edge of the city (see Figure 3.1).

Burgess was also interested in the way the zones changed over time. He developed the ideas of **invasion** and **succession**. As new groups of immigrants entered the city they would obtain homes in the lower quality zone close to the city centre. The existing residents would move outwards and *invade* the next zone. They would, in turn, eventually *succeed* or come to dominate that zone which would force the original residents of that zone to move further outwards. In other words, migration into the city creates a 'ripple effect' changing the character of existing zones, causing each population group to move closer to the edge of the city, and causing the city to expand outwards.

Similar criticisms to these can be levelled at the sector and multiple nuclei models. It can be argued that the main problem with all three classical models is that they have been used inappropriately. They have been used as though they are appropriate for all cities in more economically developed countries in all decades since the 1920s. In fact, they are models devised by geographers who were analysing a particular set of circumstances at a particular time. Nevertheless, as the exercises at the end of this chapter illustrate, they can still be used as a starting point for analysing the morphology of modern cities in countries such as the UK. Also, it can be argued that the ideas of human ecology, such as invasion and succession, continue to be relevant.

Attempts to modify the classical models

Mann's model of a British city

Since the 1940s, a number of geographers have attempted to draw up models which are more appropriate to contemporary circumstances or to specific groups of countries. For example, in 1965 Mann devised a model which he felt was more applicable to British cities (see Figure 3.4). Mann studied a number of cities in northern England and his model is an attempt to describe the patterns he found. It shows elements of both the concentric and sector models but at the same time attempts to take into account the importance of council housing in British cities. The age of the housing and the age of the people living in those houses tend to follow a concentric pattern, while tenure (and therefore the cost and status of the housing) tends to follow a sector pattern.

A Middle-class sector
B Lower middle-class sector
C Working-class sector (and main sector of council estates)
D Industry and lowest working-class sector

1 Central business district
2 Transitional zone
3 Zone of small terraced houses in sectors C and D; larger housing in sector B; large old houses in sector A
4 Post-1918 residential areas, with post-1945 housing on the periphery
5 Commuter towns

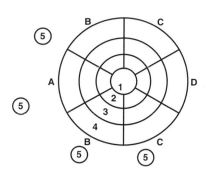

FIGURE 3.4 Mann's model of a British city

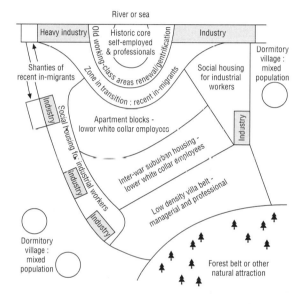

FIGURE 3.5 A model of Western European Cities outside the UK

FIGURE 3.6 High density housing in central Paris – Continental European cities generally have a far higher residential population in their central areas than British cities

A model of western European cities

The model in Figure 3.5 aims to be applicable to all cities in western Europe outside the UK. Elements of the concentric, sector and multiple nuclei models can be detected but there are some notable differences compared to the other models described in this chapter. For example, the city centre is identified as a residential zone. The central core dominated by historic buildings is a residential zone for middle class and self-employed people while the outer areas of the city centre provide working-class housing, some of which has been gentrified by middle-class people. This is in contrast to the models based on the USA and UK which assume that there is no housing in the city centre. Also, areas of social housing (the equivalent of council housing) are shown on the periphery of the city. Like Mann's model this is overcoming the failure of the classical models to take into account housing provided by the State.

The 'California School'

A number of American geographers have recently developed new models to describe the morphology of large American urban areas at the beginning of the twenty-first century. These show the impact of large-scale sprawl on urban morphology (see Figure 11.4 in Chapter 11).

Change in urban morphology

As Burgess and the other authors of the classical models acknowledged, the morphology of cities changes over time. It is possible to draw up models which highlight change. Figure 3.7 is one such model designed to show how British cities have changed since the early twentieth century.

FIGURE 3.7 A model of change in a British city during the twentieth century

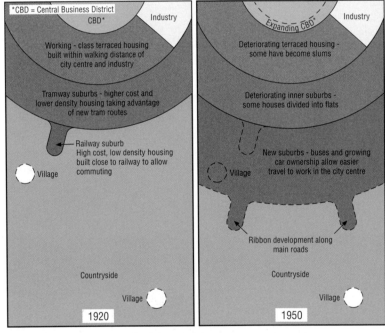

CASE STUDY

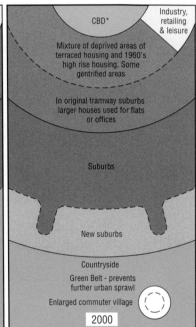

Urban models and the morphology of Sheffield

The concentric and sector models

Urban models aim to tell us about variations in the type and quality of residential areas within a city and also about variations in the socio-economic characteristics of residential areas. Figure 3.8 shows simplified concentric and sector models.

FIGURE 3.8 Simplified concentric and sector models

A group of Geography students has been asked to carry out a field work exercise designed to test the following *hypothesis*: **'Sheffield has elements of both the concentric and sector models'.** The students have been asked to study two transects in Sheffield. Both transects run from the edge of the city centre to the periphery of the urban area. One runs westwards and the other southwards. Along each transect seven locations have been selected. Each location consists of a single *enumeration district* (the smallest size of area for which census data can be obtained). Figures 3.9 and 3.10 show the transects that the students studied.

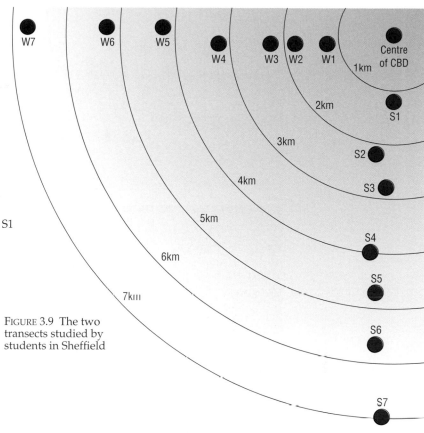

FIGURE 3.9 The two transects studied by students in Sheffield

S1

S2

S3

S4

S5

S6

FIGURE 3.10 The 14 locations studied by students in Sheffield, *cont . . .*

S7

W1

W2

W3

W4

W5

W6

W7

	1	*2*	*3*	*4*	*5*	
low value housing					✓	high value housing
housing in poor condition					✓	housing in good condition
housing allows little privacy				✓		housing allows total privacy
housing has no gardens					✓	housing has large gardens
a grey environment					✓	a green environment
an ugly environment					✓	an attractive environment
no trees				✓		well wooded
congested					✓	spacious
a lot of litter					✓	no litter
a lot of vandalism					✓	no vandalism
probably unsafe at night				✓		probably safe at night
noisy					✓	peaceful

Total score = 57

FIGURE 3.11 A biopolar evaluation matrix completed for one of the 14 locations

For each of the 14 enumeration districts the students have succeeded in obtaining three types of data
1 1991 census data (three census indicators have been calculated for each location: the unemployment rate, the percentage of houses which are owner-occupied and the percentage of households owning two or more cars)
2 Housing type and age
3 An environmental quality score.

FIGURE 3.12 Data collected for the 14 locations

The students have obtained the census information by visiting their local library. Housing type and age, and environmental quality were recorded when they visited the 14 locations. The environmental quality score was obtained by using a **bipolar evaluation matrix**. Figure 3.11 shows the matrix designed by the students and completed for one location. In this matrix the lowest possible score an area can obtain is 12 and the highest is 60. This particular matrix shows the score obtained for one of the locations on the western transect.

Figure 3.12 shows all the data collected by the students for each of the 14 enumeration districts.

Location	Distance from the edge of the city centre (km)	Age of housing	Type of housing	Environ- mental Quality Score	% unem- ployment rate	% of houses which are owner- occupied	% of households with two or more cars
W1	1.1	post-1960	tower block	15	45	1	1
W2	1.8	pre-1914	detached	35	11	68	20
W3	2.3	pre-1914	terraced	26	14	66	5
W4	3.2	pre-1914	terraced	33	8	72	13
W5	4.2	pre-1914	detached	57	7	70	37
W6	5.3	1918–39	semi and detached	55	3	96	47
W7	6.7	post-1960	semi-detached	49	3	98	26
S1	1.1	post-1960	terraced	22	24	13	3
S2	2.2	pre-1914	terraced	21	26	41	9
S3	2.8	pre-1914	terraced	33	14	80	9
S4	4.0	pre-1914	terraced	30	8	83	13
S5	4.8	pre-1914	terraced	36	7	85	13
S6	5.8	1918–39	semi-detached	45	6	100	23
S7	7.0	post-1960	terraced and tower block	29	17	16	6

FIGURE 3.13
Four scatter graphs

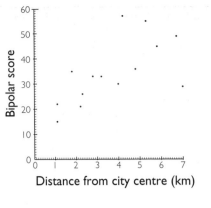

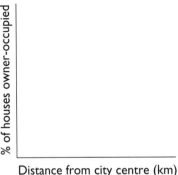

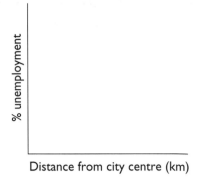

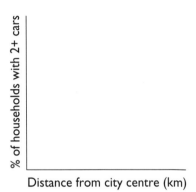

Who are the urban decision-makers?

This chapter looks at a variety of models of urban morphology and urban change but who actually *decides* how a city is organised? Who *controls* the land use in a city? Who makes the decisions which affect the layout and appearance of cities? The answer to these question is very complex because so many different groups are involved. They include:

■ private sector firms
■ national government
■ local government
■ public sector agencies
■ the voluntary sector (e.g. community groups)
■ the local population

Think about the roles played by each of these groups. Cities are in fact a product of both public sector and private sector decisions. In other words, they are a product of both government intervention and market forces. The relative power of each of these groups varies between cities and between countries. There is certainly no single group of decision-makers who are responsible for the layout and organisation of our cities.

STUDENT ACTIVITY 3.1

Study all the information about the transects carefully and then answer the following questions.
1   To what extent does there appear to be a relationship between distance from the city centre and the age and type of the housing?
2   Suggest reasons for the relationship you have identified in question 1.
3   Draw four scatter graphs as shown in figure 3.13. You may wish to distinguish the two transects by using two different colours.
4   What relationships between distance and the socio-economic indicators are revealed by your graphs? Suggest reasons for these relationships.
5   What similarities and differences do you notice between the two transects in terms of the type of housing, the age of the housing and the socio-economic characteristics?
6   With the help of your answers to questions 1 to 5 assess the extent to which the evidence supports or rejects the hypothesis that 'Sheffield shows elements of both the concentric and sector models'.
7   Critically evaluate the methods *and* data used by the students. Suggest how they could have been improved. (You should comment on the effectiveness of bipolar evaluation as a method of assessing an area, the choice of characteristics measured in the bipolar evaluation, and the choice of census indicators.)

Models of urban growth and change

Figure 3.14 is a **place specific model** for Sheffield which aims to show us how this particular city has developed over time.

FIGURE 3.14 Growth and change in Sheffield.

Location	Description	Named example OS grid reference (1:50,000 sheet 110)
A	*From the late eighteenth to early twentieth centuries industry located along the valleys of the Don and Sheaf to take advantage of flat land, valley routes and water availability. From the 1980s large areas became derelict with the large-scale closure of industry.*	*3688 to 3990*
B	*Working-class housing built adjacent to the industry. Much of the terraced housing built in the late nineteenth and early twentieth centuries remains.*	*Darnall: 3988*
C	*Affluent high status housing built in the late eighteenth and nineteenth centuries. Many of the houses were built by industrialists who made their wealth from the steel and related industries. During the second part of the twentieth century many of these large houses have been divided into flats or converted to offices.*	*Broomhall: 3486*
D	*Inter-war council housing built on vacant land not in demand from private house builders.*	*Manor: 3885*
E	*Inter-war higher status owner-occupied housing.*	*Ecclesall: 3284*
F	*Inter-war lower status owner-occupied housing.*	*Frecheville: 3983*
G	*Inter-war very high status owner-occupied housing built around an old village core.*	*Dore: 3081*
H	*1960s council estates including tower blocks and maisonettes built originally to house people from inner city demolition schemes.*	*Stannington: 3088*
I	*1960s council redevelopment schemes built on the site of demolished terraced housing. These areas include tower blocks and deck access flats. Poor design and social problems caused some of this housing to deteriorate. Some blocks have now been demolished and replaced by conventional housing.*	*Parkhill: 3687*
J	*Improved or gentrified inner city terraced housing.*	*Hunters Bar: 3385*
K	*Post-1960 medium status owner-occupied housing estates.*	*Mosborough townships: 4382*

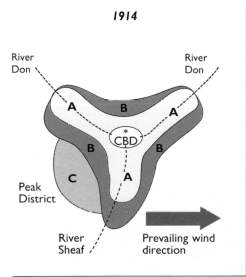
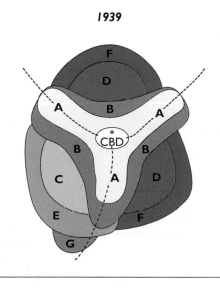
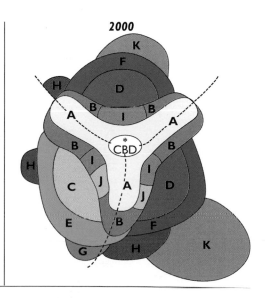

*CBD = Central Business District

4
DYNAMIC CITIES: POPULATION MOVEMENT WITHIN CITIES

Key Ideas

- Cities are dynamic. They are continually changing. The movement of population within cities is an important part of this change.
- The main population movements affecting cities in more economically developed countries

are suburbanisation, counterurbanisation, filtering, inner city decline, and gentrification.
- These processes are interrelated and have a variety of socio-economic, environmental and political impacts.

The main population processes

Cities are **dynamic**. In other words, they experience continual change. This change is driven by a variety of processes (a process being a sequence of events over time). One important set of processes involves the movement of population. This chapter focuses on five main population processes. Urbanisation is not included because in most economically developed countries it only happens on a small scale or has been replaced by counterurbanisation (see page 3).

FIGURE 4.1 The main urban population processes in more economically developed countries

Suburbanisation and urban sprawl

Suburbanisation is the construction of new housing on green field sites on the periphery of the city or around commuter villages close to the city. The term can also be used to refer to the construction of non-residential developments on green field sites, such as shopping centres and industrial estates. The term '**urban sprawl**' is also used to describe the spreading of urban areas into the surrounding countryside.

Counterurbanisation

Counterurbanisation is occurring when the number of people moving out of a city exceeds the number of people moving in (i.e. there is net **out-migration**). Counterurbanisation will occur when people decide, for whatever reason, that living in smaller towns or rural areas is preferable.

It can be difficult in reality to separate *suburbanisation* and *counterurbanisation*. If, for example, new suburbs are being built just beyond a city boundary, census statistics may indicate that the city is losing population while the adjacent rural area containing the suburbs is gaining population. This might suggest that *counterurbanisation* is occurring. However, in geographical terms the new suburbs are part of the city and so the process occurring is *suburbanisation*, rather than counterurbanisation. On the other hand, the term suburbanisation can also include new housing built around commuter villages close to the city. This may involve a net migration out of the city to

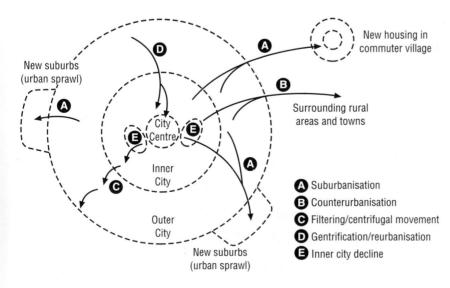

New suburbs (urban sprawl)

New housing in commuter village

Surrounding rural areas and towns

City Centre

Inner City

Outer City

New suburbs (urban sprawl)

- Ⓐ Suburbanisation
- Ⓑ Counterurbanisation
- Ⓒ Filtering/centrifugal movement
- Ⓓ Gentrification/reurbanisation
- Ⓔ Inner city decline

adjacent rural areas and so could also be defined as counterurbanisation.

To avoid this confusion some urban geographers use the concept of the **urban region** to define suburbanisation and counterurbanisation. This concept is explained in Figure 4.2. Some use the terms **decentralisation** or **deconcentration** to encompass both suburbanisation and counterurbanisation.

Counterurbanisation does not affect all cities in more economically developed countries but it has been a feature of many North American and north-west European cities since the 1970s. There is evidence, however, that the process is slowing or even reversing in European cities.

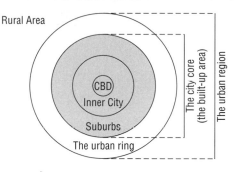

FIGURE 4.2
Suburbanisation and
Counterurbanisation

Migration from the CORE to the RING = **SUBURBANISATION:**
Migration from the URBAN REGION to the RURAL AREAS or smaller towns = **COUNTERURBANISATION:**

The city core: The built-up area of the city.

The urban ring: Semi-rural area around the city containing countryside, villages and perhaps small towns.

The urban region: This comprises the core and the ring. This is the area bound together by the daily flows of commuters and by movements

Urbanisation in 19th Century Britain

Although Britain's larger cities have been experiencing counterurbanisation since the 1970s the process of urbanisation has clearly been important in the past. In 1750 only about 15% of the population lived in towns of 10,000 or more. Rapid urbanisation began in the late eighteenth century and continued through the nineteenth century. For example, Birmingham grew from 71,000 in 1800 to 233,000 in 1850. Bradford grew eight fold in the same period from 13,000 to 104,000. This rapid growth was partly a result of overall natural increase with Britain's total population quadrupling from 10 million to 40 million between 1800 and 1900. However, it was also a result of industrialisation and economic development. New technology such as steam power led to the industrial revolution and the development of factories. People migrated from rural areas to work in the new factories and this accelerated the process of urbanisation. So while much of the less economically developed world has been undergoing industrialisation and urbanisation over the last few decades of the twentieth century the process in the most economically advanced countries occurred between the late eighteenth century and mid-twentieth century.

Filtering or Centrifugal Movement

Burgess referred to this process of movement outwards in his concentric model (see pages 9 and 10) although he used the terms *invasion* and *succession*. Burgess saw the outward movement of households towards the periphery of the city as an 'invasion' by people of an adjacent concentric zone.

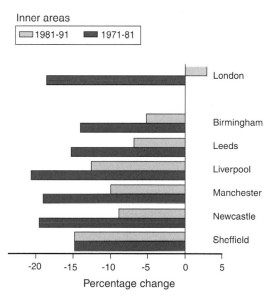

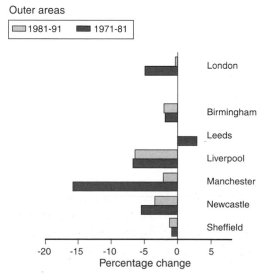

FIGURE 4.3 Population change in inner and outer areas of several British cities, 1971–1991

FIGURE 4.4 The life cycle model

Stage in life cycle	Housing needs/aspirations
1 Pre-child stage	Relatively cheap, central city apartment
2 Child-bearing	Renting of single family dwelling close to apartment zone
3 Child-rearing	Ownership of relatively new suburban home
4 Child-launching	Same areas as (3) or perhaps move to higher status area
5 Post-child	Marked by residential stability
6 Late life	Institution/apartment/live with children

Notice that in stages 1 and 2 the inner city is the most likely location for a home since most cheaper rented housing is found in the inner city. Stages 3, 4 and 5 are most likely to be in the outer city. However, it is important to note that the right hand column is headed 'housing needs or aspirations'. In other words, it shows the type of housing people may desire but not necessarily achieve.

There are two main 'driving forces' behind centrifugal movement.
1 Changes in lifestyle associated with the **family life cycle** (see Figure 4.4).
2 The desire for a better quality environment and a higher socio-economic status.
Figure 4.5 shows how filtering relates to the processes of suburbanisation and migration into a city.

Inner City Decline
Inner city decline refers to the decline of population in inner city areas caused by suburbanisation. The term is also used in a wider sense to refer to the economic and environmental deterioration of inner city areas. This is one of the most serious problems facing cities in more economically developed countries.

Gentrification or Reurbanisation
Gentrification is the reverse of filtering and the reverse of inner city decline. It is the movement of high income middle-class or professional households into inner city neighbourhoods. The importance of gentrification as a process varies greatly from city to city and may only affect small parts of an inner city. The term '**reurbanisation**' can also be used to describe this process, although reurbanisation could involve the movement of *any* socio-economic group into the inner city or the city centre.

Relationships between the processes
The five processes described are inter-related. For example:

■ the processes of counterurbanisation, suburbanisation and filtering can all contribute to inner city decline by shifting population and resources away from the inner city.
■ inner city decline can, in turn, encourage further counterurbanisation, suburbanisation and filtering.
■ gentrification counteracts suburbanisation, counterurbanisation, filtering and inner city decline.

FIGURE 4.5 The relationship between suburbanisation and filtering, or centrifugal movement

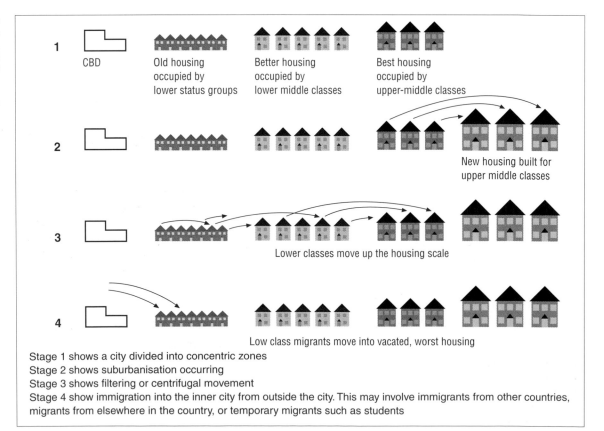

Stage 1 shows a city divided into concentric zones
Stage 2 shows suburbanisation occurring
Stage 3 shows filtering or centrifugal movement
Stage 4 show immigration into the inner city from outside the city. This may involve immigrants from other countries, migrants from elsewhere in the country, or temporary migrants such as students

Process	Examples of socio-economic impacts	Examples of environmental impacts	Examples of political impacts	You can find out more about this process in:
Suburbanisation	Resources have to be allocated to providing new infrastructure, such as roads and water supply in the new suburbs. Creates greater inequality in cities as those on higher incomes move to the new suburbs while low income households are 'trapped' in the inner city.	Loss of rural environment as new housing is built on green field sites. Increase in traffic as growing numbers of people commute from commuter villages and new suburbs into the city each day.	Opposition to new housing estates from local communities who live on the edge of the city. Political pressure from developers to allow building on Green Belts and other protected countryside	Chapter 11
Counterurbanisation	Middle-class migrants from the cities change the socio-economic structure of the rural population. May create tension between indigenous rural residents and new migrants from urban areas.	Change in the appearance of villages as newcomers improve or modernise rural housing. Increase in traffic in rural areas as growing numbers of people commute to the city for work or for services.	Changing voting patterns in rural areas. People from urban areas are traditionally less likely to vote for the Conservative Party.	Chapter 11
Filtering or centrifugal movement	In extreme cases, may contribute to the creation of ghettos as the more mobile households move out of inner city areas and ethnic minorities concentrate in the inner city.	Lack of investment in inner city housing since inner cities are dominated by low income groups or by people who intend to move to the outer city in the near future. Housing deteriorates.		Chapter 7
Inner city decline	Concentration of deprived households in the inner city. A demoralisation of the inner city community as the better qualified and more affluent groups move out.	Dereliction as housing and industrial buildings are abandoned. Poorly maintained infrastructure.	Political pressure to allocate greater government funding to inner city areas. Government concern about unrest and crime in the inner city.	Chapter 7
Gentrification	Tension between the traditional working class inhabitants and the middle-class newcomers. A change in the nature of shops, pubs, and other services as the local population becomes more professional or middle class.	Improvement in the standard and maintenance of inner city housing. Greater investment in the environment of local shopping centres.	Inner city population may become more politically influential on the local council as more educated and articulate groups move in.	Chapter 10

FIGURE 4.6 An overview of the main urban population processes

CASE STUDY

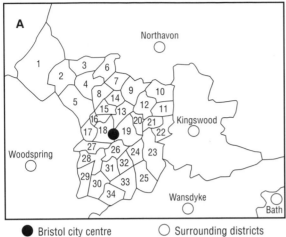

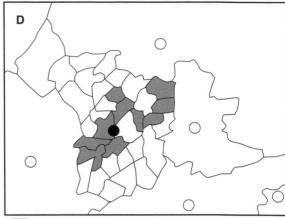

Areas with a 50% or greater increase in the proportion of households in socio-economic group I (professional) (1981 - 91)

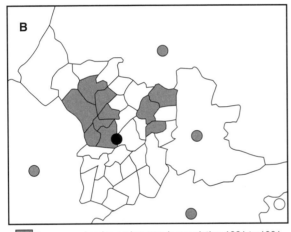

Areas experiencing an increase in population 1981 to 1991

Areas experiencing an decrease in population 1981 to 1991

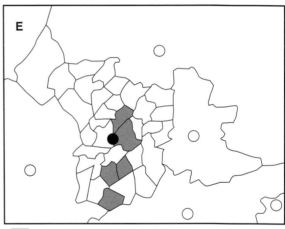

Areas with the worst unemployment: an indicator of deprivation or poverty

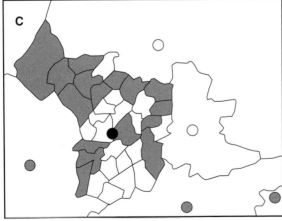

Areas where the proportion of people aged 60 or over is greater than the Bristol average

FIGURE 4.7 Population data for Bristol: Map A, the Bristol wards; Map B, population change 1981 to 1991; Map C, percentage population aged over 60; Map D, percentage of households in socio-economic group 1 (professionals); Map E, unemployment

STUDENT ACTIVITY 4.1

Study Figure 4.7 which shows demographic (i.e. population) data for the Bristol area. The data for the city of Bristol is shown at *ward* level, while the data for areas outside the city is shown at *district council* level. Map E provides an indication of the most deprived wards in the city.

1   Is there any evidence to either support or reject the presence of the following processes in the city?:
(a) Suburbanisation
(b) Counterurbanisation
(c) Inner city decline
(d) Gentrification
2   What, if any, additional data would you need to be certain whether or not these processes are occurring in the city?
3   Is there any evidence in Figure 4.7 to support the Family Life Cycle model?

5

UNFAIR CITIES: URBAN INEQUALITY

Key Ideas

■ All cities contain considerable inequality. Many cities are highly divided or segregated because affluent groups and deprived groups tend to concentrate in different areas within a city.

■ Some deprived areas experience a range of economic, social and environmental disadvantages. These areas suffer from *multiple deprivation*.

■ A variety of indicators can be used to measure and map inequality.

Urban inequality

All cities contain considerable inequality. This inequality is a reflection of national inequalities. For example, Figure 5.1 shows income inequality in the UK. In the UK 50% of the population owns 93% of the wealth leaving the poorest 50% with just 7% of the wealth. Poverty is also concentrated geographically or spatially (see Figure 5.2). In a society showing such inequality it is not surprising that enormous contrasts in quality of life can be found within individual cities.

Why do the wealthy and poor concentrate in particular districts?

In any city there may be a complex set of reasons why wealthy and poor areas are found in particular locations. Clearly, many of the reasons are related to the type of housing. Developers, planners, architects and other decision-makers design and build houses with a particular market in mind. Also, wealthy groups have the freedom to 'shop around' for the most desirable housing and environments, while the poorest have no option but to live in the least desirable housing. Wealthy groups in society are often willing to pay more for locations well away from areas of deprivation in order to set themselves apart from the urban poor.

The location of the types of housing likely to appeal to those who can shop around is related to the way in which cities develop over time. The urban models described in Chapter 3 help here because they are concerned with the processes which lead to the location of different types of residential area.

The type of housing, however, is only a partial explanation since:

■ the socio-economic groups living in a particular neighbourhood will change over time (think, for example, of a large detached house built in the nineteenth century for a wealthy family which is now in an inner city location, has been poorly maintained and is sub-divided into rented flats).
■ it is often possible to find two neighbourhoods comprising housing of a similar type and age yet one is deprived while the other is relatively affluent.

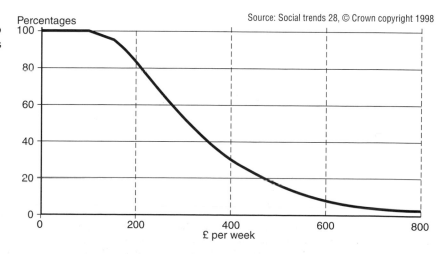

FIGURE 5.1 Proportion of full-time employees earning above different gross weekly earnings in the UK

1. Liverpool
2. Newham
3. Manchester
4. Hackney
5. Birmingham
6. Tower Hamlets
7. Sandwell
8. Southwark
9. Knowsley
10. Islington
11. Greenwich
12. Lambeth
13. Haringey
14. Lewisham
15. Barking and Dagenham
16. Nottingham
17. Camden
18. Hammersmith
    & Fulham
19. Newcastle
    upon Tyne
20. Brent
21. Sunderland
22. Waltham Forest
23. Salford
24. Middlesbrough
25. Sheffield
26. Hull
27. Wolverhampton
28. Bradford
29. Rochdale
30. Wandsworth
31. Walsall
32. Leicester
33. Oldham
34. Hartlepool
35. Doncaster
36. Coventry
37. Blackburn
    with Darwen
38. Bolton
39. Blackpool
40. Leeds
41. City of Westminster
42. Kensington & Chelsea
43. Burnley
44. Preston

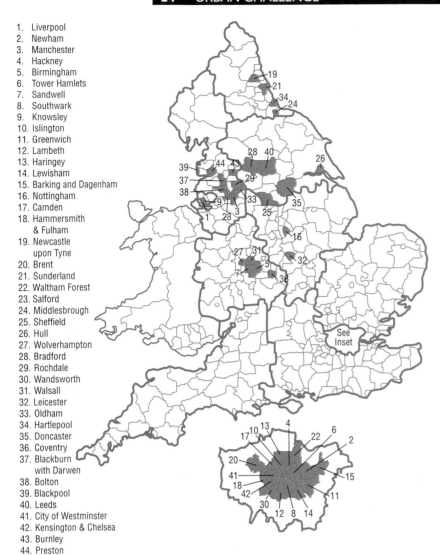

Produced by the GIS Unit, Dept. of Environment, Transport & the Regions. Crown Copyright 1998.

FIGURE 5.2 The 44 most deprived local authorities in the UK according to the 1998 Index of Local Deprivation – the districts are listed in descending order of deprivation

FIGURE 5.3 Urban poverty in New York

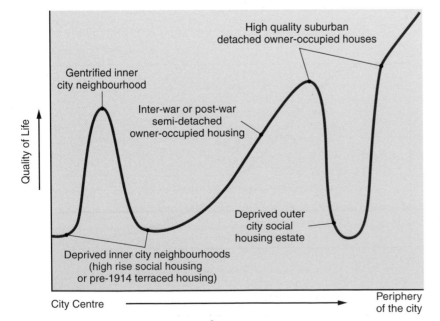

FIGURE 5.4 Urban inequality: a model of variations in quality of life within a British city

An understanding of processes such as inner city decline (Chapter 7) and gentrification (Chapter 10) is also needed if we are to explain why specific neighbourhoods become poor or wealthy.

Types of inequality

Figure 5.5 shows an example of geographical or spatial inequality. Wealth and income are only two aspects of inequality. Four broad categories of inequality can be identified:

1 Economic
2 Social
3 Environmental
4 Political.

Figure 5.6 defines each of these categories and suggests ways in which each type could be measured or mapped. In reality, it may be difficult to obtain precise data for some of the indicators without specialist research, but some data is readily available. The case study in Chapter 3 shows how data can be obtained and used to map and measure quality of life variations in a city.

Some important terms

When analysing urban inequality a number of key terms are useful.

Standard of living

This refers to a household's level of income and their ability to pay for consumer goods, housing, leisure and services.

Quality of life

This is usually used to refer, not only to a household's standard of living, but also to the quality of the environment in which they live. For example, high levels of pollution or a high incidence of burglary can lower the quality of life.

Poverty

There are a variety of definitions of poverty. Peter Townsend, a well known social scientist, has defined it as follows:

> *Individuals, families and groups in the population can be said to be in poverty when they lack the resources to obtain the types of diet, participate in the activities and have the living conditions and amenities which are customary, or at least widely encouraged or approved, in the societies to which they belong. Their resources are so seriously below those commanded by the average individual or family that they are, in effect, excluded from ordinary living patterns, customs and activities.*
>
> P. Townsend (1979) *Poverty in the UK*

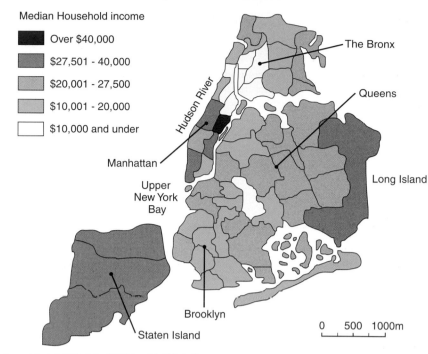

Median Household income

- Over $40,000
- $27,501 - 40,000
- $20,001 - 27,500
- $10,001 - 20,000
- $10,000 and under

The Bronx

Queens

Hudson River

Manhattan

Upper New York Bay

Long Island

Brooklyn

Staten Island

0   500   1000m

From: J Borja & M Castells (1997) Local & Global: Management of Cities in the Information Age, Earthscan

FIGURE 5.5 Inequality in New York City

Deprivation

A deprived area is one in which the population has a quality of life which is below the minimum regarded as acceptable by a particular society at a particular time.

Multiple deprivation

A neighbourhood suffering from multiple deprivation is one in which the population is deprived in a range of different ways.

Social segregation

This is the spatial or geographical separation of different social groups. It is where wealthy groups live in separate areas to poor groups.

FIGURE 5.6 Categories of inequality

Category of inequality	Definition	Examples of indicators which can be used to measure or map inequality within a city
Economic	Inequality in the ownership of wealth or income	1. Percentage of the population relying on State benefits 2. Percentage of the population living in owner-occupied housing
Social	Inequality in lifestyle or opportunity	1. Percentage of the population suffering from poor health 2. Percentage of the population aged over 16 in full-time education
Environmental	Inequality in the environmental quality of residential areas	1. Incidence of litter, graffiti and vandalism 2. Levels of atmospheric pollution
Political	Inequality in access to decision-making processes	1. Percentage of the electorate voting in elections 2. Percentage of the population participating in the local community (e.g. being a school governor)

Ethnicity and inequality

In many cities inequality and ethnic differences are closely linked. Ethnic minorities often suffer from discrimination in the job and housing markets which means that they are more likely to be unemployed, more likely to be on low incomes and more likely to be living in poor quality housing. This issue is examined in more detail on pages 36–38.

Consequences of inequality

Views on inequality vary. Those on the right of the political spectrum see inequality as an inevitable and desirable consequence of living in a free market economy, even if they do accept that the government should help the poorest groups. Those on the left see it as undesirable and believe that the government has a clear responsibility to reduce inequality. Most agree that extreme inequality and poverty can have a damaging effect on *social cohesion* and has the potential to cause crime and social disorder.

CASE STUDY

Key Map

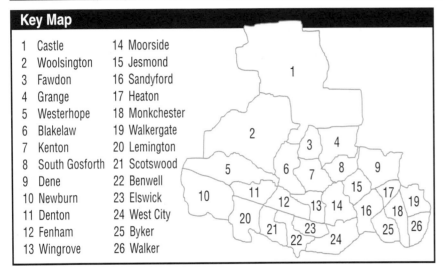

1	Castle	14	Moorside
2	Woolsington	15	Jesmond
3	Fawdon	16	Sandyford
4	Grange	17	Heaton
5	Westerhope	18	Monkchester
6	Blakelaw	19	Walkergate
7	Kenton	20	Lemington
8	South Gosforth	21	Scotswood
9	Dene	22	Benwell
10	Newburn	23	Elswick
11	Denton	24	West City
12	Fenham	25	Byker
13	Wingrove	26	Walker

Inequality in Newcastle-upon-Tyne

Study Figure 5.7 which maps 12 indicators of inequality in Newcastle-upon-Tyne.

FIGURE 5.7 Inequality in Newcastle-upon-Tyne

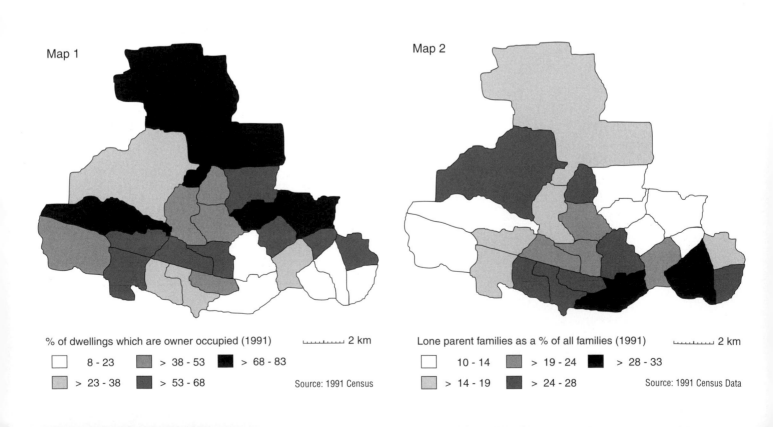

Map 1

% of dwellings which are owner occupied (1991)   ⌐⌐⌐⌐⌐ 2 km

☐ 8 - 23	
☐ > 23 - 38	
▨ > 38 - 53	
▦ > 53 - 68	
■ > 68 - 83	

Source: 1991 Census

Map 2

Lone parent families as a % of all families (1991)   ⌐⌐⌐⌐⌐ 2 km

☐ 10 - 14	
☐ > 14 - 19	
▨ > 19 - 24	
▦ > 24 - 28	
■ > 28 - 33	

Source: 1991 Census Data

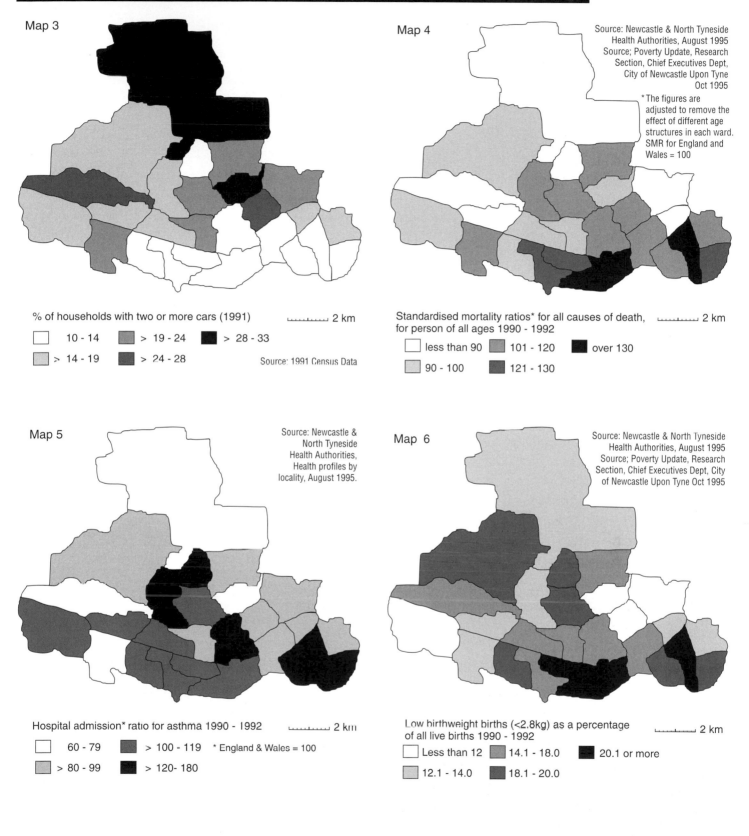

Map 3

% of households with two or more cars (1991)   ⌐⌐⌐⌐⌐⌐ 2 km

☐ 10 - 14   ▨ > 19 - 24   ■ > 28 - 33

▨ > 14 - 19   ▨ > 24 - 28   Source: 1991 Census Data

Map 4

Source: Newcastle & North Tyneside
Health Authorities, August 1995
Source; Poverty Update, Research
Section, Chief Executives Dept,
City of Newcastle Upon Tyne
Oct 1995

* The figures are
adjusted to remove the
effect of different age
structures in each ward.
SMR for England and
Wales = 100

Standardised mortality ratios* for all causes of death,   ⌐⌐⌐⌐⌐⌐ 2 km
for person of all ages 1990 - 1992

☐ less than 90   ▨ 101 - 120   ■ over 130

▨ 90 - 100   ▨ 121 - 130

Map 5

Source: Newcastle &
North Tyneside
Health Authorities,
Health profiles by
locality, August 1995.

Hospital admission* ratio for asthma 1990 - 1992   ⌐⌐⌐⌐⌐⌐ 2 km

☐ 60 - 79   ▨ > 100 - 119   * England & Wales = 100

▨ > 80 - 99   ■ > 120- 180

Map 6

Source: Newcastle & North Tyneside
Health Authorities, August 1995
Source; Poverty Update, Research
Section, Chief Executives Dept, City
of Newcastle Upon Tyne Oct 1995

Low birthweight births (<2.8kg) as a percentage   ⌐⌐⌐⌐⌐⌐ 2 km
of all live births 1990 - 1992

☐ Less than 12   ▨ 14.1 - 18.0   ■ 20.1 or more

▨ 12.1 - 14.0   ▨ 18.1 - 20.0

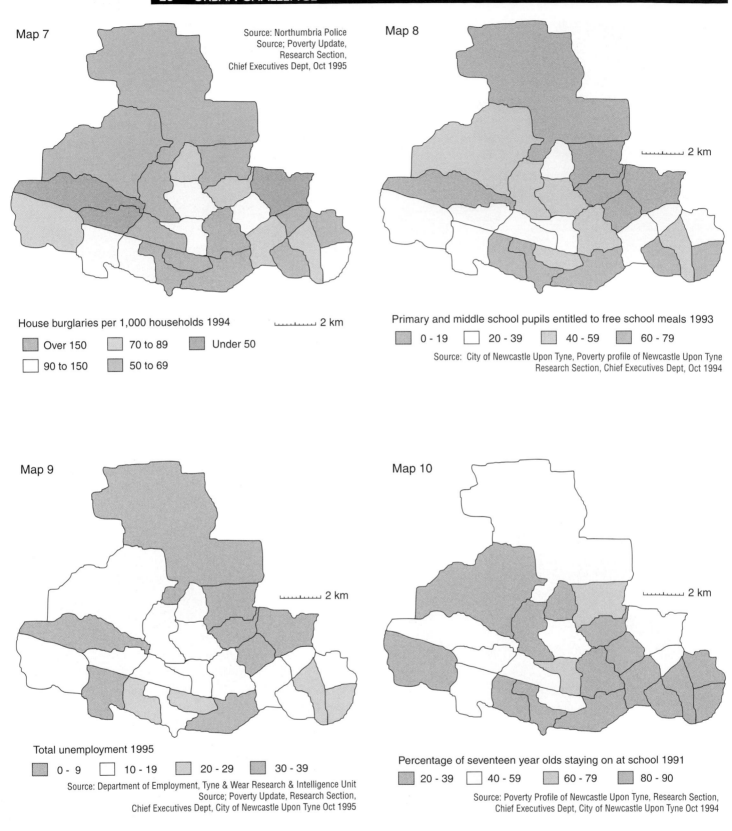

Map 7

Source: Northumbria Police
Source; Poverty Update,
Research Section,
Chief Executives Dept, Oct 1995

House burglaries per 1,000 households 1994 ⊢⊣⊢⊣⊢⊣ 2 km

- Over 150
- 90 to 150
- 70 to 89
- 50 to 69
- Under 50

Map 8

⊢⊣⊢⊣⊢⊣ 2 km

Primary and middle school pupils entitled to free school meals 1993

- 0 - 19
- 20 - 39
- 40 - 59
- 60 - 79

Source: City of Newcastle Upon Tyne, Poverty profile of Newcastle Upon Tyne
Research Section, Chief Executives Dept, Oct 1994

Map 9

⊢⊣⊢⊣⊢⊣ 2 km

Total unemployment 1995

- 0 - 9
- 10 - 19
- 20 - 29
- 30 - 39

Source: Department of Employment, Tyne & Wear Research & Intelligence Unit
Source; Poverty Update, Research Section,
Chief Executives Dept, City of Newcastle Upon Tyne Oct 1995

Map 10

⊢⊣⊢⊣⊢⊣ 2 km

Percentage of seventeen year olds staying on at school 1991

- 20 - 39
- 40 - 59
- 60 - 79
- 80 - 90

Source: Poverty Profile of Newcastle Upon Tyne, Research Section,
Chief Executives Dept, City of Newcastle Upon Tyne Oct 1994

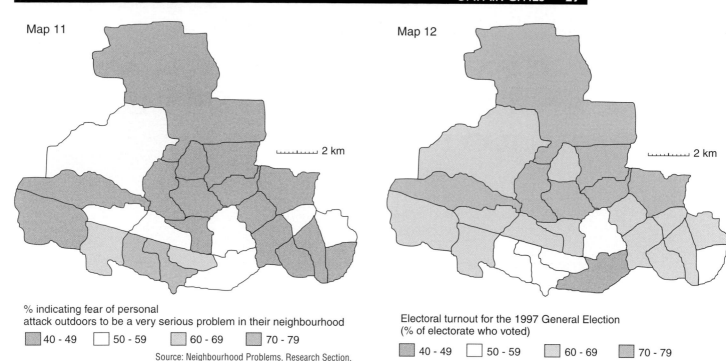

Map 11

% indicating fear of personal
attack outdoors to be a very serious problem in their neighbourhood

⬛ 40 - 49   ⬜ 50 - 59   ▨ 60 - 69   ▦ 70 - 79

Source: Neighbourhood Problems, Research Section,
Chief Executive's Dept., City of Newcastle Upon Tyne April 1995

Map 12

Electoral turnout for the 1997 General Election
(% of electorate who voted)

⬛ 40 - 49   ⬜ 50 - 59   ▨ 60 - 69   ▦ 70 - 79

Source: City of Newcastle Upon Tyne Electoral Registration Office

---

STUDENT ACTIVITY 5.1

1 Categorise the maps shown in Figure 5.7 into economic, social and environmental indicators.
2 Analyse the spatial patterns of inequality revealed by the maps. Your analysis should include reference to:
- the areas with the highest quality of life
- the areas with the lowest quality of life
- any areas suffering from multiple deprivation
- the extent of social segregation in the city
- possible reasons for the patterns
3 Using either a scatter graph or a statistical method (such as Spearman's Rank Correlation Coefficient) evaluate the relationship between unemployment and the Standard Mortality Ratio in the city (see Figure 5.8). Suggest reasons for the relationship you find.
4 What are the possible consequences of the inequalities you have described?

Ward	% unemployment (1995)	Standard Mortality Ratio* (1990–92)
Benwell	18	123
Blakelaw	10	107
Byker	18	111
Castle	5	73
Dene	8	76
Denton	11	85
Elswick	28	130
Fawdon	16	87
Fenham	12	90
Grange	8	102
Heaton	13	87
Jesmond	9	107
Kenton	14	103
Lemington	9	108
Monkchester	23	131
Moorside	20	101
Newburn	10	97
Sandyford	18	102
Scotswood	22	93
South Gosforth	5	93
Walker	24	130
Walkergate	12	107
West City	39	138
Westerhope	5	75
Wingrove	15	90
Woolsington	16	96

Average Standard Mortality Rates for England and Wales = 100

FIGURE 5.8
Unemployment and mortality in Newcastle upon Tyne

6
URBAN REVOLUTION: CHANGE IN CENTRAL AND EASTERN EUROPEAN CITIES

Key Ideas

■ Between 1945 and 1989 most countries in Central and Eastern Europe were run by communist governments. Communist cities were planned in such a way as to promote equality and collectivism.
■ A number of important differences emerged between Western European and Eastern European cities during the period of Communism.

■ Since the collapse of the communist system in 1989 the cities in Eastern Europe have changed rapidly. They are increasingly similar to cities in Western Europe. This rapid change has brought considerable benefits but has also created serious problems.

Communist Eastern Europe

For most of the period between the end of the Second World War and 1989, Europe was divided by a heavily defended frontier referred to as the **Iron Curtain**. To the west of the Iron Curtain countries were run on capitalist and democratic principles. The countries to the east of the Iron Curtain had centrally planned economies and communist systems in which individualism was discouraged and personal freedom was severely limited.

The Collapse of Communism

By the late 1980s Communism had developed major weaknesses. These weaknesses led to a very rapid and largely peaceful collapse of Communism throughout Eastern Europe in 1989 and in the Soviet Union in 1991. In place of Communism the new governments adopted the political and economic ideas of Western Europe and their countries underwent a revolution in the way in which they were organised.

Communist urban planning

Communist urban planners were operating under a very different system to their counterparts in Western Europe.

One of the biggest differences was that in Eastern Europe the State owned and managed most of the economic activity, infrastructure, property and land. In Western Europe and most other more economically developed countries private companies or individuals own most of the industrial activity, shops, housing and land. In Eastern Europe most of the housing built before the communist take-over was nationalised (i.e. taken over by the government) and all new property was built by the State. This meant that city planners had complete control over new development and existing property.

FIGURE 6.1 A model of an Eastern European communist city 1945–89

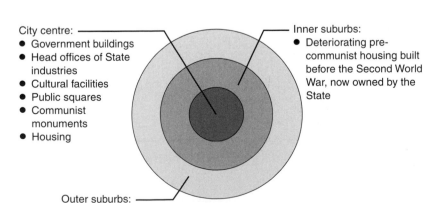

City centre:
● Government buildings
● Head offices of State industries
● Cultural facilities
● Public squares
● Communist monuments
● Housing

Inner suburbs:
● Deteriorating pre-communist housing built before the Second World War, now owned by the State

Outer suburbs:
● Communist high-rise housing estates - each with its own shopping, education, health and community facilities
● Industrial zones

State ownership also meant that there was no free market in land and property. Land could not be bought and sold by individuals or firms and most housing was rented from the State. This meant, in effect, that housing and land had the same value throughout the city. This was very different to cities in free market countries where housing and land in more desirable locations command a higher price.

Urban planners in Eastern Europe had the task of redesigning cities in order to promote communist ideology. Communist planners gave very little attention to the needs or desires of individuals. They were interested in encouraging **collectivism**, meaning that society or the community was given more importance than the individual. They also wanted to promote equality in housing and other services.

For these reasons Eastern European cities had a number of distinctive features:

■ All housing was cheap. Rents were subsidised by the government so that everybody, regardless of their income, could afford a dwelling. (In any case, wage differentials were a lot smaller than in Western Europe and everybody was guaranteed a job.) All new housing was built to similar standards so that, for example, a university professor or doctor would live in a similar dwelling to an unskilled manual worker.

■ Most housing built after the communist take-over was in the form of high-rise estates. The planners believed that such estates would promote a strong community and discourage individualism.

■ The State was not interested in encouraging **consumerism**. They felt that a large choice of goods in the shops would encourage inequality and individualism. City centres in Eastern Europe contained very few large shops. Instead, city centres were dominated by government offices, housing, cultural facilities such as museums, and monuments celebrating Communism. Large public squares were also built for parades and other State sponsored events.

■ Private cars were discouraged. Instead, the planners developed cheap public transport systems. Traffic congestion was not a problem in Eastern European cities.

■ The communist planners did little to maintain older buildings which they believed did not reflect communist ideas. This meant that many historic buildings in the central areas of cities were allowed to deteriorate and pre-communist housing was also poorly maintained.

The collapse of Communism and its impact on cities

When the communist system collapsed in 1989 and the political and economic ideas of Western Europe were adopted by the new governments it was inevitable that cities would undergo rapid change. The features of Eastern European cities which had distinguished them from cities in Western Europe started to disappear:

■ land, housing and firms have been privatised. In other words, they have been taken over by private companies or individuals

■ a market in land and property has emerged. Land and buildings in the more desirable locations are fetching high prices while those in less attractive locations are much cheaper. This is increasing social segregation as wealthier people move to the most desirable neighbourhoods and poorer households are excluded from better quality housing

■ city centres have changed particularly rapidly. A thriving consumer economy has developed. Large numbers of new shops have opened. Advertising hoardings, which were unknown under Communism, are now commonplace

■ in some cities, such as Prague and Budapest, international tourism has grown rapidly. New restaurants and hotels have opened. Many of the hotels are owned by transnational firms

■ car ownership is growing. Traffic congestion and pollution are increasing

■ many factories have closed. The ending of State subsidies and the opening of Eastern Europe to international competition has meant that many Eastern European enterprises were forced to close. This has created unemployment in societies which are used to full employment.

CASE STUDY

Prague, capital of the Czech Republic

Prague had developed since the 1940s as a typical communist city. However, it has to be remembered that the *appearance* and *morphology* of the existing areas of the city remained largely unchanged even though much of the existing housing was nationalised (i.e. taken over by the State). Housing built after the 1940s was designed according to communist ideology and consisted of large high rise estates or 'new towns' in the outer suburbs.

The collapse of Communism in Czechoslovakia in 1989 is known as 'The Velvet Revolution'. (Czechoslovakia split into two countries, the Czech Republic and Slovakia, in 1993). Since the Velvet Revolution, Prague has experienced rapid change as Communism has been replaced by capitalism and the free market has taken over from State planning.

FIGURE 6.2a Old Town Square in Prague's historic core

FIGURE 6.2b View from Prague Castle in Central Prague

FIGURE 6.2c High rise housing on the outskirts of Prague

FIGURE 6.3 Proportion of households with the main wage earner in a manual occupation

Zone	1930	1960	2000
Historic Core	26%	40%	?
Inner Suburbs	26%	40%	?
Outer Suburbs	44%	47%	?

FIGURE 6.4 Alternatives for 2000 in Figure 6.3

	A	B	C
Historic Core	40%	40%	25%
Inner Suburbs	40%	55%	55%
Outer Suburbs	45%	35%	30%

HISTORIC CORE
Population: 65,000
This zone has more than 1400 protected historic buildings and was designated as being of world-wide importance by UNESCO (a branch of the United Nations) in 1992. Many of the historic buildings are threatened by decades of poor maintenance during the communist period, lack of resources for renovation, atmospheric pollution and unsympathetic commercial development. Environmental quality is also threatened by the growing use of cars.

Most of the dwellings in this zone are flats in historic buildings and many lack basic amenities. Their poor quality meant that during the communist period the local population was dominated by elderly people and poorer families. More mobile or better paid residents moved out to the new estates in the outer suburbs.

This zone has recently seen considerable redevelopment and renovation for new hotels, shops and restaurants. Average rents for commercial premises were 50 times greater in 1992 than in 1989. Some buildings have been refurbished to create expensive high quality flats. Many of these have been taken by migrants from Western Europe.

The area attracts millions of foreign tourists each year and can become very congested.

PRAGUE:
Since 1989 100,000 properties have been returned by the government to their pre-communism owners. Others have been sold to individuals or private firms.

70% of journeys to work are by public transport including the underground metro network.

About 80 million tourists visit the Czech Republic each year and most of these stay in Prague (only London and Paris have a greater number of tourists). In 1996 they spent £4 billion. Between 1989 and 1997 the number of hotel beds increased from 12,000 to 60,000.

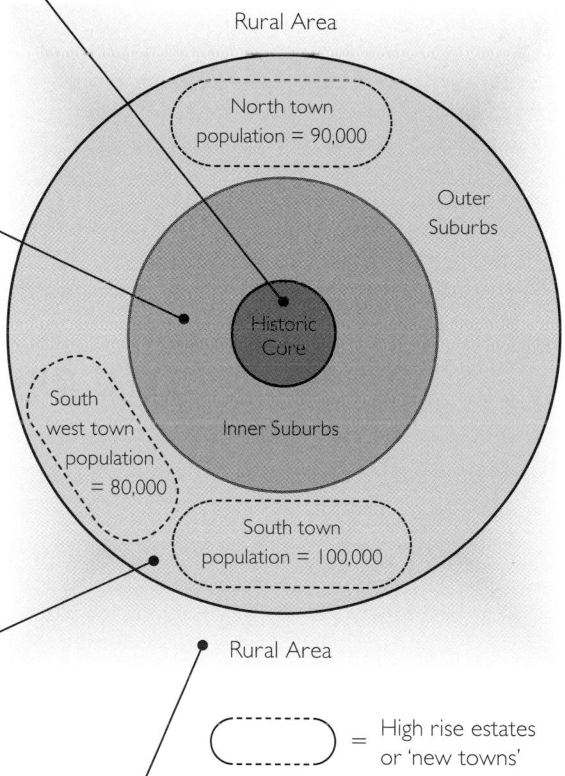

INNER SUBURBS
Population: 600,000
This zone has a declining population and largely consists of high density housing in need of modernisation. This buildings mainly date from the 1850 to 1940 period. Average housing rents are three times greater than they were before the Velvet Revolution.

OUTER SUBURBS
Population: 500,000
This area is dominated by the three large high rise housing estates or 'new towns' built in the 1950s and 1960s by the communist government. These estates were planned to encourage 'collective living' and were socially mixed with manual workers and people in high status occupations sharing the same blocks. The estates are visually monotonous and unattractive.

Rents increased three fold between 1989 and 1992. With the emergence of a free market in housing it is likely that people with higher paid jobs will move out of these estates.

The outer suburbs also contain individual family houses. The number of these is now rising as the demand for owner-occupied houses increases.

Some of the new houses are too expensive for most local people and they are being purchased by migrants from Western Europe.

FIGURE 6.5 Urban change in Prague

Rural Area

North town population = 90,000

Outer Suburbs

Historic Core

South west town population = 80,000

Inner Suburbs

South town population = 100,000

Rural Area

= High rise estates or 'new towns'

SURROUNDING RURAL AREA
In the countryside around Prague there are 140,000 cottages owned by Prague residents and used for holidays and weekends. More than 25% of Prague households own a rural cottage.

7
ESTATES OF THE EXCLUDED: SOCIAL HOUSING ESTATES AND GHETTOS

Key Ideas

■ All cities contain neighbourhoods where there is a concentration of poverty and deprivation. These areas are usually either (i) inner city or outer city social housing estates or (ii) run-down old inner city districts.
■ In many cities the outer city social housing estates now have the worst levels of deprivation and these estates pose severe problems for residents and for decision-makers.
■ Deprived housing estates suffer from a range of interconnected social, economic and environmental problems. Residents and decision-makers have found it difficult to reverse the resulting cycle of decline.

■ As the estates have declined those residents who are able to move out have done so. Only those residents who are unable to move out due to poverty or other disadvantages remain. The remaining residents may feel excluded from mainstream society.
■ In extreme cases outer city social housing estates and inner city districts may become ghettos when a large proportion of the residents are from ethnic minorities. Ghettos are formed as a consequence of a range of processes which increase the spatial concentration of ethnic minorities.

Inner city and estate decline

The 'Inner City'

Until the 1970s the most deprived urban neighbourhoods were found almost entirely in the inner city. These slum neighbourhoods consisted of sub-standard nineteenth-century housing (or older in some European cities). Most residents rented their houses from private landlords, many of whom let the housing deteriorate. By the 1970s the term **inner city** had become linked in most British people's minds to deprivation, decline and unrest. This image was strengthened when, in the early 1980s, a series of riots erupted in inner cities across Britain.

In the 1950s and 1960s decision-makers attempted to tackle the 'inner city problem' by demolishing much of the sub-standard housing and replacing it with up-to-date **social housing**. Social housing is rented housing provided by the government, local authority, housing association or other public agency. Some of this social housing was built in the inner city on land cleared of old

housing but much of it was built as outer city or peripheral housing estates. However, during the 1970s and 1980s many of these social housing estates also began to experience serious problems.

By the end of the 1990s the pattern of deprivation in most British cities had changed significantly compared to the 1970s. In many cities it is the outer city social housing estates as well as the inner city areas that are showing serious social, economic and environmental problems. Nearly all of the major disturbances or riots in the early 1990s occurred in outer city estates. Particularly serious were the disturbances in Meadowell in Tyneside and in Blackbird Leys in Oxford, both in 1991. While some of the poorest and most disadvantaged housing areas continue to be found in the inner city, they also are predominately found in social housing estates built in the 1950s and 1960s rather than older areas. By 1991 only 40% of the heads of households in British social housing estates were earning an income from work compared with 70% in other types of housing.

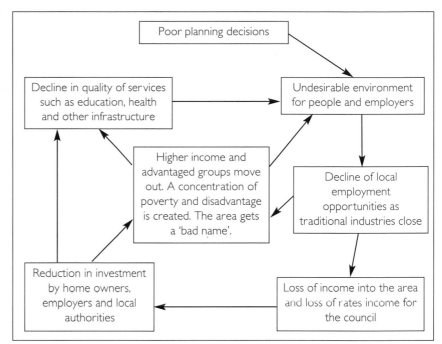

FIGURE 7.1 The process of inner city decline

The term 'inner city' continues to be used but it tends to be used in a 'looser' sense to refer to all deprived areas whether they are geographically in the inner or in the outer city. Much of this chapter focuses on social housing estates but the problems and many of the processes which are outlined can also apply to old inner city neighbourhoods.

Why do estates decline?

Figures 7.1 and 7.2 illustrate the circular or cyclical nature of the processes which lead to a 'downward spiral' in deprived areas. They show the close linkage between social, economic and environmental factors.

Specific reasons for the serious decline of many social housing estates in Britain include the following:

■ Since the early 1980s council tenants have had the right to buy their council houses but buyers have only been interested in the better quality housing in the more popular estates. This has meant that people who have no choice but to live in social housing are increasingly concentrated in the worst housing on the least popular estates.

■ The worst estates acquire a 'bad name'. In other words, they become **stigmatised** and residents who are able to move out do so as soon as they can. This further increases the concentration of disadvantaged families. This can lead to a process sometimes called '**addressism**'. This is where residents of a particular estate find it difficult to get a job because employers discriminate against them on the basis of their address.

■ Many social housing tenants depend on unskilled manual work because of their lack of qualifications and experience. However, the number of these jobs has declined particularly rapidly during the 1980s and 1990s due to deindustrialisation and cuts in local council services.

■ Most social housing estates were built in the 1960s using new prefabricated building methods and new types of design. By the 1980s design faults and inadequate maintenance meant that much of this housing was suffering structural and other problems.

■ Social housing estates have an above average proportion of single parents and teenagers, and as in the rest of society the number of single parent households is rising. In Easterhouse in Glasgow, for example, the number of single parent households increased from 1072 in 1981 to 2567 in 1991 despite a falling population in the estate. This reduces the proportion of adults who can contribute most to the community, limits opportunities for obtaining employment since child care is more difficult to organise, and increases dependency on State benefits. In a few estates adult authority has broken down and groups of teenagers are out of control.

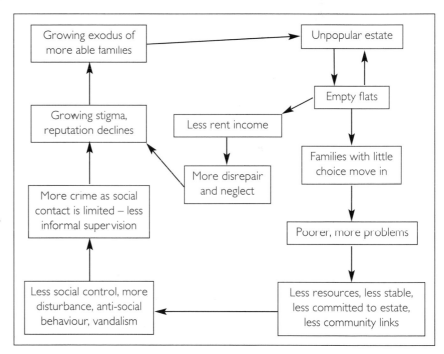

■ The increase in the proportion of jobs which are part-time or insecure and the increase since the early 1980s in the amount of long-term and recurrent unemployment have also had a damaging effect on the poorest estates.

■ Disadvantage and deprivation tends to be passed on to the next generation as young people are more likely to fail in the education system. In 1994 an average of 8% of 16-year-olds in England and Wales failed to obtain any GCSE qualifications, but the figure for schools linked to social housing estates was 23%. Truancy rates are also generally higher on the estates.

FIGURE 7.2 The downward spiral in a social housing estate

Deprived estates in French cities

Many other cities in more economically developed countries have similar problems. For example, 15% of the population of Paris live in large peripheral social housing estates called **grands ensembles**. The estates were built in the 1960s and typically contain about 10,000 dwellings. Many have concentrations of ethnic minority groups and the unemployed. The more affluent residents have moved to the more popular suburbs of owner-occupied housing. For example, the Sarcelles estate on the northern edge of the city gained a poor reputation almost as soon as it was built in the 1960s. Problems included poor transport links to the city centre, inadequate shopping and community facilities, badly designed housing and inadequate maintenance. Boredom, alienation and depression became common ailments on the estate and sufferers became known as 'Sarcellites'.

Other French cities have experienced similar problems. In the 1960s and early 1970s five giant peripheral housing schemes were built around the city of Lyon. One of these estates, 'Les Minguettes', contained 63 17-storey tower blocks and a number of eight-storey 'long blocks'. In 1981 and 1982 rioting erupted on the estate as groups of North African youths fought with police. While racial tensions were partially responsible for the violence a major factor was also the quality of life on the estate. The riots led to a range of government measures to tackle the estate's problems but this did not stop similar rioting breaking out in other estates in 1990 and 1994.

Social exclusion and the 'underclass'

Social exclusion is a term which is used to refer to the problems faced by the residents of deprived estates. People suffering from social exclusion can be defined as *people who are excluded from full participation in society because of their social or physical circumstances*. They may be excluded from jobs because of inadequate education, excluded from decent housing because of poverty, and excluded from a satisfactory quality of life because of a poor environment and high levels of crime. Social exclusion can lead to a sense of hopelessness which in turn can lead to a variety of other social problems such as crime, vandalism, social unrest and drug and alcohol abuse.

Social exclusion can also be linked to the concept of an **underclass**, although there is a controversy over whether an underclass really exists in Britain. An underclass can be defined as *a section of the population experiencing long-term exclusion from mainstream society*. In particular, people are excluded from the labour market. This may be due to inadequate experience, education and skills or because they choose not to seek appropriate employment. The underclass can be seen as a threat to the rest of society due to their dependence on illegal forms of income, their alienation from mainstream society and their disrespect for authority.

Ghettos

The formation of ghettos

In the USA the terms 'underclass' and 'social exclusion' are particularly associated with poor black Americans (or African Americans) living in ghettos. A ghetto can be defined as *an area of a city where the population is almost exclusively made up of an ethnic or cultural minority*.

Two of the most well known ghettos of the twentieth century have been The Bronx and Harlem, both black ghettos in New York. Ghettos have existed in American cities for many decades. In 1930 over 90% of the black population lived in areas where they formed 80% or more of the total population and levels of **segregation** (i.e. ethnic separation) remain similar today. Some sociologists and geographers use the term **hypersegregation** to describe the situation in some American cities.

Most European cities also show evidence of the concentration of ethnic minorities in particular neighbourhoods, although whether the level of concentration is high enough for them to be genuine ghettos is questionable.

Ghettos are often, but not always, concentrations of severe deprivation and social exclusion. Racism and discrimination cause higher levels of unemployment and lower income levels amongst ethnic minority groups, so they are more likely to be found living in poor housing. Ghettos are often located in neighbourhoods which have been abandoned by more affluent households. Levels of crime and unrest are often higher. For example, black American adolescents, many of whom live in ghettos, are nine times more likely to be murdered than their white counterparts.

The processes which create ethnic minority neighbourhoods are complex and the degree of racism and discrimination varies from country to country. Figure 7.3 summarises the main causes. The diagram indicates that some of the causes are a result of ethnic minorities 'opting' for segregation or separation from the majority population. However, this does not mean that they are necessarily *freely choosing* segregation, but rather that they may see segregation as the best response to racism. Ghettos tend to be fairly stable in their location and size but changes can occur over time. Some members of ethnic minority groups will obtain higher paid jobs or become more integrated into the majority population. This will give them the opportunity to move out of the ghetto to the more prosperous suburbs. This process can lead to the gradual 'outward spread' of the ethnic minority population, a process sometimes called **spillover**.

A process known in American cities as 'white flight' can also occur. If a small number of people from the ethnic minority population move into a residential area the existing majority population may fear that the value of their houses will fall as a result of racist attitudes. In an attempt to beat this fall in property prices a number of residents may put their houses on the market. The resulting glut of houses for sale leads to a rapid fall in prices. This will put more of the houses within reach of the poorer ethnic minority population from other neighbourhoods. This can lead to accelerating 'flight' of white people from the area and the eventual creation of a new ghetto.

Are there ghettos in British cities?

Figures 7.4 to 7.7 give an indication of the extent of ethnic segregation in British cities. Some of the tables use a measure called the **Index of Dissimilarity** (ID) to assess levels of segregation. IDs run from 0 (zero segregation) to 100 (total segregation).

Figure 7.5 shows that at ward level the highest concentration of ethnic minorities is found in Northcote ward in Ealing in London where 90% of the population is from ethnic minorities. Two other wards in the country (Spinney Hill in Leicester and Glebe in Ealing) have percentages above 80%. As Figure 7.5 indicates, concentration levels are lower when individual ethnic groups are measured separately. These figures are exceptionally high and unusual for the UK but in US cities concentrations of African Americans of 80% or more are common at *census tract* level (similar to ward level in Britain).

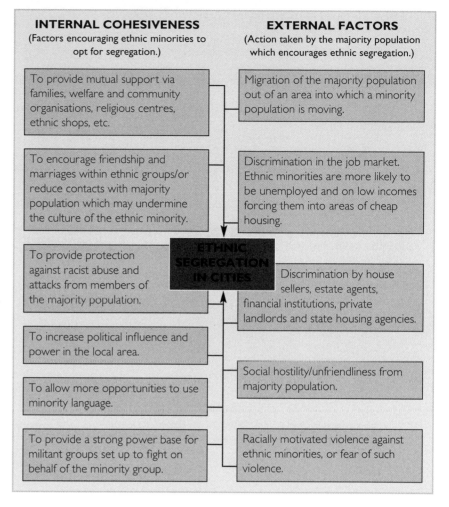

FIGURE 7.3 Causes of ethnic segregation in cities

One researcher has written:

Despite fears of following the African American model of inner-city segregation, the 1991 Census suggests rather more optimistic conclusions. Ghettos on the American model do not exist [in Britain] and, despite an unfavourable economic position and substantial evidence of continuing discrimination, the segregation trend amongst the Black Caribbean population in London is downwards.

(C. Peach (1996) 'Does Britain have Ghettos', in *Transactions of the Institute of British Geographers*)

	White	Black Caribbean	Black African	Black Other	Indian	Pakistani	Bangldeshi	Chinese
GREAT BRITAIN	94.5	0.9	0.4	0.3	1.5	0.9	0.3	0.3
Greater London	79.8	4.4	2.5	1.2	5.2	1.3	1.3	0.8
West Midlands	85.4	2.8	0.2	0.6	5.5	3.5	0.7	0.2
Greater Manchester	94.1	0.7	0.2	0.4	1.2	2.0	0.5	0.3
West Yorkshire	91.8	0.7	0.1	0.3	1.7	4.0	0.3	0.2

FIGURE 7.4 Ethnic population in four large British conurbations (1991)

FIGURE 7.5 Highest concentrations of ethnic minority population in Great Britain (1991)

Local council area with highest proportion of its population from ethnic minorities	Brent, London	45%
Ward with the highest proportion of its population from ethnic minority groups	Northcote in Ealing, London	90%
Ward with highest proportion of its population who are Black Caribbean	Roundwood in Brent, London	30%
Ward with the highest proportion of its population who are Indian	Northcote in Ealing, London	67%
Ward with the highest proportion of its population who are Bangladeshi	Spitalfields in Tower Hamlets, London	61%
Ward with the highest proportion of its population who are Indian	University ward in Bradford, West Yorkshire	53%

FIGURE 7.6 Indices of Dissimilarity (ID) for Pakistanis and Black Caribbeans in a selection of British Cities

City	Pakistani ID	Black Caribbean ID
London	54	49
Birmingham	74	54
Manchester	58	56
Sheffield	71	49
Bradford	63	47
Bristol	64	59
Glasgow	69	data not available
Leeds	64	69
Edinburgh	32	data not available
Leicester	56	38

Year	ID for people born in the Caribbean
1961	56
1971	49
1981	46
1991	41

FIGURE 7.7 Changes over time in the Index of Dissimilarity (ID) for people *born* in the Caribbean, now living in London (i.e. first generation immigrants). Calculated at ward level

Source: 1991 Census

FIGURE 7.8 Ethnic black Caribbean population as a percentage of total population in Greater London, 1991

CASE STUDY: EXAMPLES OF ESTATE DECLINE

The Ballymun Estate, Dublin and the Drumchapel Estate, Glasgow

Ballymun, Dublin

In many respects Ballymun suffers from all the problems of a typical deprived peripheral housing estate. However, within Ireland it is unique. It is the only high rise social housing estate in the country. In the 1960s and 1970s Ireland experienced rapid urban and economic growth and there was a high demand for housing. The idea of a modern high-rise estate built to tackle the housing shortage in Dublin appealed to many of the country's decision-makers. The Ballymun estate was built between 1966 and 1969 and contained seven 15-storey tower blocks, 19 eight-storey deck access blocks, 10 four-storey blocks and 400 houses. The estate was designed to house 20,000 people. Most of the new tenants came from demolished or sub-standard inner city housing.

Almost immediately the flats proved to be unpopular with a population totally unused to high rise living. Also, from the beginning the management and maintenance of the estate was inadequate. By the end of the 1970s Ballymun had gained a reputation for poor services, insecurity and deprivation. The situation was not helped by a government scheme designed to encourage social housing tenants to buy their home at a subsidised price. No one wanted to buy a flat in Ballymun and so tenants on higher incomes were keen to move to other estates to take advantage of the scheme. By 1989 there were 450 empty and boarded up flats.

The city council increasingly used the estate to house the most deprived households. Ballymun has less than 10% of the city's council housing but it housed 45% of the city's single parent families, 30% of households classed as homeless and 60% of the single male applicants for council housing. Many of the single males had previously lived in institutions of various kinds and had a long history of instability.

The high proportion of poorly supervised teenagers also created problems. Wear and tear on the estate increased and vandalism, graffiti and noise were widespread. Repair costs in the estate were much higher than on other estates in the city. The estate's shopping centre which had initially thrived became run-down and a location for drug-dealing.

In 1984 a number of local residents decided to take action against the estate's continuing decline. They formed the Ballymun Community Coalition to fight for improvements to the estate and over the following years a number of initiatives were launched to tackle the estate's problems. New lettings policies were introduced, environmental improvements carried out and a variety of projects launched to tackle the estate's social problems.

FIGURE 7.9 Ballymun, Dublin

By 1995 there had been a range of radical improvements although there were still serious problems. The estate was still dominated by deprivation and the flats were suffering from structural problems but it no longer had the reputation of being the worst estate in Dublin and there was a waiting list of people wanting to live there.

FIGURE 7.10 Partially boarded up housing in Drumchapel, Glasgow

Drumchapel, Glasgow

Drumchapel was one of a number of estates built on the edge of Glasgow in the 1950s and 1960s. Others included Easterhouse, Castlemilk and Pollok. The estates were built quickly and on a tight budget. Little attention was given to the design and layout of the estates or to the provision of local amenities.

Drumchapel's inherent problems were made much worse in the late 1970s and 1980s by the rapid deindustrialisation occurring in Glasgow and the resulting rise in unemployment and poverty. By the 1990s Drumchapel and the other peripheral estates were seen as one of the most serious issues facing the city.

Figure 7.11 is an extract from a 1997 edition of the *Scotsman* newspaper:

FIGURE 7.11 Extract from the *Scotsman* 28.11.97

It was the post-war housing scheme designed to provide stylish new homes for the people of Glasgow. The list of luxuries was endless – insulation, neat gardens and inside lavatories – and the sprawling estate promised a new way of life for hundreds of families.

When the waves of new housing were thrown up after the war, children scattered across the streets of Drumchapel playing games like 'peever' and 'kick the can'. Yesterday their grandchildren stood on the same streets, some of them trying to blind drivers with laser pens. It is hooliganism, say tenants, that is at the root of the area's problems.

Mr W., a father of five, who has lived on Invercanny Drive for three years, is desperate to get out. On the litter strewn street outside his house, in the shadow of a burned-out building, he said, "When we first moved in, it was hassle. On the first night someone set the wheelie bins alight. We want to get out as soon as possible. We're on the waiting list and can't get out soon enough."

Mrs M. – six and a half years on Invercanny Drive and heartily sick of it – said, "We've heard some places are being knocked down, but I've had nothing official from the council. But look at it", she said, sweeping her arm in front of her, "This place is a disgrace. Vandals are causing the problems. And heroin addicts. I would rather stay here in Drumchapel, but sometimes I wish I could lift my house up and put it down somewhere else. Ten years ago we didn't have the problems as we do now. There were folk taking drugs, but it was hash. Now we've got all these people taking heroin."

The community has crumbled, she said, despite the efforts of the few who remain loyal to the area. She explained, "I came here 30 years ago when I was three years old and I enjoyed living here. But now some of us are just trying to hold the community together against the odds. The council has spent thousands doing nothing. But if they are serious about sorting the area out they should build fewer, larger houses because there are all these big families cramped into terrible wee places. Either that or they should just stick a massive police station right where all the houses are – give the vandals a warning.

From the *Scotsman*, 28.11.97

Considerable amounts of money have been invested in refurbishing the estate in recent years but serious social and economic problems remain.

STUDENT ACTIVITY 7.1

1 Study figures 7.1 and 7.2 showing the process of decline in inner city and peripheral housing estates and then study the information on Ballymun and Drumchapel. Draw up two lists, one for Ballymun and one for Drumchapel, listing the factors which seem to have created problems in the estates. How similar or different are the two lists? In the light of the information on Drumchapel and Ballymun do the models shown in the figures seem to be valid?

FIGURE 7.13 Refurbished housing in Drumchapel, Glasgow

Anti-drugs protesters appeal to Government

By Frank Kilfeather

Calls on the Government to provide more resources for gardaí fighting drug pushers and for Dublin Corporation to develop more amenities in Ballymun were made at a peaceful 'anti-drug pushers' demonstration in the area last night.

A number of speakers at the demonstration stressed the harm being caused by pushers. It would not be tolerated any longer, the protesters heard. After the speeches the crowd of some 500 people marched through the Ballymun flats area, chanting 'pushers out, pushers out'.

The demonstration was organised by the newly-formed Ballymun Community Links Against Drugs Committee, which represents the Ballymun flats complex.

FIGURE 7.12 Article from *The Irish Times*, 22.10.96

8
REVIVING THE INNER CITY: POLICY IN BRITISH CITIES

Key Ideas

■ The decline of inner city areas and inner city deprivation have been a prime concern of urban decision-makers since the 1960s.
■ The approach to inner city problems used by decision-makers in British cities has changed a number of times since the 1960s.
■ Inner city policies have met with varying degrees of success.

The inner city problem

The causes of inner city decline are dealt with in detail in Chapter 7. This chapter concentrates on how decision-makers have attempted to tackle the problem. Changes in the way in which decision-makers have perceived the problem over recent decades can be summarised as follows:

1950s/ 1960s	The inner cities contained large areas of substandard terraced housing. **Slum clearance** and **redevelopment** were seen to be the priority.
1970s	Housing continued to be seen as the priority. However, growing worries about the results of large scale inner city redevelopment carried out in the 1960s meant that policy shifted to **improving or refurbishing old housing**.
1980s	*Deindustrialisation* became a major concern. Many of the large traditional industries had been concentrated in the inner cities and had employed large numbers of inner city residents. When these industries closed they left large areas of derelict land and high inner city unemployment. Unemployment and derelict land rather than housing were now seen as the major inner city problems. **Economic regeneration** became the priority.

1990s	While policies aimed at tackling unemployment and dereliction during the 1980s had brought some success many inner city areas continued to show serious decline. Social problems in particular seemed to be worsening. Also, the term 'inner city' had now widened to include the outer city social housing estates. Decision-makers now believe that policies which concentrate on one aspect of the inner city problem will only have limited success. They believe that it is necessary to tackle social, economic and environmental problems simultaneously. This 'holistic' approach to **social, economic and environmental regeneration** became the priority both in the inner city and in the outer city social housing estates.

The effects of government ideology on policy: the example of the urban development corporations

Changes in inner city policy (see Figure 8.1) reflect changes in government ideas or **ideology**. For example, in the 1960s and early 1970s there was a general consensus or agreement amongst the main political parties that state planning and state spending were the best approach to addressing social and economic problems. This formed part of the 'post-war consensus' on social policy. This meant that inner city policies such as Comprehensive Development Areas and Housing Action Areas relied largely on government spending and government or local council planning.

Date	Examples of policies	Details	Brief Evaluation	Links
1960s	**Comprehensive Development Areas**	This involved the complete clearance and redevelopment of whole inner city neighbourhoods. Old sub-standard or slum housing was replaced by new estates of council housing. Much of this new housing was in the form of maisonettes, tower blocks or deck access blocks. Some of these new estates were built on the periphery of cities to allow a more spacious layout and so whole inner city neighbourhoods were 'transplanted' in the outer city. Initially these new inner and outer city estates were popular with residents but during the 1970s serious design and social problems began to emerge.	*Successes:* ■ Replacement of old slum housing with housing with modern amenities such as central heating, bathrooms and hot running water. ■ Large numbers of new homes built quickly. *Failures:* ■ New prefabricated building techniques proved to be faulty. Structural problems were widespread. ■ Comprehensive redevelopment often destroyed existing inner city communities. ■ Poverty and unemployment not addressed.	Chapter 9
1970s	**Housing Action Areas** **Enveloping Schemes**	From 1974 local councils could designate selected inner city neighbourhoods as 'Housing Action Areas'. Grants were given to house owners for up to 75% of the cost of renovating a house. From 1979 local councils could provide the full cost of improvements to houses in the most deprived areas. Councils could also organise the contractor used for the work and therefore had full control over the design and standard of the improvements.	*Successes:* ■ Inner city communities were not broken up. ■ Traditional houses proved to be more popular than maisonettes and flats. *Failures:* ■ Improvements sometimes encouraged gentrification which put rents and house prices beyond the reach of existing residents. ■ Poverty and unemployment not addressed.	
1980s	**Enterprise Zones** **Urban Development Corporations**	Enterprise Zones were introduced in 1981. These were relatively small areas in which special incentives were offered to firms choosing to locate there. Urban Development Corporations were introduced in 11 urban areas between 1981 and 1988. This scheme spearheaded the Conservative government's regeneration policy in the 1980s. The corporations were agencies appointed by the government. They had the responsibility of planning and development in their area and their main task was to attract new firms. They did this by preparing sites for new businesses, marketing the area, investing in new infrastructure and improving the environment.	*Successes:* ■ Both policies were reasonably effective in attracting new businesses to run-down urban areas and the environment of some UDC areas was transformed during the life of the corporations. *Failures:* ■ UDCs in particular were concerned primarily with property development. This property-led approach did not necessarily do anything to tackle the social problems of the inner city and there is little evidence that the new jobs went to deprived inner city residents. ■ Most UDCs were not involved in providing significant amounts of new inner city housing.	Chapter 8
1990s	**City Challenge** **Single Regeneration Budget**	City Challenge was a scheme where cities had to compete with each other for government regeneration grants. The cities which could propose the 'best' schemes would be awarded the grants. The government selected the schemes on the basis of whether they would be successful in involving a range of local organisations including businesses, educational institutions and local community groups. The Single Regeneration Budget replaced City Challenge in 1994. In many respects it is similar to City Challenge but it pulled together 20 budgets which had originally been run by a variety of government departments. It was felt that this would increase the effectiveness of government funding in the inner cities.	*Successes:* ■ Regeneration programmes are likely to be more successful because bids have to be well thought out if they are to succeed against the competition ■ These policies have probably been more successful in developing partnerships between the different agencies operating in the inner city. *Failures:* ■ Local councils have to put a lot of effort into preparing bids for government money. This effort is wasted if the bid is not successful. ■ Some areas which used to receive funding on the basis of need no longer receive funding because their bid was unsuccessful. ■ Resources are thinly spread over large areas.	Chapter 9
2000s	**New Deal for Communities** **Regional Development Agencies**	This programme, announced by the Labour government in 1998, will concentrate funding on the 17 most deprived estates in the country. Regional Development Agencies (RDAs) were set up in 1999. Each region of the country has its own RDA. They are government agencies with the responsibility of co-ordinating New Deal for Communities, the SRB and a variety of other regional and regeneration programmes.	It will not be possible to evaluate these schemes until later in the decade.	

FIGURE 8.1 A summary of changes in British inner city policy since the 1960s

In 1979 the new Conservative government led by Margaret Thatcher set about ending the post-war consensus. They believed that state spending and state intervention were bad for the British economy. Public spending was to be cut, private businesses were to be given much more freedom, and the free market would be allowed to operate much more widely. They also believed that people had become too reliant on the government and needed more encouragement to be independent and self-supporting. She wanted to 'roll back the frontiers of the State' and allow the private sector (i.e. businesses) to have a much greater role. The Urban Development Corporations (and Enterprise Zones) were a result of this new ideology.

CASE STUDY

The London Docklands Development Corporation

The Urban Development Corporations spearheaded government inner city policy until the mid-1990s. The London Docklands Development Corporation (LDDC) was the 'flagship' of the UDCs in that it covered the largest area (nearly 9 square kilometres), had by far the largest budget and was the Conservative government's most important experiment in using market forces and private business to drive inner city regeneration.

There is controversy over just how successful the LDDC has been in regenerating this part of London's inner city. The LDDC, as with the other UDCs, relied heavily on *property-led regeneration* to transform the environment and the economy of the docklands. Some people believe that this has been damaging to the local community.

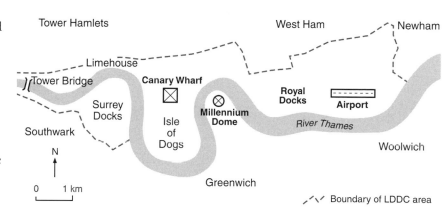

The successes and failures of the LDDC can be summarised as follows:

FIGURE 8.2 The London Docklands

Successes

■ Overall there has been a stunning transformation in the visual appearance of the area.
■ £1.7 billion of public sector investment attracted a further £6.1 billion of private sector investment, mainly in new businesses, office developments and housing.
■ The population of the area increased from 39,000 in 1981 to 68,000 in 1995.
■ £140 million was spent on reclaiming a total of 7 square kilometres of derelict land.
■ £950 million was spent on improving access to the area, including new roads, the Docklands Light Railway and the London City Airport.
■ The number of businesses located in the area increased from 1000 in 1981 to 2350 in 1995 and the number of jobs from 27,000 to 66,000.
■ 19,000 new homes were built.
■ 7700 council houses were refurbished.

Failures

■ Most of the new housing built with the encouragement of the LDDC is very expensive and is well beyond the reach of the original inner city residents. This has led to major gentrification.
■ Although 7,700 council houses were refurbished, relatively little was done for locals particularly in the early years of the LDDC.
■ Most of the new jobs (in areas such as financial services and the media) need highly skilled or experienced people. Few opportunities have opened up for the relatively unskilled inner city population.
■ The influx of a highly paid professional population has increased inequality and highlighted the poverty in the social housing estates.
■ The rapid changes have destroyed the traditional closely-knit 'Eastenders' community.
■ Inadequate public expenditure on transport infrastructure means that transport links to the area are inadequate. The construction of the Jubilee Line extension in the late 1990s linking the area to London's underground system has helped but many feel that this should have been constructed much earlier and that it highlights the problems of relying on private businesses to regenerate an area.

CASE STUDY: INNER CITY REGENERATION IN MANCHESTER

TRAFFORD PARK DEVELOPMENT CORPORATION

Dates of operation: 1987–1998

Type of policy: Urban Development Corporation

Public sector investment: £275 million

Private sector investment: £1,800 million

Details:
By the mid-1980s this was a declining industrial area with no resident population. The TPDC claimed to have transformed the fortunes of the area by attracting 37,000 new jobs and an additional 990 firms by 1998, bringing the total employment in the area to 50,000. Investors included US, Taiwanese and Japanese firms.
The TPDC also aided the £600 million Trafford Centre (a new shopping and leisure complex) and the new Imperial War Museum North. It reclaimed 2 km² of derelict land and planted 900,000 trees.
£4.5 million was allocated to a job training programme focused on deprived neighbourhoods in Salford, Trafford and Manchester. The programme included the creation of 'Job Shops' to advise local people on how to apply for jobs in Trafford Park and a free jobs newspaper distributed to 100,000 households.

SALFORD QUAYS (INCLUDING THE LOWRY CENTRE)

Dates of operation: 1984 onwards

Type of policy: Salford Quays has not been developed using a specific inner city initiative. A partnership between Salford City Council and a private development company raised the necessary funding. Government grants were provided through existing programmes such as the Derelict Land Grant scheme. European funds were also provided.

Public sector investment: £40 million

Private sector investment: £250 million including lottery funding for the Lowry Centre.

Details:
Salford City Council reclaimed the derelict Manchester Ship Canal docks. It then sold sites to private developers for building. Much of the land has been used for office development although about 500 waterside dwellings have also been built by housing associations for rent. 4000 new jobs have been created and job training has been provided for local people to allow them to take advantage of the opportunities.
The Lowry Centre is a more recent project. It will form a waterfront complex comprising a theatre, exhibition space and 'The National Industrial Centre for Virtual Reality'.

EASTLANDS COMMONWEALTH GAMES FACILITIES

Dates of operation: The games will take place in 2002. The venue was chosen in 1995.

Type of policy: an example of regeneration based on an event.

Public sector investment: Precise figures are not known. Central government has helped to fund the construction of the new facilities.

Private sector investment: Precise figures are not known. The organisers are hoping to attract more than £50 million in private sponsorship.

Details: The Eastlands Centre will comprise a new 60,000 seat stadium, the National Cycling Centre, venues for badminton and table tennis, and the Games Village. The organisers claim that up to 4000 permanent jobs will be created as a result of inward investment attracted by hosting the games. In addition, there will be a large number of temporary jobs.

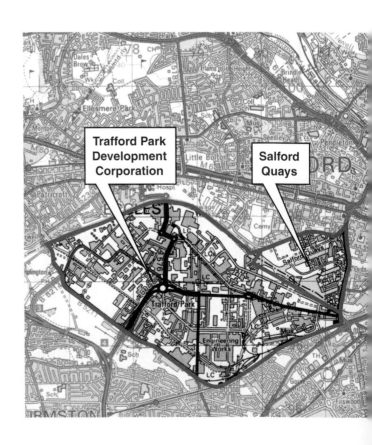

REGENERATION OF HULME

Dates of operation: 1992–2002 approx.

Type of policy: City Challenge

Public sector investment: £38 million (1992–1998) from City Challenge and more than £15 million from other sources.

Private sector investment: total not yet known but will considerably exceed £60 million.

Details:
Until the 1960s Hulme was a traditional inner city neighbourhood of densely packed terraced houses. In the 1960s the terraced housing was cleared and replaced by a council estate of deck access flats and tower blocks housing a much smaller population of 12,000.
Within a few years the new blocks were suffering from a variety of defects including dampness, pest infestation and inadequate heating. The blocks were ugly and many residents felt isolated and alienated. Although a large area of public open space had been provided in the estate it lacked a clear use and suffered from poor maintenance. By the early 1980s the physical problems of the housing combined with the social problems faced by the residents had stigmatised the estate. According to some indicators the estate was one of the worst in Europe. In 1991 unemployment was 40%, 60% of the residents depended on state benefits and 80% of households lacked a car.

In 1991 Manchester City Council won City Challenge funding to redevelop and regenerate the area. The project was to be run by Hulme Regeneration Ltd whose board included council representatives, local residents and representatives of AMEC (a construction company with expertise in inner city redevelopment).
The blocks of flats had all been demolished by 1998. The new development has the following characteristics:
■ Low rise housing following a more traditional design.
■ An emphasis on streets and squares to encourage a stronger sense of community.
■ A mixture of house designs and types of tenure.
■ Creation of a shopping high street for Hulme to help create a sense of community. The high street's focus will be a new Asda store.
■ Provision of new community and job training facilities.
■ Creation of a new park.
■ Workshops and offices will be mixed with housing to encourage firms and jobs into the area.

Successes already include:
900 new homes
600 homes refurbished
540 jobs created (building contractors are encouraged to recruit local people and local people receive training and advice on setting up small businesses)

FIGURE 8.3 Inner city regeneration initiatives in Greater Manchester

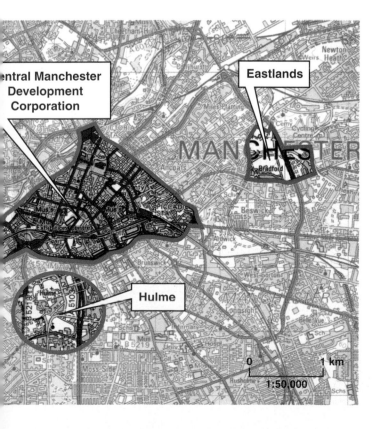

CENTRAL MANCHESTER DEVELOPMENT CORPORATION

Dates of operation: 1988–1996

Type of policy: Urban Development Corporation

Public sector investment: £80 million

Private sector investment: £350 million

Details:
The CMDC area comprised the southern part of Manchester city centre. This was not the most deprived part of the city and the resident population was very small.
Projects aided by the CMDC included:
1 The Castlefield Urban Heritage Park
This was a derelict industrial area comprising the Bridgewater Canal Basin, massive Victorian railway viaducts and disused Victorian warehouses and factories. Many of the buildings have been restored and are now being used for offices and cafe-bars. The area also includes the Museum of Science and Industry and the Castlefield Outdoor Events Arena. Funding for building restoration also came from the European Regional Development Fund and English Heritage.
2 The Bridgewater International Concert Hall
Built at a cost of £43 million and partially funded by the CMDC.
3 New city centre housing
2500 new dwellings were provided, partially funded by the CMDC. Nearly half of these are student flats in converted warehouses.

CASE STUDY

FIGURE 8.4 The Trafford Centre opened in 1998, part of the Trafford Park Development Corporation area until 1998

FIGURE 8.5 Canal warehouses converted to offices, Cattlefield Urban Heritage Park, part of the Central Manchester Development Corporation area until 1996

Pages 44 to 45 provide a summary of key inner city regeneration projects in Manchester, Salford and Trafford from 1984 onwards. You should read this information with Figure 8.1 in mind.

STUDENT ACTIVITY 8.1

You are to adopt the role of a civil servant in the Department of Environment Transport and the Regions (DETR) who has been asked to prepare a brief report for a government minister. The minister has responsibility for urban policy and intends to visit Greater Manchester on a 'fact finding' mission. The minister is interested in evaluating the success of past and current regeneration initiatives in Greater Manchester. His findings will influence government policy over the next few years.

Your report should be divided into two sections:

1 A comparison of the relative success of the five projects described on pages 46–47. *You should use an appropriate technique to compare the projects.* You should consider criteria such as:

- cost
- 'leverage' (i.e. how much private sector investment has been attracted by each pound of public expenditure)
- likelihood of future investment and spending in the area
- job creation
- number of people benefiting from the project
- education and training
- housing provision
- visual impact
- infrastructure
- impact on levels of deprivation
- sustainability (i.e. are the benefits short-term or long-term?)
- any other criteria you think are important.

2 A summary of the characteristics which, in your opinion, seem to be possessed by successful inner city regeneration policies. You should highlight about five key characteristics. Remember, your views could influence the shape of future policies and initiatives adopted by the government.

9
CHALLENGING DEPRIVATION: THE SINGLE REGENERATION BUDGET

Key Ideas

■ In the 1990s British urban regeneration policy has been designed to simultaneously tackle economic, social and environmental deprivation. This more *holistic* approach is an important feature of the Single Regeneration Budget (SRB) launched in 1994. The SRB is now the main tool of inner city policy in England and Wales.
■ Cities have to compete with each other to win government funds by submitting regeneration schemes. Only the 'best' schemes win funding.

The Single Regeneration Budget

The SRB was launched in 1994 *'to encourage local communities to develop local regeneration initiatives to improve the quality of life in their area'*.

By the early 1990s it was felt that there were two main weaknesses with inner city policy:
■ too much emphasis had been put on *economic* regeneration and not enough on *social* regeneration
■ there was poor co-ordination between different government departments working in deprived areas.

The government brought together 20 separate urban programmes run by five different government departments and created the Single Regeneration Budget.

The SRB will continue to run at least until 2005, but from 1999 it has been run in conjunction with the 'New Deal for Communities' programme (see page 42).

Who gets SRB funds?

In order to get SRB Challenge Funds cities have to present their proposals to the government for approval. The government selects the proposals which it considers to be the best and gives grants to fund the chosen schemes. This means that some cities will be disappointed.

The SRB demands that schemes are submitted and run by a **partnership** of different organisations. The partnership has to include a public sector organisation (such as the local council), businesses and community groups. Sometimes the partnership will form a company to run the scheme.

The SRB funds schemes for between one and seven years. Grants have ranged from as little as £30,000 up to £60 million.

The government states that successful schemes must show that they will:
■ enhance the employment prospects, education and skills of local people
■ encourage economic growth by improving the competitiveness of the local economy
■ improve the environment and infrastructure
■ improve housing
■ tackle crime
■ enhance the quality of life and capacity of local people to contribute to local regeneration by improving health, cultural and sports facilities.

Problems with the SRB

Some urban decision-makers have criticised the SRB. They argue that:
■ because cities have to bid for funds in competition with other cities there is a good chance that many bids will fail. In the first round only 200 of the 600 bids received funding.
■ because SRB funds are awarded to the most impressive bids rather than on the basis of need some very deprived areas no longer receive government funding for regeneration.
■ the SRB claims to give local people the opportunity to influence regeneration policies in their area. In reality it is the government that controls policies because they have the final say on which schemes go ahead.
■ the SRB claims to address economic, social and environmental problems. In at least some cases economic regeneration is still seen as the priority. For example, an SRB bid in central London in 1994 stated: *Street homelessness is bad for London. People in shop doorways represent a barrier to business confidence and tarnish London's image – they also represent a high waste in human resources.*

High Rise Housing

One problem facing decision-makers who are trying to improve the quality of life in deprived areas is how to deal with high-rise blocks of flats. These were largely built between the late 1950s and early 1970s. The decision to build tower blocks and deck access flats (i.e. blocks where the access to each flat is via an overhead walkway) was made for a number of reasons:

■ there was a severe shortage of housing and high rise buildings could be built quickly
■ they were built using prefabricated techniques which reduced cost
■ they allowed high housing densities while still leaving room for open space and landscaping
■ high-rise housing was popular at the time with architects
■ central government offered larger grants to local authorities building high blocks.

By the 1970s and 1980s major problems were emerging in many high rise estates. Problems included:

■ poor design and construction which meant that many flats suffered from damp and poor insulation
■ poorly maintained open space between the blocks
■ children could not play outside while being observed by parents
■ vandalism and crime increased, particularly in lifts, stairwells, overhead walkways and hallways
■ traditional contact between neighbours disappeared and social cohesion was weakened.

Some researchers have argued that high rise housing actually encourages crime. For example, one American researcher, Oscar Newman, developed the concept of *defensible space* in the 1970s. He argued that households living in high rise estates lack defensible space. No individual or family feels responsible for the estates' public areas in the same way as they feel responsible

for their own garden or yard. Similarly, Alice Coleman investigating high rise housing in the 1980s came to the conclusion that 'indicators of social malaise' such as graffiti and vandalism show a positive correlation with design features found in high rise estates (see Figure 9.1).

By the early 1970s opinion had swung against high rise blocks and most cities stopped building them. However, this did not tackle the problems being experienced in many of the existing blocks. A variety of policies have been tried:

■ complete demolition
■ removal of the top storeys
■ refurbishment including improved heating and exterior recladding
■ creation of private gardens around blocks
■ change of ownership (for example, selling blocks to private housing companies)
■ improved security (using receptionists, video surveillance, phone entry systems and improved lighting)
■ specialised use (for example, elderly persons blocks or student accommodation)
■ improved management using block or estate managers.

By the late 1990s there was evidence that the popularity of some high rise estates was growing due at least partly to such policies (see Figure 9.2).

FIGURE 9.2 from *The Guardian* 6.2.99

High-rise makeovers give inner cities a key to towering success

Martin Wainwright

The renaissance of the tower block took another step forward yesterday with tenants in one of Britain's biggest cities accepting a £3 service charge hike to refurbish sought-after high rise flats.

Waiting lists for three groups of 16-storey blocks in central Leeds, which were threatened with demolition less than 10 years ago, have grown to the stage where investment in security, shared heating and communal gar-dens have proved "irresistible".

"People are gradually giving up the attitude of 'tower block equals the big sixties mistake'," said Richard Lewis, chairman of housing in Leeds, where a third of the 148 towers – from five to 25 storeys – are oversubscribed. "There are still unpopular blocks which may be only half let. But there's much more potential than anyone would have though just a few years ago."

FIGURE 9.1 The relationship between the number of dwellings per entrance (an indicator of the size of the high rise block) and the incidence of a range of social problems. (The horizontal axis has a logarithmic scale.)

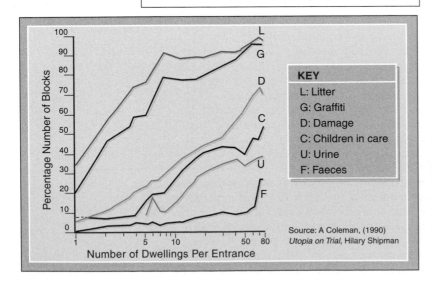

KEY

L: Litter
G: Graffiti
D: Damage
C: Children in care
U: Urine
F: Faeces

Source: A Coleman, (1990)
Utopia on Trial, Hilary Shipman

CASE STUDY

The SRB in Sheffield

Sheffield received SRB grants in four successive years:

- Round 1 (1995): £38 million
- Round 2 (1996): £36 million
- Round 3 (1997): £17 million
- Round 4 (1998): £7 million

In each case the money is to be spent over a seven year period so Round 4, for example, will be spent between 1998 and 2004. As Figure 9.3 indicates, SRB funding forms only part of the new investment. It is intended that the SRB funds will attract further public and private sector funding, a process called **leverage**. Although some of this funding is being spent on city-wide initiatives, most has been allocated to four specified deprived areas. Figure 9.7 gives details of these areas while Figure 9.3 to 9.6 provide detailed information on funding and expenditure.

The SRB in Sheffield is run by a partnership called 'Sheffield SRB Company Limited'. This partnership includes:

- Sheffield City Council
- Sheffield TEC (TEC stands for Training and

Enterprise Councils, organisations which have been set up by the government to fund and run job training. They are dominated by business interests.)
- Sheffield Chamber of Trade and Commerce
- Sheffield Black Community Forum
- Voluntary Action Sheffield (a co-ordinating body for Sheffield voluntary and community groups).

The SRB schemes in Sheffield are extremely complex and so it is worth focusing on one area to illustrate the type of initiatives which the SRB is funding.

The North-West Inner City Area (Round 1)

As Figure 9.3 indicates, it is intended that £36 million of SRB funding will have 'levered in' a further £86 million over the period 1995 to 2001. The spending of this very large sum of money will be co-ordinated by Sheffield SRB Co. Ltd. and also by a North-West inner city local management board comprising three local councillors, three local business representatives and six representatives of the local community.

Figure 9.10 illustrates the work being carried out with the help of SRB funding.

	Round 1	Round 2	Round 3	Round 4
SRB	36	36	17	7
Other public sector (1)	35	40	38	15
Private sector (2)	51	32	45	4
TOTAL	122	108	100	26

FIGURE 9.3 Total expenditure on SRB schemes 1995 to 2004 (£ millions)

(1) Public sector sources include Sheffield City Council, Sheffield TEC, European Union, South Yorkshire Police, Government departments, Sheffield College, National Lottery, etc.
(2) Private sector sources include local businesses, charities, churches, etc.

	Target 1997/98	Achieved 1997/98
No. of jobs created	470	810
No. trained into jobs	280	290
Nos. involved in youth crime prevention schemes	730	1450
New businesses in area	230	250
Private houses built/refurbished	50	50
Council houses built/refurbished	290	340
Housing association houses built/refurbished	110	100
No. of childcare places created	260	400
No. of voluntary or community groups assisted	430	640

FIGURE 9.4 Sheffield SRB performance indicators for 1997/98

FIGURE 9.5 Allocation of
Round 1 SRB funds
(1995–2001)

Housing	£19.6 million
Community/health care	£0.9 million
Employment & training	£1.7 million
Environmental improvements	£2.0 million
TOTAL FOR NORTH-WEST INNER CITY AREA	£24.2 million
City-wide initiatives	£11.8 million
TOTAL	**£36.2 million**

FIGURE 9.6 Estimated
annual funding
allocations for Round 1
SRB funds

Year	Funding allocation
1995	£2.7 million
1996	£5.0 million
1997	£5.3 million
1998	£6.5 million
1999	£6.5 million
2000	£6.0 million
2001	£4.0 million
TOTAL	**£36.0 million**

FIGURE 9.8 Refurbished maisonettes, North–West Inner
City SRB area, Sheffield

FIGURE 9.9 Derelict maisonettes, North-West Inner City
SRB area, Sheffield

ROUND 1 (1995 to 2001)
The North-West Inner City Area (Netherthorpe, Upperthorpe and Kelham)
Netherthorpe and Upperthorpe are areas of council housing, mainly tower blocks and maisonettes, built in the 1960s. Until the mid-1990s the Upperthorpe area also contained Kelvin flats, a massive high rise deck access block, but this has now been demolished. Kelham is an old industrial area on the River Don containing a number of active businesses, an industrial museum and a number of disused or derelict factories and workshops.

ROUND 2 (1996 to 2002)
Norfolk Park and Sheaf Valley (Norfolk Park, Highfield, Lowfield, Heeley and Sharrow)
This area contains considerable variety. Norfolk Park is primarily 1960s council housing. Lowfield, Heeley and Sharrow are mainly areas of late nineteenth century or early twentieth century terraced housing. Highfield is a neighbourhood of 1970s council houses. Highfield and Sharrow have a large ethnic minority population.

ROUND 3 (1997 to 2003)
Manor and Castle
The inter-war Manor council estate forms the bulk of this area. Despite considerable investment in housing refurbishment over recent years it continues to be one of the most deprived neighbourhoods in the city. Unemployment is very high and youth crime has been a particular concern.

ROUND 4 (1998 to 2004)
Burngreave, Darnall, Tinsley and Attercliffe
These neighbourhoods are adjacent to the Lower Don Valley which has been transformed by Sheffield Development Corporation. However, these continue to contain some of the most deprived communities. Much of the housing is old terraced housing built a century ago.

FIGURE 9.7 The four
Sheffield SRB areas

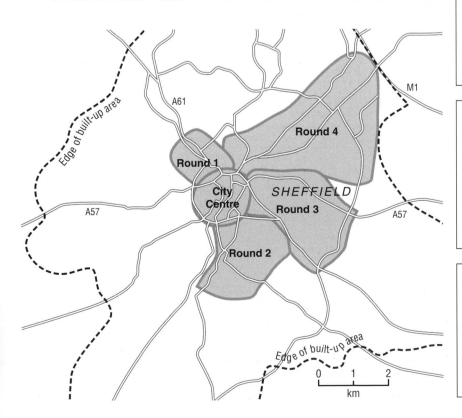

FIGURE 9.10 A selection of projects in the North-West Inner City SRB area

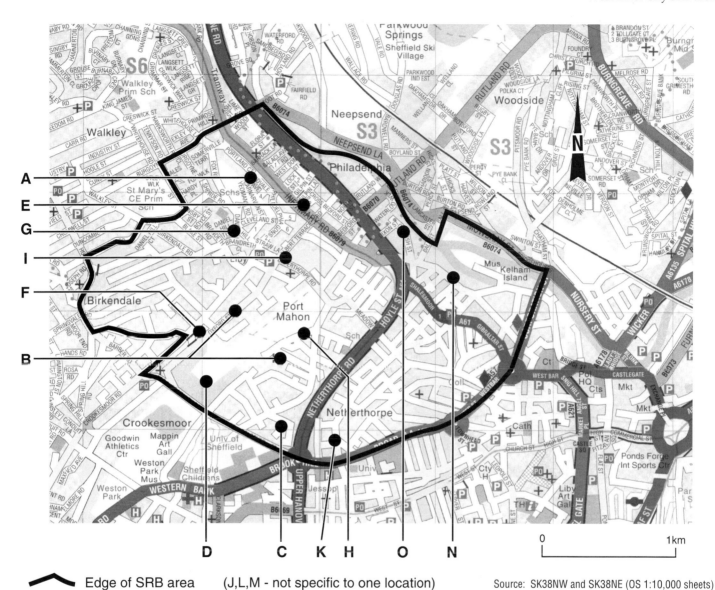

Edge of SRB area   (J,L,M - not specific to one location)   Source: SK38NW and SK38NE (OS 1:10,000 sheets)

STUDENT ACTIVITY 9.1

1 Using the information in this chapter to complete one of the following tasks:

(a) Produce the draft of a publicity leaflet to be distributed to residents of the North-West Inner City Area which explains what the SRB is and how it will affect them.

(b) Prepare a brief financial report on the SRB in Sheffield. Your report should deal with both sources of funding and expenditure. It should also describe the geographical and chronological allocation of money and the effectiveness of the expenditure. Use a variety of graphs to support your text.

(c) Write a brief report outlining the likely benefits and drawbacks of the SRB in Sheffield.

A   130 new housing association and owner-occupied homes built on the site of the demolished Kelvin deck access flats

B   Refurbishment of 1960s maisonettes in Upperthorpe and Bramwell Street including improved security and insulation, improved heating systems and replacement of flat roofs with pitched roofs.

C   Refurbishment and recladding of Netherthorpe tower blocks.

D   New play area and other environmental improvements on the Ponderosa open space.

E   Refurbishment of Infirmary Road shops

F   Refurbishment of former Crookesmoor School building for use as a training centre.

G   The Sunnymeade Centre: a community centre comprising swimming pool, library and meeting room.

H   Improvements to Netherthorpe Village Centre.

I   Upgrading of Upperthorpe shopping centre.

J   Education Business Programme: setting up links between businesses and schools in the area.

K   The Beet Street Nursery (run by a local co-operative).

L   Support for Somali and Yemeni young people.

M   NWICA Mental Health Project.

N   Kelham Riverside Development Agency: a partnership aiming to regenerate an area of disused historic factories and workshops for industry, housing and leisure.

O   Cornish Place: Refurbishment of an historic cutlery works for residential, commercial and leisure use.

10
INNER CITY PIONEERS: GENTRIFICATION AND REURBANISATION

Key Ideas

- Gentrification is the process whereby affluent groups move into poor inner city neighbourhoods. The term reurbanisation is also used to describe the process of people choosing to live in the inner city or city centre rather than in the suburbs or in commuter villages.
- Gentrification contradicts the classical urban models.

- Gentrification occurs for a variety of social, economic and environmental reasons. It can be a consequence of individual choice and market forces or it can be a result of planning by urban decision-makers.
- Gentrification can completely change the character of inner city neighbourhoods. The process has both positive and negative impacts.

Gentrification and Reurbanisation

According to the classical urban models, affluent people live in the outer suburbs or in commuter villages outside the city. The models assume that, through the process of filtering, people who have a high enough income to have a choice in where they live will move outwards in stages from the inner city towards the edge of the city. According to the models, people living in the inner city will either be immigrants, younger people or new families living in their first house, or people on low incomes who cannot afford to move closer to the outer suburbs.

However, most cities in more economically developed countries now show evidence of a process which contradicts the classical models. This process is known as **gentrification**. Gentrification can be defined as *the process of affluent middle-class households moving into poor inner city neighbourhoods.*

Households involved in gentrification may have moved from the outer suburbs into the inner city or they may be new households who are on a high enough income to afford to live in the outer city but who *choose* to live in the inner city.

Only a small number of inner city neighbourhoods may be affected but nevertheless the impacts can be very significant. Once higher earners start to move into an inner city neighbourhood property prices rise. This in turn prevents poorer families from moving into the area and may encourage existing poorer tenants to move

out. It also encourages private landlords to sell their housing to the highest bidder and this cuts the availability of cheap rented housing.

Gentrification can contribute to the process called **reurbanisation**. This can be defined as *the net in-migration of population into the inner city or city centre.* A recent trend in British cities, for example, has been the provision of housing in the inner city or city centre for single people, particularly students. This is significantly raising population densities in some central areas and so is contributing to reurbanisation.

Why does gentrification happen?

All of the following factors may play a part:
- **The Rent Gap** – this is the name given to a situation in which the price of land or property has fallen below its real value. In other words, there is a 'gap' between its actual price and its potential price. This can happen where a neighbourhood has been allowed to deteriorate due to lack of maintenance and investment. The housing can only fetch a low price but because of its size, design or character it may have the potential to attract a high price if money is spent on renovation. So, for example, a run-down house could be bought for £30,000 but sold for £90,000 following a £20,000 renovation. This represents a huge profit on each house which would be very attractive to builders, property developers or individual householders.

The Rent Gap concept sees capital or profit as the main motivation behind gentrification.

■ **New types of household** – most industrialised countries are seeing a growth in the proportion of their populations living in single or two person households without children. Such households have different housing needs and are more likely to see advantages in living close to the city centre. Two words emerged in the 1980s to describe these groups. 'Yuppies' ('Young Upwardly Mobile Professionals'), who were seeing a steady rise in their incomes in the 1980s, and 'Dinkies' ('Dual Income and No Kids') who are couples where both partners are in full-time jobs but they do not have the costs of raising children. Families with children are more likely to be concerned about the attractions of the suburbs such as larger gardens, more attractive parks, a more peaceful environment, front drives and garages, and higher achieving schools.

■ **High commuting costs** – commuting from the outer suburbs or commuter villages can be stressful, time consuming and costly, particularly in larger cities. For people who work in the city centre the prospect of cutting these costs by living in the inner city can be attractive.

■ **The 'pioneer' or 'frontier' image** – this is an explanation for gentrification based on the idea that some people enjoy the 'challenge' of moving into a deprived inner city area which to outsiders may appear threatening or even dangerous. It is claimed that gentrifiers see themselves as 'pioneers' or 'colonisers' helping to 'tame' and 'civilise' a run-down 'wilderness' dominated by 'hostile natives'. It is an explanation of gentrification which is probably of more importance in North American cities than in European cities, but it almost certainly plays a part in all cities. There is evidence that particular categories of people are motivated by this kind of

frontier mentality. Artists, designers, people with radical political views, and other groups who want to be seen as different are often involved. For example, artists form an important part of the communities in the Lower East Side in New York, in Prenzlauer Berg in eastern Berlin and in Gas Town in Vancouver. In San Francisco gays have played an important part in gentrification. By converting inner city buildings such as warehouses, workshops and large houses into unconventional but carefully designed dwellings these groups can emphasise their difference from mainstream society.

■ **Government or local authority action** – in some cases local decision-makers deliberately plan to gentrify an area as a way of regenerating a run-down neighbourhood. In the London Docklands, for example, the London Docklands Development Corporation actively encouraged developers to build very expensive housing in the area. The aim was to encourage investment by building firms to bring high earners into the area to help boost the local economy.

The effects of gentrification

You couldn't even get a decent camembert when I first came here ... Now there are delicatessens all over the place.

The above comment made by a gentrifier in Islington in north London illustrates the type of change experienced in gentrifying neighbourhoods. The process affects not only the housing and the socio-economic character of the local population but also the shops and services. There is often a decline in low order shops such as greengrocers and an increase in high order specialist shops and restaurants. Local pubs also change their decor and image to cater for the tastes of the new population.

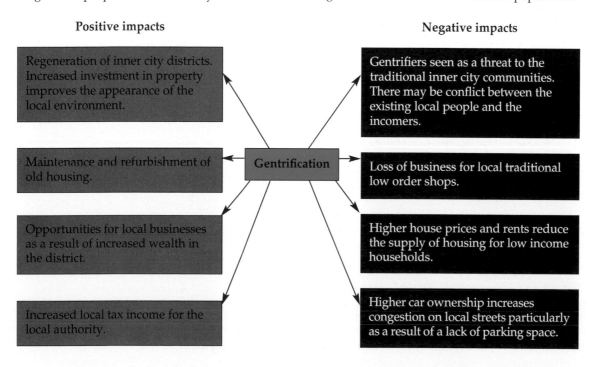

Positive impacts		Negative impacts

Regeneration of inner city districts. Increased investment in property improves the appearance of the local environment.

Maintenance and refurbishment of old housing.

Opportunities for local businesses as a result of increased wealth in the district.

Increased local tax income for the local authority.

Gentrification

Gentrifiers seen as a threat to the traditional inner city communities. There may be conflict between the existing local people and the incomers.

Loss of business for local traditional low order shops.

Higher house prices and rents reduce the supply of housing for low income households.

Higher car ownership increases congestion on local streets particularly as a result of a lack of parking space.

FIGURE 10.1 The positive and negative impacts of gentrification

CASE STUDY

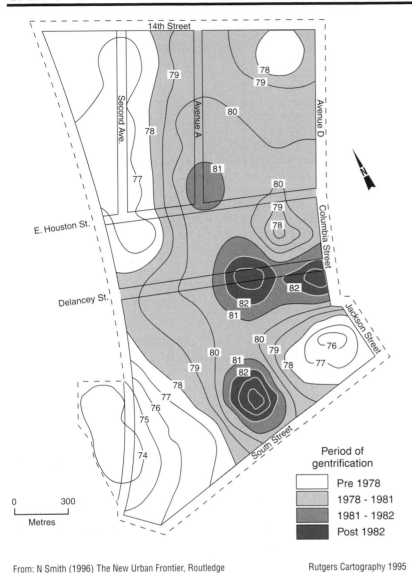

From: N Smith (1996) The New Urban Frontier, Routledge   Rutgers Cartography 1995

FIGURE 10.2 The process of gentrification in the Lower East Side of New York in the 1970s and 1980s. This map was produced by analysing the extent of rent arrears in each part of the district in each year. Researchers have found that with the onset of gentrification there is a fall in the numbers of properties where rent is in arrears

New York

One of the most thoroughly documented examples of gentrification is the Lower East Side in New York. The process began in the 1970s and many of the pioneers of gentrification were artists who romanticised the area's deprivation. The attraction of the area to these artists was summarised by one journalist as its *'unique blend of poverty, punk rock, drugs and arson, Hell's Angels, winos, prostitutes and dilapidated housing that adds up to an adventurous avant-garde setting'*. However, during the 1980s the area became established as a more respectable location for studios and galleries. This encouraged a more conventional middle class population to move in. As gentrification progressed the original population of poor African Americans, Poles, Ukrainians and Puerto Ricans declined. However, in 1980 25% of the district's population was still living below the poverty line.

Paris

In Paris gentrification has had an impact on a number of districts, most of them consisting of very old housing built between the sixteenth and eighteenth centuries. One of the most well known gentrified districts is the Latin Quarter. The area now includes expensive fashion shops, specialist food shops and up-market cafes and restaurants. Few of the current residents were born in Paris. A small two room flat costing 20,000 Francs in 1970 cost 300,000 Francs by 1995. Some of the larger apartments fetch 5 million Francs.

On the opposite bank of the River Seine lies the Marais, another gentrified district. This area was originally built as a high class district for the aristocracy and nobility but it experienced a steady decline for two centuries until gentrification began in the 1970s. The construction of the Pompidou Centre, an internationally famous art centre, and the construction of a new indoor shopping centre called Les Halles encouraged a wave of gentrification.

CASE STUDY

Gentrification in Battersea and Barnsbury, London.

Battersea and Barnsbury are both districts which have experienced gentrification. Barnsbury was a relatively early example of gentrification with the process mainly occurring in the 1970s. Battersea has gentrified more recently and house prices were continuing to rise in the late 1990s as demand for the area increased.

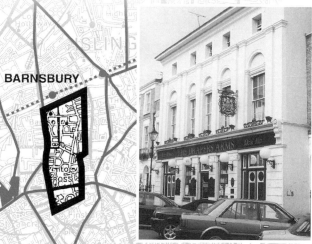

FIGURE 10.3 Barnsbury and Battersea in London

STUDENT ACTIVITY 10.1

Study the photographic and map information on Barnsbury and Battersea and attempt the following questions.

1   Why do you think these two districts have attracted gentrifiers? Try to think of environmental and locational reasons.

2   What evidence is there that high income households live in these districts?

3   What evidence is there for continuing property and environmental improvements?

4   Is there any evidence that council spending on environmental improvements rises in response to gentrification? If so, why do you think this would happen?

11
SPRAWLING CITIES: SUBURBANISATION AND EDGE CITIES

Key Ideas

- Urban sprawl or suburbanisation is the process of cities spreading outwards into the surrounding countryside.
- Suburbanisation and urban sprawl accelerated in the second half of the twentieth century as growing car ownership and improved public transport gave people the freedom to live further away from the city centre.
- Cities in more economically developed countries have had only slowly growing or falling populations since the 1970s but this has not halted urban sprawl.
- Developers prefer to build new housing on 'green field sites' on the edge of the city rather than on reclaimed or 'brown field' sites within the city.
- The growth in popularity of out-of-town shopping centres and suburban leisure facilities in recent decades has also contributed to urban sprawl.
- Urban sprawl occurs on a particularly large scale in the USA. This is leading to a new type of urban settlement known as 'edge cities'.
- Urban sprawl can have a negative impact both on the countryside around a city and on the social, economic and environmental conditions in the inner city. Decision-makers often try to limit urban sprawl by the use of planning controls.

What is urban sprawl?

When a city spreads outwards the process is called **urban sprawl**. Urban sprawl may be a consequence of population growth or it may be the consequence of the suburbanisation of population or economic activity. In many cities of the world, particularly in less economically developed countries, the process is unplanned and out of control. However, in most more economically developed countries planners have the legal power to control and plan urban sprawl. There is often tremendous pressure from other decision-makers, particularly private developers, to allow new building around cities. The area around a city where the countryside may become increasingly urbanised is known as the **urban-rural fringe**.

In the case of British cities urban sprawl has been an important process throughout the twentieth century. Although urban populations had grown rapidly in the nineteenth century the lack of any transport for most of the population meant that sprawl was relatively limited. Most people had to live within walking distance of their place of work and the centre of the city. The arrival of mass public transport in the early decades of the twentieth century in the form of trams and buses, and more recently the growth of car ownership, have given people the freedom to live well away from the city centre. Also, the growth, for much of the twentieth century, in the proportion of the population who can afford their own suburban semi-detached or detached house with a garden has meant that new housing has been built at a lower density. This increases the rate of urban sprawl since each house takes up a larger area. This and other factors encouraging suburbanisation are summarised in Figure 11.1.

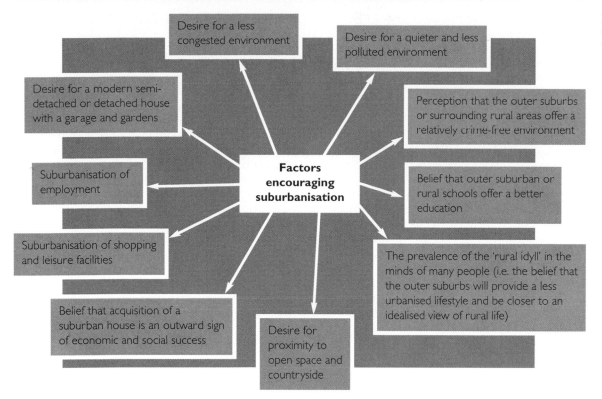

FIGURE 11.1 Factors
encouraging
suburbanisation

Is urban sprawl a good thing or a bad thing?

This depends on your point of view. Negative consequences include:

■ loss of countryside and rural habitats
■ 'swallowing up' of villages
■ reduction in resources available for the inner cities as decision-makers have to provide new infrastructure to service the new suburbs
■ increasing social segregation of cities as the more wealthy sections of the population move to the new suburbs and the poor are 'trapped' in the inner city
■ impact on urban sustainability (see Chapter 16).

Positive consequences include:
■ the increased availability of high quality housing in attractive locations close to the countryside
■ the lowering of house prices as the supply of housing is increased.

Although the negative impacts appear to outweigh the positive impacts there is no doubt that urban sprawl is a consequence of providing low density housing. To stop urban sprawl would be to limit the availability of the type of housing which so many people desire.

Urban sprawl in the USA

American cities have seen urban sprawl on a particularly large scale since the 1950s. Many American urban areas have sprawled well beyond the city boundary to form large urbanised regions. There are a number of reasons for this including:

■ a perception that there is plenty of space in North America. Many decision-makers felt there was no need to prevent urban sprawl because of the vast areas of available countryside
■ the high car ownership rate means that most people are more mobile. They are more willing to travel large distances for work, shopping or leisure. Also, petrol is relatively cheap in the USA

FIGURE 11.2 Urban sprawl in Los Angeles

■ there is a greater reluctance to control new development. Many people believe it is unacceptable for decision-makers to obstruct developers who want to build around cities. They believe that market forces should be allowed to operate freely.

There are two particularly important consequences of this large-scale urban sprawl in the USA:

1. **Extreme social segregation** – In many cities only the poorer and disadvantaged sections of society remain within the city boundary. The more wealthy groups have moved to low density suburbs beyond the city boundary. Some American geographers have particularly highlighted this fragmentation of cities into segregated communities divided according to wealth and ethnicity and have described these sprawling cities as 'constellations' of individual communities.
2. The creation of **edge cities** – in some cases new self-contained suburbs have emerged beyond the

city boundary which are effectively cities in their own right.

Edge Cities

Edge cities have no clear centre or clear structure but they have their own shopping malls, leisure facilities and employment and the residents may rarely, if ever, visit the original core city. Some geographers regard edge cities as a completely new type of urban settlement with their own distinctive characteristics. They are a consequence of high car ownership. Building densities are very low with residents often driving long distances to large indoor shopping malls or to linear shopping and leisure areas alongside highways. Employment is dispersed throughout the edge cities in suburbanised offices and factories. Edge cities are often administered by a number of different local authorities because they have developed across existing local government boundaries.

FIGURE 11.3 Arguments in favour of urban sprawl [Source: *The Mackinac Center for Public Policy, USA*]

Urban Sprawl: Michigan's Bogeyman of the 1990s

There's a new bogeyman in town. Its very name sounds ominous. It's called 'urban sprawl'.

Just take the following sampling from recent newspaper stories and statements about sprawl in Michigan:

'Sprawl is a plague on the land.'
'People are looking for ways to tame the monster called suburban sprawl.'
'From planning experts to community leaders to farmers, people in Michigan are alarmed at how fast sprawl is gobbling up open land.'
'As bulldozers plow their way through more farmland in southeast Michigan . . . agriculturists, environmentalists and homeowners are trying to find new ways to stop suburban sprawl.'

First, what is sprawl? It is rarely defined except in the broadest of language that's often loaded with negatives. It is usually thought of a uncontrolled growth, a flight from the cities, the transformation of rural land into suburban neighbourhoods and shopping malls. In fact, a public consensus on urban sprawl simply doesn't exist.

Benefits to sprawl? You bet. Despite vocal objections to it, sprawl reflects social progress more than decline.

More importantly, suburbanisation represents a significant improvement in the quality of life for movers. Most people who move out of their older homes do so because their needs have changed. Suburban and rural areas often meet these new needs

better than older, more densely populated central cities.

In *Selling Cities*, planning professors David Varaday and Jeffrey Raffel found people move to the suburbs because those communities offer environments better suited for raising families. The key qualities for movers include larger houses, more housing diversity, enough land to provide private yards for their children, safe neighbourhoods and high quality schools. Because many of our cities no longer offer these amenities and often pile on a much higher tax burden to boot, people are looking for greener pastures. That suggests that instead of imposing Big Brother restrictions on sprawl, maybe we should encourage our cities to change the policies that send people and businesses packing in the first place.

What sprawl represents is the creation of new communities and the transformation of old ones: The farming community gives way to the rural–residential community; the rural–residential community gives way to a full-fledged suburb; the suburb may even grow into a larger, economically and socially diverse city.

So, what's the problem?

The political problem is one of managing change. People grow up and move to certain communities because they like them. The political problem emerges when existing residents and new residents use the political system to prevent the further evolution of their community. They want, in essence, to close the gates after they get in.

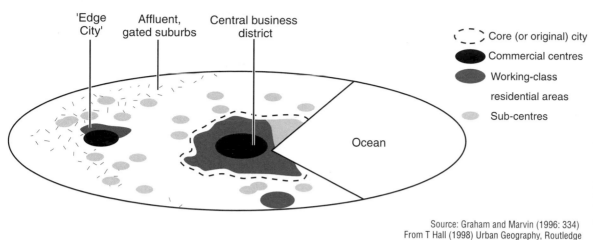

'Edge City'   Affluent, gated suburbs   Central business district

Core (or original) city
Commercial centres
Working-class residential areas
Sub-centres

Ocean

Source: Graham and Marvin (1996: 334)
From T Hall (1998) Urban Geography, Routledge

FIGURE 11.4 A model of a suburbanised city based on Los Angeles. It shows an edge city with its own commercial area surrounded by 'gated suburbs' (ie wealthy private housing areas which have high levels of security). The original core city has a central business district which acts as a 'global command centre'. The rest of the core city consists mainly of poor working-class residential areas.

CASE STUDY

Urban sprawl in the USA and the formation of edge cities

Los Angeles

The classic example of a sprawling low density urban area containing a number of edge cities is Los Angeles. Los Angeles city itself has a population of 3.5 million and is about 30 kilometres across. However, this 'core city' is surrounded by an urban region of 14.5 million people more than 100 kilometres across at its widest point. This urban region comprises more than 150 towns and cities with their own local authorities, 15 of which have a population of 500,000 or more. These are the edge cities of the Los Angeles urban region.

San Francisco

San Francisco has similarly sprawled outwards to form an urban area extending 100 kilometres from north-west to south-east. Figure 11.6 illustrates the growing importance of the suburbs or edge cities in providing employment for the residents of the San Francisco urban region.

Detroit

The growth of Detroit, in the state of Michigan, has been closely linked to the development of the US car industry. Between 1900 and 1920 the city quadrupled its population from 285,000 to over 1 million as the production of cars increased. However, after 1945 new car plants were built on green field sites around the edge of the city and this encouraged more general suburbanisation and the loss of population from the Detroit core city. This trend accelerated in the late 1950s as retailing also started to move to the suburbs. The relocation of Kern's, Detroit's second largest department store, from the city centre to the edge of the city in 1959 was a key turning point in the development of the city. In the 1960s offices joined the migration to the suburbs, the most notable being Ford's global headquarters.

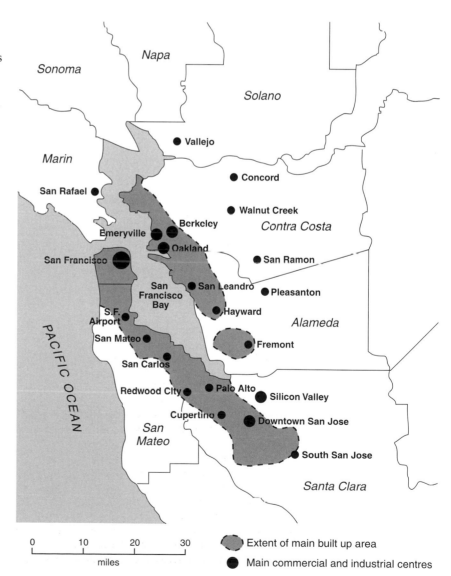

FIGURE 11.5 The San Francisco urban region

Extent of main built up area
Main commercial and industrial centres

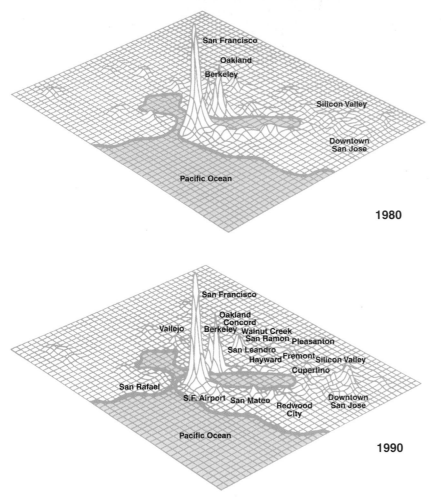

FIGURE 11.6 A 3-dimensional model of employment density in the San Francisco urban region. The diagram shows that employment continues to grow in the suburbs and edge cities of San Francisco, indicating that suburbanisation is a continuing process

(From: R Cervero & K.Wu (1997) Sub-centring & Commuting: Evidence from the San Francisco Bay Area, 1980-90, in Urban Studies Vol 35 (7) pp1059-76.)

Another key turning point was the creation of separate local authority administrative areas in the new suburbs in the 1950s. This meant that the city of Detroit lost local tax revenue, especially as it was the wealthiest households and businesses paying the highest taxes which moved to the suburbs. The city went into decline as the local authority could no longer afford high quality services. This decline in services in turn encouraged more people to move out of the city. This situation continued to worsen over the following decades as the poorest families who were unable to move to the suburbs were left behind. A growing proportion of the city's population comprised poor and ethnic minority families. The crime rate increased and Detroit became known as 'murder city'. In 1967 riots erupted killing 40 people and destroying 1300 buildings. This intensified the migration of better off white families and by 1990 80% of Detroit's population was black, compared with 30% in 1960. By 1990 30% of the city's population were living in poverty.

Between 1950 and 1990 the population of the core city of Detroit fell from 1.8 million to 1 million as a result of suburbanisation. In the same period the greater Detroit urban area had become spatially segregated with the edge cities being predominately prosperous and white and the core city predominately poor and black.

Preventing urban sprawl

In the UK planners have seen the control of urban sprawl as a priority since 1945. Britain has a very high population density and decision-makers have taken the view that, without strict controls, urban areas in some parts of the country would grow rapidly and eventually merge. In regions of particularly high population density such as south-east England little true countryside would remain. This would not only be environmentally damaging but would also limit opportunities for rural leisure and recreation.

The main tool for controlling sprawl in Britain has been **green belts**. A green belt is an area of land encircling an urban area within which it is very difficult to obtain planning permission for new development. The policy was introduced in 1955 around London and most British cities now have a green belt. The green belt policy went hand in hand with the construction of new towns beyond the green belts (particularly around London) to house the 'overspill' population from the cities.

Are green belts successful?

There is no doubt that green belts have been very effective in controlling urban sprawl but not all decision-makers are entirely happy with the concept. They point out the following drawbacks:

■ the type of countryside found in the green belts is often not particularly attractive or environmentally important. Meanwhile, higher quality countryside beyond the green belt may be left unprotected

■ green belts simply encourage new development to 'leapfrog' over the green belt to the countryside beyond. While urban sprawl is prevented immediately around the city suburbanisation beyond the green belt continues unabated. This has the secondary effect of forcing commuters to travel further to work or shop in the city and thereby increasing the amount of traffic

■ by restricting urban sprawl the green belts restrict the supply of housing within the city. This forces up house prices in the city and prevents people on lower incomes from purchasing a house

■ one of the arguments in favour of green belts is that by restricting the availability of green field sites close to the city developers are encouraged to build on more expensive 'brown field' sites in the inner city. Critics argue that there is little evidence at the moment that green belts do in fact encourage inner city development. They are more likely to encourage developers to build in smaller towns or rural areas elsewhere

Green wedges

One compromise solution might be to replace green belts with **green wedges** (see Figure 11.7). However, at the moment green belts continue to have considerable public support, particularly from people living close to the existing edges of cities. Decision-makers would find it politically difficult to end the green belt policy.

Brown field versus green field

In the UK this issue became particularly controversial in the second half of the 1990s. The controversy was intensified in 1998 when the government announced that 4.4 million new homes would be needed by 2016. These would be needed mainly because of changing household structure. The number of small families is growing (because of a rising number of older households where children have left home, rising numbers of one or two person childless families, and rising numbers of separated couples) and so more homes are needed for each 1000 people in the population.

The government stated that only 40% of these new homes would be built on green field sites. The other 60% would be built on brown field sites within existing urban areas. However, many people doubt whether this 40:60 split can be maintained without a special tax on green field sites to make them more expensive, or a government subsidy for brown field sites.

Counterurbanisation

One of the driving forces behind urban sprawl is the desire of many people to live in a less crowded and less urbanised environment. Very similar preferences are encouraging some people to leave

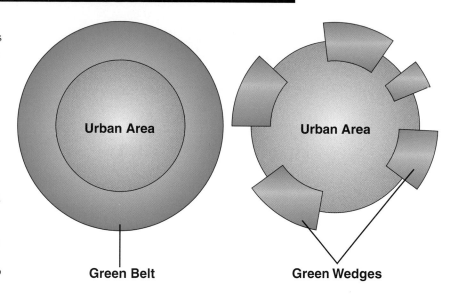

urban areas completely and move to smaller towns or rural areas well outside the city. Where this process leads to a net decline in the city's population it is known as **counterurbanisation**. Counterurbanisation first appeared in a number of western European countries in the 1970s and continued throughout the 1980s and into the 1990s. In the 1980s and early 1990s a common view was that counterurbanisation would lead to the long-term decline of European cities and a growth in the importance of rural areas and smaller towns.

The most recent data suggests that the pace of counterurbanisation may be slowing down in European cities and this throws into doubt the view that all cities are facing long-term decline. Cities may have begun to experience an **urban renaissance**, and some experts are even arguing that a process of **reurbanisation** or **reconcentration** is now emerging in some countries, with a net movement back into some urban areas. The evidence for this change is strongest in Germany. Only when data from the 2001 census is published will we know the true extent to which counterurbanisation continues to be a significant process in the UK and whether reurbanisation is occurring.

FIGURE 11.7 Alternative models for controlling urban sprawl

CASE STUDY

The West Midlands conurbation

The West Midlands conurbation comprises a number of originally separate urban areas which merged due to urban sprawl in the nineteenth and early twentieth centuries (see Figure 11.8). Sprawl and suburbanisation continued around the periphery of the conurbation throughout the

twentieth century, although after 1945 it was rigorously controlled by decision-makers. These controls included the creation of a green belt.

The maps (Figures 11.9 and 11.10) and photographs provide information on sprawl on the south-eastern periphery of the conurbation in the Solihull area.

Figure 11.8 A diagrammatic map of the West Midlands conurbation or agglomeration

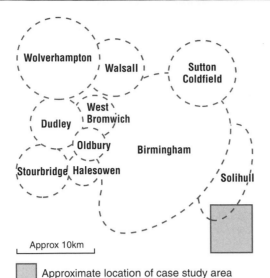

Wolverhampton

Walsall

Sutton Coldfield

West Bromwich

Dudley

Oldbury

Birmingham

Stourbridge   Halesowen

Solihull

Approx 10km

Approximate location of case study area

STUDENT ACTIVITY 11.1

Use the information provided to:
1 Estimate how many square kilometres of countryside were lost between 1974 and 1996.
2 Use the photographs to describe the main features of the sprawl.
3 Using evidence from the maps evaluate the success of the green belt in the area.
4 Suggest why this area is likely to continue to be attractive to developers and potential house buyers.

Figure 11.9 The south-eastern periphery of the West Midlands conurbation in 1974, showing the extent of the green belt

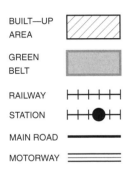

BUILT—UP AREA

GREEN BELT

RAILWAY

STATION

MAIN ROAD

MOTORWAY

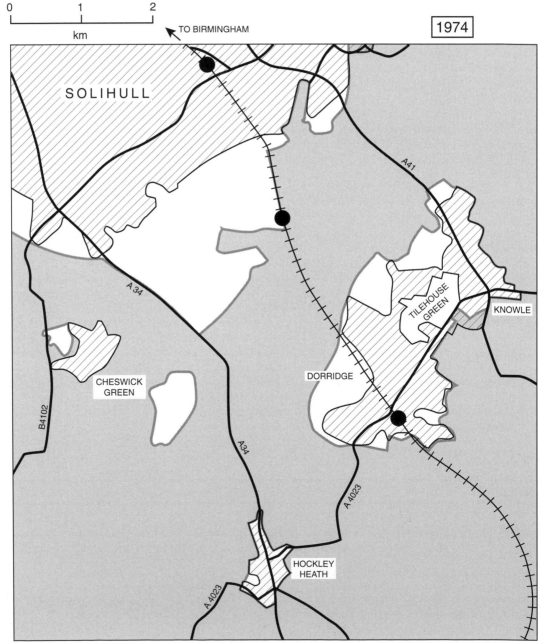

1974

0   1   2

km

TO BIRMINGHAM

SOLIHULL

A41

A34

B4102

CHESWICK GREEN

TILEHOUSE GREEN

KNOWLE

DORRIDGE

A34

A4023

HOCKLEY HEATH

A4023

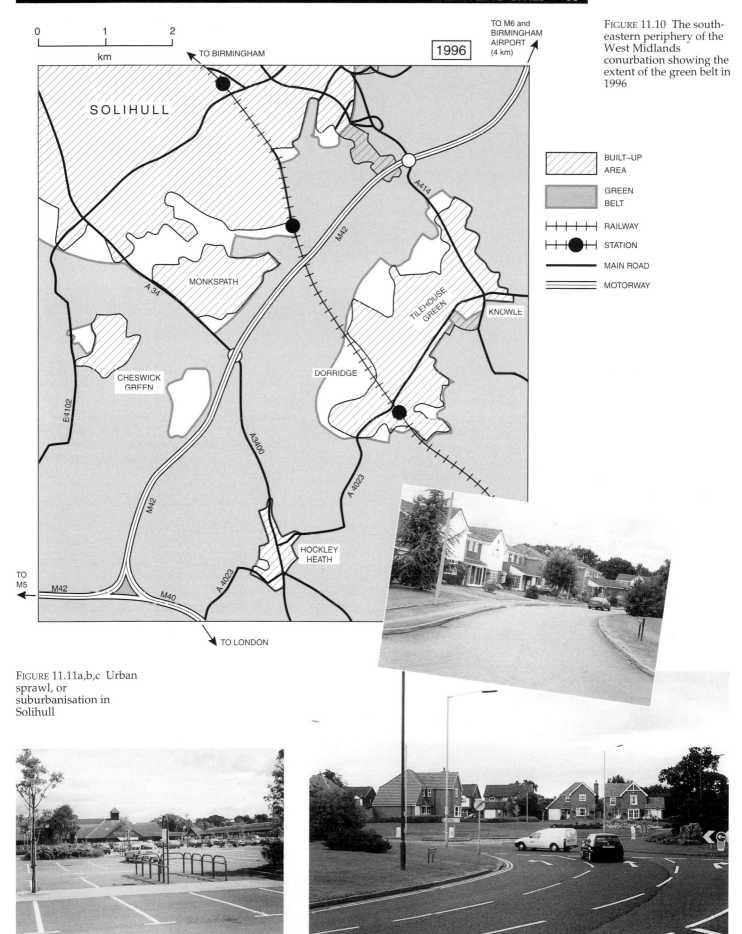

1996

0   1   2
km

TO BIRMINGHAM

TO M6 and
BIRMINGHAM
AIRPORT
(4 km)

SOLIHULL

A414

M42

MONKSPATH

A 34

TILEHOUSE
GREEN

KNOWLE

CHESWICK
GREEN

E4102

DORRIDGE

A3400

M42

A 4023

HOCKLEY
HEATH

TO
M5

M42

M40

A 4023

TO LONDON

BUILT–UP
AREA

GREEN
BELT

RAILWAY

STATION

MAIN ROAD

MOTORWAY

FIGURE 11.10 The south-eastern periphery of the West Midlands conurbation showing the extent of the green belt in 1996

FIGURE 11.11a,b,c Urban sprawl, or suburbanisation in Solihull

12
THREATENED CENTRES: CHANGING PATTERNS OF RETAILING AND THE FUTURE OF CITY CENTRES

Key Ideas

■ Shopping behaviour and shop location have seen considerable change over recent decades. There has been a rapid growth in the number of suburban or out-of-town shopping centres.
■ Shopping behaviour and types of shop have changed in response to wider social and economic change.
■ In recent years new out-of-town shopping centres have attracted shoppers away from city centres. This has posed a threat to the future role of city centres as important shopping locations.
■ Offices have also shown a growing preference for suburban and green field locations and this is posing a further threat to the future of city centres.
■ Decision-makers are now using a variety of strategies to attract shoppers, retailers and offices back to city centres.

Changes in shopping behaviour

Changes in shopping behaviour are a result of wider social and economic changes over recent decades. Rising incomes have led to higher car ownership and a greater demand for a wider range of more sophisticated goods. More women are in employment and have the use of a private car. Advertising and fashion have a wider influence than ever before. Over the same period increased levels of ownership of domestic appliances such as freezers and microwaves have had an impact on the types of food demanded.
Shoppers now:

■ are more likely to shop by car
■ are willing to travel further to shop and are less likely to shop locally
■ shop less frequently for low order goods (i.e cheaper goods purchased frequently), particularly food, but buy greater quantities during each trip
■ demand a greater choice of goods within each shop
■ choose to shop at 'non-traditional' times such as Sundays and the late evening
■ are less likely to choose the city centre when shopping for higher order goods (i.e. expensive or specialist goods purchased infrequently) such as clothes, furniture or electrical goods
■ often prefer indoor shopping centres or 'malls' where they are protected from the weather.

Retailers have responded to these changes in a variety of ways:

1 Many local neighbourhood shops such as green grocers and butchers have closed as the number of customers choosing to use them has fallen.
2 There is a continuing rise in the number of large supermarkets and retail parks comprising a range of retail 'warehouses'.
3 Large retailers, particularly supermarkets, have increasingly preferred less congested suburban locations offering plenty of free parking space.
4 Large retailers are keen to locate in regional indoor shopping centres on the periphery of urban areas.
5 An increasing number of shops open at 'non-traditional' hours such as Sundays and late evening.

It is arguable whether changes in consumer behaviour have *caused* these changes in retailing or whether the reverse is true (i.e. the decisions made by retailers have forced or encouraged consumers to change the way they shop). Both processes are probably occurring. What is certainly true is that some groups in society, such as the elderly and those without cars, now have poorer access to shops because there are considerably fewer local neighbourhood shops within walking distance of their home.

The growth of out-of-town shopping centres, malls and hypermarkets

The biggest change in retailing in recent years has been the appearance of large out-of-town shopping malls. The USA was the first country to experience this trend in the 1950s and 1960s and it has been one of the factors that has led to the decline of American city centres.

France was one of the first European countries to see the emergence of the similar concept of out-of-town hypermarkets (large supermarkets selling a wide range of low and high order goods under one roof), with the first being opened by Carrefour in 1963. The number of hypermarkets grew rapidly during the 1960s and 1970s and by the 1980s there were nearly 600, with most French towns having at least one.

In the UK some of these out-of-town shopping centres are of regional importance. The Trafford Centre in Greater Manchester, the Bluewater Centre in Kent, the Metro Centre in Tyneside and the Meadowhall centre on the edge of Sheffield have very large catchment areas. Other well known centres include Merry Hill in Dudley and Brent Cross in London.

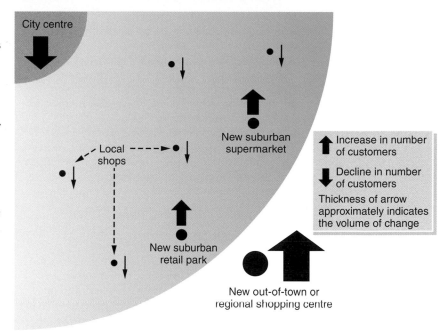

FIGURE 12.1 A model of retail change in a sector of a British city in the 1990s

Why are out-of-town shopping centres thriving?

Many consumers like using out-of-town centres because:
■ their location in the suburbs or on the edge of urban areas allows shoppers to avoid inner city traffic congestion and, if they are travelling from outside the city, they can avoid the city completely
■ the centres are often located close to motorways or other main routes allowing fast access from other areas

FIGURE 12.2 From *The Guardian*, 18.2.99

Welcome to the pleasure dome

There it is, as you come over the breast of the Kentish hill, crouched in the chalk pit beneath you: a sprawling shopping-pod that looks like it has dropped out of a next-door galaxy. What you are looking at is the Last Shopping Centre in England. When it opens in March, Bluewater will be the largest shopping centre in Europe, expecting 30 million visitors a year, and having cost £350 million to build. All the figures for Bluewater look like this: everything is the biggest, the longest, the best. So much work has been put into creating the perfect "retail and leisure experience" that it almost seems a shame that no one in this country will be able to copy it.

It's an architectural extravaganza. American architect Eric Kuhne has gone to town with the lakes, the welcome halls, the winter garden (the largest greenhouse built in this country this century), the revolving dance floor, the long avenues (with natural light coming in through the distinctive ceiling: Kuhne

borrowed the design from traditional Kent coasthouse roofs) and flagship stores for John Lewis, Debenhams and Marks & Spencer, all of whom have agreed to be more adventurous than usual store designs.

Then there are the details: parent and child toilets, for those poor dads trying to take their daughter to the loo without being called a pervert; 25 per cent extra space for each car; "male crèches" in which to park bored boyfriend with a beer and some TV sport; roundabouts with just three exits, to save tired shoppers from having to make "significant traffic decisions".

So why will this supermall be the last one? Because in Europe, the High Street is the thing: Britain recently adopted a policy that discourages large out-of-town retail developments, and "planning laws on the Continent are even more ferocious than they are here," says Clive Vaughan of Corporate Intelligence on Retailing. "The planning laws here aim to get retail investment back into the high street."

■ they have large free car parks
■ a large variety of shops are located in a compact area
■ they feel safe and secure because of security guards and video surveillance and because of the traffic free environment
■ they are protected from the weather by the air-conditioned environment.
■ a variety of other entertainment and leisure facilities such as restaurants, cinemas and creches are available on the same site allowing a 'family day out' to be combined with shopping.

Government policy and out-of-town shopping centres

Over recent years there has been growing concern about the damaging impact of out-of-town shopping centres on city centre retailers and on traffic volumes. As a consequence, governments in a number of European countries, including Britain, have introduced policies to limit their development. It is likely that the Bluewater Centre in Kent opened in 1999 will be the last large regional centre to be built and new investment in the future is likely to be steered back into city centres (see figure 12.2).

Suburbanising offices

With the growth of tertiary employment since the 1970s there has been a growing demand for office space. City centres have traditionally been the main location for offices in cities because:
■ city centres have, at least until recent years, been more accessible for workers and clients because transport routes focus on the city centre
■ the concentration of offices in city centres allows easy personal contact between firms
■ city centre addresses traditionally have had more status or prestige.
    However, offices are showing a tendency to locate in the suburbs or on the periphery of cities rather than in the more traditional city centre locations. This is a similar trend to the one shown by retailing. The reasons for this new locational preference include:
■ very high rents in some city centres
■ cheaper land on green field sites
■ space for free car parking
■ the availability of imaginatively designed offices in new landscaped or semi-rural 'office parks' on the edge of urban areas
■ avoidance of city centre congestion.
    In many circumstances, however, city centre locations continue to be more attractive for organisations locating offices. For example, most leading financial firms in the City of London still prefer locations within the 'Square Mile' (the main concentration of international financial firms in London). A City address brings prestige and the opportunity for contact between firms. Similarly firms needing access to a wide variety of clients often prefer a central location. It also gives them cheaper access to high quality telecommunications networks. A central location in any of the World Cities (see page 6) and other leading urban areas continues to attract firms who can afford the high rents.

The threat to city centres

So city centres face two main threats to their commercial future:
1   The loss of leading retailers to out-of-town shopping centres.
2   The loss of offices to suburban or peripheral locations.
Decision-makers are concerned that city centres face a spiral of decline, similar to that experienced in many cities in the USA, unless preventative action is taken.

Does the decline of city centres matter?

This really depends on your point of view. Those who prefer using out-of-town or suburban facilities, and who dislike the less controlled environment of city centres, may argue that city centres should be allowed to decline.
    However, many decision-makers believe it is vital to retain city centres as thriving and lively places used by the whole of a city's population. They point to the potential problems of run-down city centres being deserted by most of the population in the evening and becoming blighted by crime and vandalism. They believe that high quality city centres help build a positive image for a city. A rundown and poorly used centre will discourage inward investment. They also argue that city centres should be an important cultural and social meeting place. Without a thriving city centre, cities will become more fragmented with different sections of the population, such as rich and poor and different ethnic groups, keeping to their own parts of the city. The lack of a thriving centre is also likely to encourage urban sprawl.

Reviving the city centres

A number of strategies are being used by decision-makers to revitalise city centres and to help them compete against the out-of-town centres. These strategies include:
■ marketing city centres by publicising their attractions
■ pedestrianisation of shopping streets to improve safety and to provide a more attractive shopping environment
■ encouraging the construction of indoor shopping arcades within the city centre
■ encouraging the location of new leisure, cultural and entertainment facilities within the city centre
■ improving public transport links to the city centre and providing 'park and ride' schemes

■ planning the provision of car parking in order to balance ease of access to the city centre with the need to control traffic congestion and pollution levels

■ introduction of video surveillance to reduce crime and improve personal safety.

The following section examines one further strategy in more detail.

24 hour cities

British urban decision-makers have been worried about the way in which people have traditionally used and perceived city centres. Many residents perceive the late evening and night time to be threatening and unsafe. During the day decision-makers are aware of an 'in and out syndrome' with shoppers leaving as soon as they have completed their planned shopping rather than seeing it is a place of leisure or as a place to enjoy. There is also a 'dead' time between about 5.00 and 8.00 pm.

Decision-makers are concerned about this for the following reasons:

■ they feel that if city centre shops can be encouraged to stay open later in the evening and if leisure facilities attracting a wider range of users can be created, then the local economy would benefit from higher spending

■ they feel that if city centres were seen as lively and attractive places throughout the evening and night more visitors from outside the city would be encouraged which would benefit the local economy

■ crime is a problem in some areas of city centres during 'dead' periods and at night. If city centres were busier at all times and attracted a wider range of users there is evidence that crime would decline.

So decision-makers want to extend the use of city centres so that they are used by a wider range of people for a longer period each day. This concept is known as **24 hour cities**. In many other parts of Europe, particularly Mediterranean countries, this is less of an issue. The warmer climate and the much stronger tradition of families going out at

night mean that in many respects these countries already have 24 hour city centres.

How can decision-makers encourage the emergence of 24 hour city centres in Britain? A wide range of measures have to be taken such as:

■ relaxing licensing laws

■ encouraging better public transport provision in the evenings and at night

■ encouraging a wider range of leisure facilities such as cafe-bars, restaurants, clubs, music venues, hotels, theatres, cinemas, art galleries and other cultural venues

■ the installation of camera surveillance to improve personal safety

■ promoting 'street life' by, for example, encouraging street cafes, markets and street entertainment

■ encouraging longer shop opening hours.

Such measures need a partnership between the local council and private firms if they are to succeed.

FIGURE 12.3 Creating a more attractive city centre environment: public art in Birmingham city centre

CASE STUDY

Revitalising Southampton City Centre

The vision for Southampton is that it should be ... the main centre in southern England for shopping, leisure and business. The city centre should have a range and quality of shops and facilities which are set in an attractive environment and be easily accessible by all sections of the local and sub-regional community, creating a prosperous, dynamic and vibrant European city.

Southampton City Council, City Centre Action Strategy.

Along with most cities in more economically developed countries, Southampton has been concerned in recent years with threats to the future of its city centre. Four recent developments in particular have become the centrepiece of the city council's drive to guarantee the city centre's future:

1 The West Quay shopping development has been built by private developers at a cost of £200 million on a city centre site. It is an integral part of the city centre shopping area and comprises a covered shopping mall with about 60 shops and restaurants.

The centre is designed to become the region's main shopping attraction and to attract new retailers to the city.

2 A swimming and diving complex – this £10 million centre was completed in 1998 and was funded by the city council and lottery funds.

3 A 'multi-leisure complex' was built by Rank Leisure at a cost of £27 million and completed in 1997. This includes a multi-screen cinema, bowling centre, nightclubs and restaurants.

4 A retail park on the edge of the city centre contains a number of retail warehouses.

However, the city is not relying on these developments alone. The city now has a 'City Centre Management' initiative run by a management board which includes representatives of the city council and the managers of branches of NatWest Bank, Boots and Marks and Spencer. City Centre Management has basic funding of about £80,000 a year. The funding comes from the city council, central government, retailers and developers. This money is used to pay the salary of a city centre manager and for funding small projects. The aim of the board is to attract much greater funding from the city council and firms. City Centre Management has two main objectives supporting the city council's vision quoted above:

1 To improve the perception of the city centre as an attractive, lively, successful place where people want to shop, visit and enjoy themselves in an accessible, safe and high quality environment.

2 To further the development of Southampton as the regional capital by encouraging new investment together with partnership between the private and public sectors for the purpose of enhancing and promoting the city centre.

Figure 12.4 shows details of the main features of Southampton city centre and the key recent and current developments. Figure 12.8 lists a selection of the projects planned or implemented by Southampton City Council and City Centre Management between 1996 and 1999. For the purposes of the following exercise it will be assumed that they are all being considered for a single year.

FIGURE 12.4
Southampton city centre

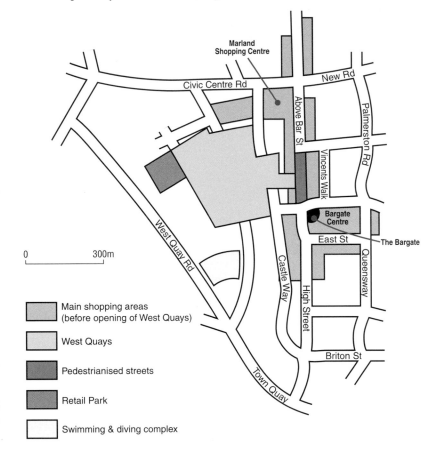

FIGURE 12.6 West Quays shopping centre in Southampton, under construction in 1998

FIGURE 12.5 CCTV surveillance cameras, Southampton city centre

FIGURE 12.7 City centre skateboard park Southampton

Marketing and promotion

Extension of area with Christmas lighting	£40,000
Switching on of Christmas lighting with celebrities	£2,000
Radio and press advertising for Christmas shopping period	£30,000
Christmas street entertainment	£15,000
Promotion of late evening shopping on Thursdays	£6,000
Floral displays including hanging baskets and planters	£15,000
Sunday shopping launch	£16,000
Finger signs for 'hidden' shopping streets (5 posts)	£5,000
Street entertainment throughout the year	£90,000
Illumination of the Bargate Monument	£10,000

Improvement and maintenance of physical environment

Cleaning of stonework of historic buildings on Bargate	£100,000
Maintenance of historic monuments in the Old Town	£105,000
Improvements to street cleaning programme	£120,000
Employment of a 'City Centre Ranger' to co-ordinate a more rapid response to problems	£20,000
Refurbishment of public toilets	£80,000
Townscape enhancement including landscaping, improved street furniture and repaving	£1.5 million
Upgrade of Guildhall Square including paving, flower beds and public art	£150,000
Encouragement of privately funded street cafes	£3,000

Improvement of accessibility for all

Introduction of free car parking from 4.30 pm onwards on Thursday evenings to encourage office workers to stay in the city centre for late evening shopping	£33,000
Improved bus shelters with enhanced information and lighting	£385,000
Cycle parking (parking racks and bays)	£50,000
Pedestrian priority scheme on Above Bar Street (including wider pavements and closure to cars during shopping hours)	£1.5 million

Safety improvements and anti-crime measures

Upgrading of city council multi-storey car parks with with improved barrier control systems and installation of CCTV cameras	£1 million
CCTV camera installation on main shopping streets	£280,000
Briefing of shop staff about the 'Truant Watch' scheme	£1,000

Encouragement of retail and commercial developments

Marketing to attract new businesses to the city centre	£21,000
Publication of guidance on shop front design for retailers	£10,000

Training and support for city centre businesses

Taxi driver training (taxi drivers to be trained in helping visitors in the city and in knowledge of city centre facilities)	£1,000
Customer care training for car park staff	£3,000
Support for organisations representing city centre businesses	
Employment of a city centre manager	£40,000

TOTAL COST OF ALL THE SCHEMES LISTED	**£5,631,000**

FIGURE 12.8 Southampton City Centre Management Projects

13
POST-INDUSTRIAL CITIES: FINDING A NEW ECONOMIC ROLE FOR CITIES

Key Ideas

■ Most cities in more economically developed countries have experienced deindustrialisation since the 1970s or 1980s. Traditional secondary industries have either declined or have become more capital-intensive and so employ less people.
■ Tertiary and quaternary industries have grown in importance in most more developed countries but the increase in employment in these industries has not made up for the loss of jobs in secondary industry. The result is that total unemployment has increased.

■ Many of the newer jobs in the tertiary sector are part-time or temporary. As a result the income of many households is now less secure.
■ The location of economic activity in cities is changing. Economic activity is undergoing suburbanisation.
■ Many cities are actively promoting new types of industry to help combat the impacts of deindustrialisation. Cities are also actively promoting themselves as attractive locations for new firms.

FIGURE 13.1 Industrial monument in a post-industrial city: preserved dockyard crane in Glasgow

Deindustrialisation in the 1970s and 1980s

During the 1970s and 1980s western industrialised societies began a new phase in their development. Primary and secondary industries which had formed the basis of their economies since the nineteenth or early twentieth centuries rapidly declined. Countries were becoming increasingly dependent on newer tertiary activities for both employment and wealth creation. They were becoming **post-industrial societies**.

These changes have had enormous social and economic impacts, posing particularly severe problems for cities which had been reliant on traditional industries such as steel-making, ship-building, textiles and heavy engineering. The problem was worsened by the rapid pace of change.

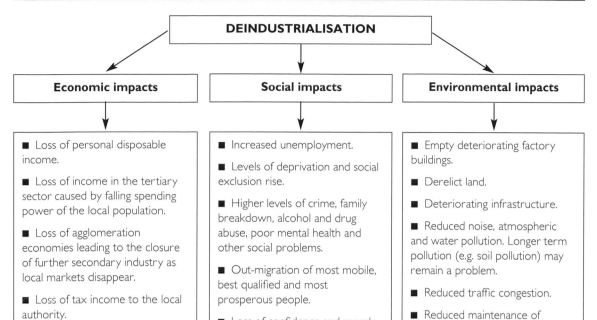

FIGURE 13.2 The impact of deindustrialisaion on an urban area

The term post-industrial society is not really accurate because manufacturing industry continues to be important despite the decline. A more useful term is **deindustrialisation**. This is the loss of manufacturing industry. However, even this term is ambiguous because it can be defined in different ways:

(a) A decline in the *proportion* of a country's wealth (or Gross Domestic Product) created by manufacturing industry.
(b) An *absolute* decline in manufacturing output. (This is potentially more serious than (a) because it means a real decline rather than a decline relative to other sectors of the economy.)
(c) A decline in the *number of people employed* in manufacturing industry.

For individual cities (c) is probably the most important definition because it is the loss of jobs which has created the biggest problem. For example, between 1961 and 1991 the number of manufacturing jobs in the city of Glasgow declined from 227,000 to 49,000. Between 1970 and 1985 Barcelona, one of Spain's leading industrial cities, lost 40% of its manufacturing jobs.

Reasons for deindustrialisation

Reasons for the decline in the number of jobs in the traditional industries can be summarised as follows:
■ automation and mechanisation have increased productivity (i.e. the amount each worker can produce). Less workers are needed for each unit of output. Most firms can produce their goods more cheaply and efficiently by becoming more capital-intensive (ie. more automated) and less labour-intensive
■ there is greater foreign competition from outside the western industrialised countries (particularly from rapidly industrialising countries such as Taiwan, South Korea, India and China)
■ there is also reduced demand for traditional products as new materials and technologies are developed.

In Western Europe and North America deindustrialisation occurred mainly in the 1970s and 1980s. In Eastern Europe, however, the process occurred in the 1990s. Before 1989 the Communist goverments had heavily subisidised their industries and protected them from global competition. When Communism collapsed this protection disappeared and the industries proved to be too out-dated to compete.

Deindustrialisation has been accompanied by changes in the organisation of secondary industry. This has been described as a change from **Fordist** production methods to **post-Fordist** production methods (see figure 13.3).

New types of manufacturing industry

Cities are trying to attract new types of secondary industry to replace those that have been lost. High technology industries such as telecommunications equipment, computers and biotechnology are examples of relatively new types of secondary industry. In the 1980s and 1990s some cities were successful in attracting such firms but in the 1990s it

FIGURE 13.3 The change from Fordist to post-Fordist production methods

Fordist Production Methods
These methods were favoured by large manufacturing industries in the period from 1945 to the 1970s.
The term Fordism derives from Henry Ford who began mass producing standardised cars on production lines in the USA in the 1920s.

Fordism was characterised by:
- firms which could not easily adapt to changes in demand for their products
- the mass production of standardised products
- extreme division of labour with each worker's tasks narrowly defined and each worker being highly specialised
- the use of inflexible machinery with each machine being designed for a specific task.

Post-Fordist Production Methods
Since the 1970s manufacturing firms have increasingly favoured more flexible and adaptable production methods.

Post-Fordism is characterised by:
- firms which can rapidly change in response to frequent changes in demand for their products
- the production of less standardised items (a wider variety of more specialised products are now manufactured in order to cater for customers who have become more 'choosy' in what they purchase)
- a more flexible and less specialised workforce
- more contracting out of specific tasks to specialist sub-contractors rather than employing specialist workers within the firm
- the use of more adaptable machinery which can be reprogrammed to do a variety of tasks.

Impact on Cities
Fordist firms employed large stable workforces. This provided a strong base for the local economy and a source of secure full-time jobs.

Impact on Cities
Post-Fordist firms tend to employ fewer people. They also employ more part-time and temporary workers. They are more likely to shrink or expand in response to changes in demand and so jobs are less secure. They provide a much less secure base for the local economy.

was becoming increasingly apparent that such industries would not solve the problems of high unemployment created by deindustrialisation. There were two main reasons for this:

1 Such industries are very capital intensive and employ relatively few people.

2 International competition in these industries is very intense and many high technology factories are very vulnerable to closure.

The latter problem was illustrated by the closure of a semi-conductor factory owned by Siemens in North Tyneside in 1998. It was closed because the price of semi-conductors, used in computers, fell to unprofitable levels. This was due to international competition and reduced demand caused by an economic crisis in east Asia. Other similar operations have experienced the same fate.

The growing importance of tertiary and quaternary industry

While manufacturing industry has declined, tertiary industry has grown in importance. For example, between 1981 and 1991 the number of jobs in producer services (i.e. services used by industry) increased by 54% in Leeds, 53% in Cardiff and 46% in Newcastle upon Tyne.

It is becoming increasingly useful to divide the tertiary sector into two categories:

1 tertiary activity such as financial services (e.g banking and insurance), retailing, leisure industries, transport, education and health.

2 quaternary activity which includes industries where knowledge or ideas are the main output (e.g. computer programming, software design, advertising and research).

So, why are tertiary and quaternary industries becoming increasingly important? The easy answer to this question is that cities need something to replace the secondary industries they have lost.

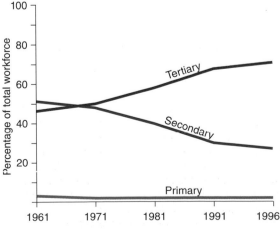

FIGURE 13.4 The changing employment structure in the UK

Most cities in the more economically developed countries grew into large urban areas as a result of industrialisation during the late eighteenth, nineteenth or early twentieth centuries. The need for large numbers of workers to run the machines in the new factories led to rapid population growth and the spread of urban areas. Other cities grew up around ports which were handling the rapidly increasing volume of imports and exports created by industrialisation. So it can be argued that most cities exist *because of* secondary industry. Cities are desperate to find a new economic role or purpose for themselves.

However, this is only part of the answer because it does not explain why the *demand* for services provided by tertiary and quaternary firms has grown. The reasons for this can be summarised as follows:

■ as societies become more technologically sophisticated they tend to become more complex and need a larger range of specialised services to keep them running
■ some sections of society, but certainly not all, have more leisure time and more disposable income than ever before. This increases the demand for services such as leisure and retailing.

Is the growth of tertiary and quaternary industry solving the problems caused by deindustrialisation? Clearly the creation of new jobs in the tertiary and quaternary sectors of the economy is helping cities to reduce unemployment and create wealth but they are only providing a partial solution. This is for the following reasons:

■ in most cities the growth in tertiary jobs is not great enough to make up for the loss of secondary jobs.
■ many of the new tertiary jobs are part-time or temporary
■ many men who lost jobs through deindustrialisation continue to suffer from long-term unemployment because women are finding it easier than men to obtain jobs in the tertiary sector. In a number of cities more women than men are now in employment.

The changing location of economic activity

It is not just the overall decline of employment in secondary industry which has caused problems for cities. The *location* of industry is also changing. Two trends can be identified:
1 **The suburbanisation of economic activity** – over recent decades firms have favoured locations in the suburbs or on the edge of cities rather than the more traditional inner city locations.
2 **Urban-rural shift** – some firms are preferring to locate in small towns or villages rather than in larger urban areas.

One of the reasons for these trends is the increasingly 'footloose' nature of industry (for example, firms can take advantage of telecommunications to reduce the need to locate in a specific area). The result is that inner cities continue to suffer from economic decline and industrial land and buildings are left abandoned and derelict.

Attracting new types of economic activity

So, in summary, cities have to find ways of overcoming two problems:
1 The economic, social and environmental effects of deindustrialisation and the fact that the growth of tertiary industry has been insufficient to meet the demand for employment.
2 The abandonment of inner city locations by many secondary and tertiary firms. They now prefer locations outside the large urban areas. This has led city decision-makers to look for new types of economic activity which actually prefer inner city locations or which exploit new markets and create new jobs. Chapter 14 looks at the ways in which some cities are marketing themselves in order to attract new types of industry and Chapter 2 looks at the importance of city league tables in this process. The rest of this chapter looks at one city which is encouraging new types of economic activity to help tackle the problems brought by deindustrialisation.

CASE STUDY

The Cultural Industries Quarter, Sheffield

The problem facing decision-makers in Sheffield

Sheffield has been a metal-working centre for centuries. Iron ore was mined in the area as early as the thirteenth century. By the sixteenth century increasing numbers of metal smiths and cutlery makers were importing iron from elsewhere and using water power from a number of local fast flowing rivers for their forges and grinding wheels.

However, the real 'take off' of the industry occurred in the eighteenth and nineteenth centuries when new methods of making steel were developed and exploited, and Sheffield could make use of the nearby coalfield. By 1850 there were 135 steel-making firms in the city. Sheffield's economy was now based on the two linked activities of (a) steel-making in large factories and (b) the manufacture of cutlery and tools in hundreds of small workshops. By 1920 70,000 people were employed in steel-making and 40,000 in cutlery and tool-making.

The population of the area grew in parallel with this industrial growth. In 1800 Sheffield's population was 46,000. By 1900 it was 400,000.

Deindustrialisation occurred in the early 1980s for three main reasons:

1 competition from low-cost steel producers, particularly in Japan and newly industrialising countries such as South Korea
2 new capital-intensive production methods

3 the withdrawal of government subsidies by the Conservative government in preparation for the privatisation of the industry.

It would be wrong to assume that Sheffield is no longer an important steel-making centre. By the mid-1990s it was producing more specialist steel, particularly stainless steel, than at any point in its history but using methods that needed far fewer workers and far fewer factories and firms.

Decision-makers responded to the city's deindustrialisation in a number of ways. For example, an urban development corporation was created in the Lower Don Valley where most of the industry had been concentrated. One of the city council's own initiatives is the **Cultural Industries Quarter**.

What is a 'Cultural Industries Quarter'

Cultural industries include any economic activity related to film, television, drama, music, dance, computer graphics, photography, fashion, visual art or design. The city council decided that these were ideal types of economic activity. There were already some small firms located in the area involved in this type of production and they were showing considerable potential. This particular district on

FIGURE 13.5 Part of the Cultural Industries Quarter, Sheffield

FIGURE 13.6 The Cultural Industries Quarter, Sheffield

1 Site Gallery
A centre for digital imaging and photographic arts. Includes exhibition space, dark rooms, computer facilities for community and commercial use, accommodation for new commercial enterprises and a café.

2 Yorkshire Artspace Society Persistence Works
A new building with 60 arts workshops, exhibition space and café.

3 Music Garden the old Leadmill Bus Garage
A private developer is planning to convert this former bus garage into an office, leisure, food and drink complex including a central 'amphitheatre' with a video wall.

4 Audio-visual Enterprise Centre (AVEC)
Provides accommodation and shared facilities for a variety of firms involved in audio-visual production.

5 Sheffield Independent Film Ltd
Runs training workshops and courses in film and video production.

6 Wired Workplace Ltd
Manages and develops on-line computer services for businesses in the Cultural Industries Quarter and elsewhere in the city. Partially financed by European funds. Many of the businesses in the Quarter now have internet sites.

7 Showroom Media Centre
A 5-screen cinema showing a mixture of popular and specialist films. This is the largest independent cinema outside London. Includes a café-bar also used for live music. The centre also runs an educational programme.

8 Sheffield Hallam University Media School
Provides education and training for people intending to work in the media industry.

9 Red Tape Studios
Recording studios originally set up with city council assistance. The studios provide recording facilities for bands and a variety of training opportunities for local people interested in working in the music industry.

10 The National Centre for Popular Music
Built largely with lottery money but has also received sponsorship from firms such as Philips. Opened Spring 1999. Contains interactive exhibitions on all aspects of popular music and a state-of-the-art music auditorium. It also runs a wide variety of educational events and course on popular music. The centre is planned as a national visitor attraction and may employ up to 70 people.

11 Public Square for public art and live performances

12 Workstation Cultural Business Complex
Provides accommodation and shared facilities for over 30 small cultural firms.

13 Truro Works Student Housing
A converted factory providing flats for 300 students and a 7-days a week mini-market.

14 Bar Central
A private sector project including a café-bar, restaurant and 700 capacity music venue.

15 The Leadmill
A club and live music venue. 30,000 people visit the Leadmill each year.

the edge of the city centre was chosen because it included a number of empty industrial buildings, some of which were owned by the City Council, and the area was showing signs of dereliction.

It was felt that cultural firms would benefit from being located close to other similar firms within a single area. Such proximity would encourage links between firms and the exchange of ideas. It would also allow firms to share expensive equipment, secretarial support and even office space. In other words, it would provide **agglomeration economies**.

Although the Cultural Industries Quarter was launched as long ago as 1980 it was not until the 1990s that development really took off, when the area was given a significant boost by the availability of Lottery funds and European grants. The Quarter now contains a wide variety of cultural firms and important visitor attractions. The focus for the area is the National Centre for Popular Music which opened in 1999 with financial support from the Lottery and the private sector. It contains interactive exhibitions on the development of popular music and is the base for a range of education and training programmes based on popular music.

STUDENT ACTIVITY 13.1

1 Study Figure 13.8 which shows a range of economic statistics for Sheffield. Is there any evidence in these figures to support the idea that Sheffield is now a 'post-industrial city'?
2 Study the all the information in this chapter on the Cultural Industries Quarter including Figure 13.7.
(a) List the benefits the Quarter is likely to be having on Sheffield's *local economy*.
(b) Make an assessment of the extent to which cultural industries are likely to tackle the problems caused by the loss of jobs in the city's steel industry.

FIGURE 13.7 The National Centre for Popular Music

	Sheffield	UK
Unemployment rate (1997) %	8	6
% of unemployed out of work for more than 1 year (1997)	38	34
% employed in manufacturing	20	19
% employed in services	74	76

	1990	1995	2000 (projection)	2005 (projection)
MALES	114	102	96	92
full-time	106	93	84	80
part-time	7	10	11	13
FEMALES	104	105	105	105
full-time	56	57	57	57
part-time	48	48	48	48
TOTAL	218	207	201	197
full-time	162	149	142	136
part-time	55	58	59	61

	% of total output
Agriculture	0.4
Energy and water supply	2.0
Minerals, metals and chemicals	10.9
Engineering	4.7
Other manufacturing	6.5
Construction	6.3
Distribution, hotels and catering	14.5
Transport and communications	12.4
Financial and business services	16.9
Other (mainly public) services	24.9

	Sheffield	UK
1981	11%	4%
1983	9%	4%
1985	6%	4%
1987	4%	3%
1989	4%	3%
1991	4%	3%

	Sheffield
1981	27,100
1984	16,500
1987	8,600
1989	8,200
1991	7,300

	Percentage rate	As a percentage of the national unemployment rate
1975	2%	63%
1978	5%	75%
1981	9%	97%
1984	14%	119%
1987	16%	137%
1990	9%	148%
1993	13%	118%
1997	8%	141%

FIGURE 13.8 Employment patterns and trends in Sheffield
(a) Key statistics: a comparison with the UK as a whole

(b) Employees in employment in Sheffield [all figures are in thousands]

(c) Makeup of Sheffield's Gross Domestic Product (GDP) by industrial sector (1996)

(d) Local and national employment in metal manufacturing during the most severe period of deindustrialisation in Sheffield (1981–1991): percentage of total workforce in metal manufacturing

(e) Numbers employed in metal manufacturing in Sheffield during the most severe decade of deindustrialisation in the city (1981–1991)

(f) Unemployment rates in Sheffield (1975–1997)

14
REPACKAGING THE CITY: CITY MARKETING AND THE IMPORTANCE OF IMAGE

Key Ideas

■ Cities are increasingly involved in promoting leisure, tourism, sport and culture. These areas of activity offer cities a range of benefits.
■ There is a growing demand for leisure, tourism, sport and culture for a variety of economic and social reasons. Cities hope to take advantage of this growth in demand.

■ In order to attract additional visitors and new investment decision-makers are attempting to create and market more attractive images of their city.

The importance of image

A minority of cities are already seen as interesting or enjoyable places to visit and have traditionally been seen as visitor or tourist attractions. Within the United Kingdom cities such as Edinburgh, Oxford and London attract large numbers of British and international tourists largely because of their historic centres but also because of their image. For example, since the 1960s London has been seen around the world as a centre of innovative cultural development in fields such as fashion, music and lifestyle. Elsewhere cities such as Paris, Venice, Prague and Amsterdam have attracted visitors for similar reasons. However, most cities do not have this attractive image and so have to create new ways of promoting themselves if they want to attract visitors and investment. In fact, many larger industrial cities suffer from a very poor image and have to work particularly hard at trying to change the way in which they are perceived by the public.

Cities of sport and cities of culture

Many cities are now actively involved in promoting themselves as centres of leisure, tourism, sport and culture. Some have adopted marketing slogans such as 'City of Sport' or 'City of Culture'. One of the reasons for this is that there has been a growth in the demand for these activities.

FIGURE 14.1a The Guggenheim Museum, Bilbao, Spain

SPORT	**Sydney, Australia:** the 2000 Olympic Games	Over £2 billion is expected to be spent on the games (the bulk of the revenue coming from sponsorship, television rights and ticket sales) with a profit of $40 million. While not all of this will remain in the city the benefits to local businesses, and the benefits in terms of new infrastructure, sports facilities and publicity for the city are potentially enormous.
CULTURE AND TOURISM	**Bilbao, Spain:** The Guggenheim Museum (see figure 14.1a)	Bilbao, whose economy was based on steel and ship-building, experienced severe deindustrialisation during the 1980s. The Basque Regional Government spent $200 million on the Guggenheim Museum, an internationally important art gallery with a very unusual and striking design, opened in 1997. It forms part of a programme to create a new image for the city and to attract tourists. The Guggenheim Foundation, based in New York, is one of the world's most well known and wealthy art organisations and will provide the art works for the exhibitions.
CULTURE LEISURE AND TOURISM	**Liverpool, UK:** The Albert Dock	The Albert Dock, part of Liverpool's port facilities, first opened in 1846. Following a decline in trade they closed in 1972. The dock and the surrounding buildings have now been refurbished and are used for specialist shops, bars, restaurants and cafes. The dock also contains the Merseyside Maritime Museum, the Museum of Liverpool life, the 'Beatles Story' (a Beatles museum) and the Tate Gallery of the North. The dock is now a major national visitor attraction.

FIGURE 14.1b Three examples of cities being promoted through tourism, leisure, sport or culture

A number of factors have contributed to this growth in demand:

- although the populations of most more economically developed countries are either growing only slowly or declining, the number of *households* is growing more rapidly. A growing proportion of these households comprise one or two adults with no children. Such households are more likely to have disposable income and time which can be allocated to leisure
- the demand for leisure and cultural activities is now much more diverse than it was even a few years ago. The recent growth in cinema audiences demanding a greater choice of films, the interest in new sports such as snowboarding, and the proliferation of clubs catering for a variety of music, fashions and lifestyles are all examples of these changes
- more flexible working patterns mean that there is more demand for leisure at 'unconventional' times. More people work part-time, work outside the conventional 9 to 5 working hours or at weekends
- an increase in the proportion of the population aged over 50 and an increase in the number of people who have taken early retirement on a substantial pension has had an impact on the range of cultural and leisure facilities demanded
- in some cities the growth in the student population caused by the expansion of higher education has also had an impact.

Reimaging the city

Becoming a supplier of these leisure activities allows cities to promote and publicise themselves in new ways and to change people's perception of the city. This process has become known as **reimaging**. Cities are 'repackaging' themselves in the same way as a manufacturer may repackage and advertise a product to boost sales. Through reimaging, cities hope to attract not just more visitors but also more inward investment and more jobs. Successful reimaging can help to give a city a competitive edge over other cities. Sometimes cities are helped in this process in unforeseen ways. Sheffield, for instance, gained positive publicity through the film *The Full Monty* despite the images of industrial decline emphasised in the film.

CASE STUDY

The 'reimaging' of Glasgow

By the early 1980s Glasgow was facing all the problems typical of deindustrialisation. The traditional secondary industries, particularly steel, ship-building and heavy engineering, were in serious decline. Between 1961 and 1991 manufacturing employment fell from 307,000 to 121,000. By comparison the growth of tertiary jobs was small. The level of deprivation in some of the city's estates was as bad as anywhere in the United Kingdom. The city's decision-makers were desperate to attract new investment and new jobs. However, Glasgow faced a serious 'image problem'. It had a reputation as a city suffering from widespread poverty, unemployment, drabness, slums, violence and alcoholism. This was not a good recipe for attracting inward investment or tourists.

FIGURE 14.2 Reimaging Glasgow: the 'Armadillo' Conference Centre

FIGURE 14.4 Reimaging Glasgow: Versace shop, Glasgow city centre

FIGURE 14.3 Reimaging Glasgow: Upmarket indoor shopping centre, Glasgow city centre

The city's decision-makers set about changing the city's image by adopting a series of marketing campaigns and promotional events:

FIGURE 14.5 Marketing campaigns aimed at reimaging Glasgow

1983 and into the 1990s	**Glasgow's Miles Better** now adapted to **Glasgow the Friendly City**	This is a long running promotional campaign featuring the 'Mr Happy' character. The campaign is aimed at encouraging a more positive attitude from residents towards their own city and also at a national and international audience. Research suggests that the campaign has been highly successful in significantly improving the city's image. Between 1982 and 1989 the annual number of visitors rose from 750,000 to 3.5 million.
1990	**Cultural Capital of Europe**	Glasgow was selected as the focus for a series of events designed to highlight the city as a centre of internationally important cultural activity.
1996	**Festival of Visual Arts**	This comprised a programme of art exhibitions and performances throughout the year and centred on the opening of the new Gallery of Modern Art.

While 'Glasgow's Miles Better' was designed to improve the overall image of Glasgow, the 1990 and 1996 events were designed more specifically to promote Glasgow as a *cultural* centre. The city had already used the opening in 1983 of the internationally famous Burrell Art Collection in the city as a marketing tool to attract visitors. The city's decision-makers felt that such initiatives were successfully changing the commonly held view that Glasgow is a dirty industrial city. People were now more likely to see Glasgow as a leading European city with a vibrant and attractive cultural life.

UK City of Architecture and Design 1999

This apparent success encouraged an even more ambitious scheme. The British Arts Council (the agency funded by the government and the lottery to promote the arts) wanted to select a city to be the 'UK City of Architecture and Design 1999'. Glasgow competed with other cities to be selected and won. The 1999 programme aimed not just to further reimage the city as a city of culture but also to help regenerate the city economically and socially.

The Aims of the 1999 programme

■ To publicise Glasgow as a European centre of excellence in design and innovation in order to attract further inward investment.
■ To hold a Festival of Architecture and Design of international importance which will comprise a wide range of cultural events and which will involve people from all sections of society. This will include exhibitions, street parties and parades.
■ To boost the number of visitors and tourists in Glasgow by 250,000 in 1999.
■ To create 400 new jobs in design and a further 1,800 jobs in other areas of the economy.

■ To promote and encourage the design industry through exhibitions, training and grants to enable it to become an important and growing part of the local economy.
■ To boost the local economy by attracting £20 million of new investment by 2000.
■ To improve the design and quality of all new buildings built in Glasgow by highlighting the importance of good design.
■ To involve young people in schools and colleges throughout the Glasgow area in order to encourage interest in design and architecture. This will be done through designers and architects visiting schools, the development of new teaching materials and school involvement in 1999 events.
■ To create new high quality housing, public buildings and public open space.
■ To open a new arts centre in the city centre (the 'Lighthouse') to encourage interest and involvement in design and architecture and to attract visitors.

Figure 14.3 provides more detailed information on four specific 1999 initiatives.

Figure 14.6 Hundreds of initiatives are being sponsored by Glasgow 1999. The four described here illustrate the range of initiatives receiving assistance

The Lighthouse	Homes for the Future	Bishoploch Play Area	Glasgow Collective
A new architecture and design centre which will be used for exhibitions, events, teaching and conferences. The Lighthouse will also contain its own art and design galleries, art shops and restaurant. The centre will be used by schools, colleges, people working in design and architecture and businesses. It will make considerable use of new information and communications technology. The building is a renovated late nineteenth century building designed by Charles Rennie MacKintosh, a world famous architect who worked in Glasgow.	This is a new housing development located on a derelict site on the edge of the city centre. A variety of architects will work on designing 150 homes for sale and rent to be completed between 1999 and 2005. The architects will aim to design new types of housing: ■ 'solar apartments' designed to be highly energy efficient ■ 'loft apartments' which will be 'shells' to be customised to meet individual requirements ■ 'single apartments' for single people and couples ■ 'live/work apartments' providing homes with attached work space for people who want to work from home.	This is the first phase of a programme of environmental improvements for part of the deprived Easterhouse area of Glasgow and has been given a grant of £6000. The project will include closing a traffic 'rat run', constructing a childrens' play area, a cycle way and footpaths and carrying out landscaping. The play area will be designed by local residents.	This is a programme designed to encourage innovative designers based in the city. Each year for three years 15 new products designed by local individuals or businesses will be selected. They will be promoted nationally and internationally and grants given to help them reach prototype stage. Local firms will receive assistance to manufacture the products. 25% of the chosen products will be designed by graduates of design courses in Glasgow's colleges and universities.

Funding the programme

Income		**Expenditure (1996–2000)**		FIGURE 14.7 Funding Glasgow City of Architecture and Design, 1999
£5.0 million	Glasgow City Council	£7.0 million	A Development Fund to fund a variety of initiatives to help individuals and firms involved in design, to fund educational projects, and to fund projects encouraging local community involvement in design and building projects.	
£0.8 million	Glasgow Development Agency (a government backed agency designed to encourage new private sector investment in the city)			
£0.4 million	The Arts Council	£1.1 million	The Lighthouse arts and design centre	
£2.0 million	Private sector sponsorship	£1.0 million	Public relations, marketing and publicity	
£1.5 million	Other funding sources (such as the European Union and the Lottery)	£0.6 million	Management of the festival	
£9.7 million Total		**£9.7 million Total**		

Opposition to the 1999 programme

Not everybody in the city approves of this reimaging. Opponents believe that the city's decision-makers are wasting money on short-term high profile initiatives. Such initiatives, they argue, may be of interest to a middle class elite but they do little for the majority of Glasgow's population and certainly do not help the city's deprived estates. Some go further and claim that reimaging is dangerous because the city is marketing an 'illusion'. By highlighting the image of a vibrant cultural city attention is being diverted away from problems such as poverty and long-term unemployment and so even less is likely to be done to tackle such problems.

STUDENT ACTIVITY 14.1

Study all the information in this chapter about 'UK City of Architecture and Design 1999'. This information is based on the city council's original bid to the Arts Council. Write a critical evaluation of the programme. You can use the following questions to help you plan your report:
1 What are the economic, social and environmental aims of the programme?
2 Is the programme:
■ successfully attracting external funding and inward investment?
■ likely to attract new visitors?
■ improving the appearance of the city?
■ improving quality of life in the city?
■ helping to regenerate the city's economy and providing employment?
■ improving the city's reputation in the rest of the UK and abroad?
■ helping education and training in the city?
■ helping the city's population as a whole or is it only benefiting an elite interested in the arts?
3 Could the money have been spent in a better way?
4 Overall is the programme a good idea?

15
FIGHTING GRIDLOCK: URBAN TRANSPORT MANAGEMENT

Key Ideas

- Since the 1950s cities have seen a continuous rise in the use of private cars. Over the same period there has been a decline in the use of public transport. This has led to growing congestion and rising economic, social and environmental costs.
- In the period from the 1950s to the 1970s most cities responded to the growing use of private cars by building new roads and expanding the amount of land used for parking. In many cities relatively little money was invested in new public transport infrastructure.
- Since the 1980s many cities have adopted policies which are designed to discourage the use of private cars and to encourage the use of public transport. They have also introduced measures to use existing road space more efficiently while allocating less money to new road building.
- Growing use of private cars has had an impact on the morphology or layout of cities.

The rise of the private car

Car ownership began to grow rapidly in the 1950s and 1960s. The private car offered unrivalled levels of convenience and the freedom to travel opened up opportunities undreamed of by earlier generations. As average real incomes steadily increased more and more people could afford to run a car. Throughout the era of mass car ownership, the USA has seen the highest levels of car use. Relatively high incomes and cheap petrol allowed more people to afford a car and the construction of an advanced network of freeways in the 1950s and 1960s encouraged greater reliance on the private car. Car ownership in Europe is lower than in the USA but is rising steadily and will to continue to rise for the foreseeable future.

The cost of the car

Throughout the 1950s, 1960s and 1970s most cities were keen to meet the demand created by growing car use. Increasing amounts of land were used for new roads and car parking. Most cities had major road building programmes which involved carving dual carriageways or urban motorways through existing built up areas. Many cities redeveloped their city centres to cater for car use.

As car use increased, the use of public transport declined. By comparison with a private car public transport can seem slow, uncomfortable and inconvenient. This trend created a downward spiral in the quality of public transport in many urban areas during the 1970s and 1980s.

By the 1990s increasing numbers of people began to feel that the undoubted benefits of private cars were beginning to be outweighed by the costs, at least in urban areas. Environmental costs were mounting, particularly with rising noise levels, atmospheric pollution and congestion. Social costs were also increasing as rising volumes of traffic were actually reducing personal freedom, particularly the freedom of children to travel without adult supervision.

The impact of cars on urban land use

The geography of cities has been changed by the private car in a number of ways. In particular, high car ownership has allowed greater suburbanisation and urban sprawl because it has allowed people to travel greater distances for work, shopping or leisure. In the USA it has allowed the development of 'edge cities' (see Chapter 11). Residents of edge cities are totally dependent on their cars. Many journeys are now within the suburbs or between different edge cities but most public transport networks are primarily designed for travel to and from the city centre. It is very difficult to design a profitable public transport network which can cater for the complexity and variety of journeys within the suburbs.

Increasingly new shopping centres, leisure facilities, and centres of employment are planned on the assumption that most people have the use of a car. This has meant that such facilities have become more dispersed. Cities have become less compact. This dispersal of urban functions is a particular problem for those who do not have the use of a car, particularly the elderly, the young and those on low incomes. In this way high car ownership can increase social exclusion.

Approaching gridlock

It has become increasingly apparent to transport planners that the growth in traffic is outstripping their ability to supply new road space. In other words, new roads do not appear to reduce congestion. On the contrary, there is considerable evidence that new roads actually *encourage* the growth of traffic volumes. Despite the fact that American cities have sophisticated freeway networks designed to allow an average speed of 50 to 70 mph, average speeds at peak travel times are now 15 to 20 mph and falling. In 1995 it was estimated that congestion in California's urban areas was costing $6 million a day in delays and wasted fuel. It was also estimated that by the early 1990s road networks in half of the 50 largest cities in the USA had reached saturation point.

The recent response of American decision-makers has been to cut road building programmes and to shift resources to public transport. By the late 1990s the British government had also drastically cut its national road building programme having come to the conclusion that it would be impossible to meet the growing demand for road space and that an alternative solution would have to be found. Many city councils had come to the same conclusion in the 1980s or early 1990s.

Promoting public transport

Urban decision-makers around the world increasingly believe that public transport must be improved if gridlock is to be avoided. However, there are differing views on which types of public transport are best.

In Los Angeles proposals to improve public transport have created controversy over which type of public transport is most appropriate. New 'Metro Rail' lines have been opened since 1990 as part of a $130 billion rapid transit network designed to tackle traffic congestion. However, in 1998 construction work was suspended in the face of considerable opposition. This opposition came from two directions:

1 Some people in Los Angeles argue that a publicly funded rail network is out-dated in an urban area which is becoming increasingly dispersed as a result of suburbanisation. As the city spreads outwards the density of population declines and so fewer people will live close enough to metro stations to consider using it. They argue that only private vehicles are flexible enough to cope with this type of urban area.
2 Other people, who agree that a well funded public transport network is vital, argue that the new metro network is too expensive and that resources would be better spent on improving the bus network. They point out that the rail links are mainly used by wealthier outer suburban residents who can afford the higher rail fares. Meanwhile poorer inner city residents are totally dependent on buses (see figure 15.1). A Bus Riders' Union was formed in 1994 to campaign for better bus services in Los Angeles. The Bus Riders' Union argues that without bus improvements poorer city residents will be increasingly excluded from employment and leisure opportunities.

Traffic management, traffic restraint and traffic calming

Transport planners in most cities are now approaching the problem by adopting three strategies:

1 encouraging the use of public transport
2 discouraging the use of private cars
3 using existing roads more efficiently.

The relative weight given to each of these strategies varies from city to city and country to country and a range of methods are being used to implement these strategies. The rest of this section will look at three types of initiative, one for each of the three strategies.

FIGURE 15.1 A comparison of the bus and rail systems in Los Angeles

	Bus system	Rail system
Daily ridership	350 000	26 000
Ethnic composition	81% black or hispanic 19% white	50% black or hispanic 50% white
Core rider economic status	'Profoundly poor'	Middle class
Load factors	Most overcrowded in US	Running half empty
Dependability	Late/often passes you by	On time
Quality	Dirty to filthy	Clean and new
Age of capital	Oldest bus fleet in US	New and modern
Amenities	None, seat is optional	Computer racks/four seats for every three passengers
Subsidy per passenger	$0.33 to $1.17	$5 to $25

Encouraging the use of public transport: bus lanes and guided busways

If people are to be attracted on to public transport in greater numbers it is vital that public transport is seen to have advantages over private cars. One of the key problems facing bus services in many cities is that the buses are delayed by the congestion created by cars. This affects the reliability and frequency of services. Also, motorists may feel that when held up in a traffic jam they would rather sit in the comfort and privacy of their own car than in the relative discomfort of a crowded bus. Decision-makers have two options if they are to tackle this problem:

- they could construct new types of public transport network, such as underground railways or surface tramways, which are segregated from road traffic.
- they could segregate the buses from other road traffic as much as possible by creating bus lanes or constructing guided busways.

The first option has been chosen in a number of cities. Most recently tramway networks have been built in Manchester, Sheffield and Strasbourg. Underground rail networks are regarded as being essential in most larger cities such as London and Paris but this is a very expensive option and most cities and governments are unable to commit the necessary funding.

The second option is much cheaper but has very real disadvantages. Bus lanes can be difficult to enforce, can be disrupted by illegal parking and are only an option when there is adequate road space. Some London buses are now carrying video cameras to record the registration numbers of cars using the bus lanes illegally. Guided busways have the advantage of guaranteed segregation from cars and of saving space compared to a conventional bus lane (a guided busway can be narrower), but again they are only an option when space is available.

Discouraging the use of private cars: congestion pricing

Congestion pricing is based on the idea that motorists using highly congested urban roads are not paying the real costs they incur on other road users or local residents through additional delays, pollution and stress. If motorists had to pay these real costs they would be less likely to use their car and more likely to use public transport. Supporters of congestion pricing also argue that for many other services we expect to pay more during periods of high demand and less during periods of low demand (for example, holidays, telephones and electricity) and congested urban roads should be treated in the same way.

There are two main ways of implementing congestion pricing. One method is to impose tolls on cars entering an urban area. The other method involves the use of technology to measure the speed of the traffic flow. The levels of charges would vary automatically according to the traffic flow and the severity of the congestion.

The three largest cities in Norway (Oslo, Bergen and Trondheim) have central area toll systems. Between 6.00 and 10.00 am charges are up to 50% higher than at other times of the day. At night and weekends there are no tolls. Motorists can either pay manually at toll barriers or they can fit transponders to their cars which allow them to be charged electronically. The tolls have had the effect of reducing central area traffic by 10% during toll hours but increasing it by 8% outside toll hours.

Using existing roads more efficiently

This can be done in a variety of ways. The most common method is to use computer operated traffic signals in such a way as to maximise traffic flows. Some cities are currently experimenting with more unusual methods such as 'High Occupancy Vehicle' (HOV) lanes. This is where lanes are set aside on congested sections of road for vehicles carrying more than one person. Transport planners hope that this will encourage more people to share cars or to operate 'car pooling' systems.

HOV lanes have operated in California for some years and Madrid has had an HOV lane since 1995. Leeds is the first city in the UK to experiment with such a scheme. The lane in Leeds has operated on a dual carriageway in the west of the city since 1998.

FIGURE 15.2 The South Yorkshire Supertram, Sheffield

FIGURE 15.3 Guided busway, Leeds

CASE STUDY

Transport Management in Leeds

Transport policy in Leeds is now primarily concerned with restricting the growth in car use, managing the negative impacts of traffic and encouraging people to use public transport. Transport planners work in co-operation with the other urban areas in West Yorkshire (Bradford, Halifax, Wakefield and Huddersfield) and with the West Yorkshire Passenger Transport Executive (PTE) which is responsible for co-ordinating public transport in West Yorkshire. The planners have to produce an annual document called the *Transport Policies and Programme* (or TPP). This document has to be submitted to the government. It outlines the transport plans of the five councils and contains bids for central government money to fund those

FIGURE 15.4 South Leeds Supertram – an artist's impression

FIGURE 15.6 Proposed transport schemes in Leeds 1999–2000

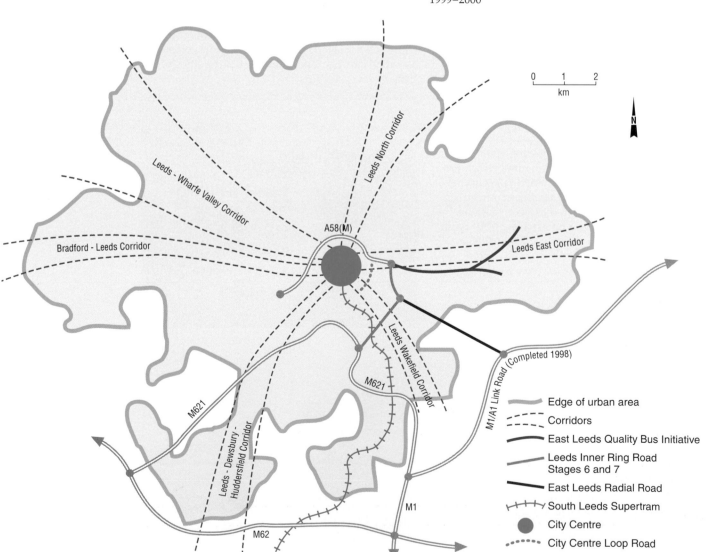

plans. Without the government funding requested in the TPP the schemes cannot go ahead. The information in this case study is based on the West Yorkshire TPP for the period 1999–2002.

FIGURE 15.5 A summary of the transport spending plans for Leeds

Scheme	Cost 1999–2002	Details
Leeds Inner Ring Road Stages 6 and 7	£32.4 million	This is the final part of a scheme started as long ago as 1967 to provide a by-pass around Leeds city centre. The existing sections of the ring road have allowed Leeds to develop one of the largest pedestrianised centres in the UK. Stages 6 and 7 will allow all remaining through traffic to be removed from the city centre. The new sections will also provide a link to the planned East Leeds Radial Road (see below).
Leeds City Centre Loop Road	£1.1 million	£5.9 million has already been spent on this scheme and some sections have already been completed. Completion of the scheme is essential for making improvements to public transport facilities in the city centre and will also allow environmental improvements in the city centre. In particular, it will allow Briggate, the city's main shopping street, to be closed to all traffic.
South Leeds Supertram	£139 million	This is the first phase of the proposed Leeds Supertram network, a tram system powered by an overhead electricity supply. The track will run along roads although the majority of the route would be segregated from other traffic. The South Leeds route would link the city centre with the developing business district to the south of the city centre, the Royal Armouries Museum and a number of suburban areas. The tram would also form the main element in a new 'Park and Ride' scheme with a 3000 space car park make next to the M1.
East Leeds Quality Bus Initiatives	£9.9 million	This scheme is designed to improve the quality of bus services in eastern Leeds. It aims to improve reliability, journey times and frequency. The scheme includes a new guided bus way, new bus lanes, junction improvements and a variety of passenger facilities such as timetable information points and bus shelters. Leeds already has a successful guided bus way operating in the north of the city. The Quality Bus Initiative is a partnership between West Yorkshire PTE, Leeds City Council, First Group and Arriva (the latter being the two bus companies involved). The bus companies will also invest in new buses.
East Leeds Radial Road	No government funding requested. The Council hopes to use private sector funding.	This 4km long dual carriageway will link the Leeds Inner Ring Road to the new M1–A1 link dual carriageway. It will reduce congestion in eastern Leeds and will also improve access to an area designated by the city council as a priority location for new businesses and jobs. £2.3 million has already been spent on preparations for the scheme from the city council's own funds. It is hoped that most of the rest of the scheme will be funded by private companies through the government's 'Private Finance Initiative'.
(i) Leeds–Wharfe Valley Corridor (NW Leeds)	£6 million	Measures include:
(ii) Leeds North Corridor	£2 million	■ bus priority schemes ■ bus stop 'enforcement' (i.e. preventing car parking)
(iii) Leeds East Corridor	£0.9 million	■ cycle routes
(iv) Leeds–Wakefield Corridor (SE Leeds)	£1.9 million	■ traffic calming ■ 'safer route to school' projects
(v) Leeds–Dewsbury– Huddersfield Corridor (SW Leeds)	£1 million	■ pedestrian routes ■ bus passenger facilities
(vi) Bradford–Leeds Corridor (W Leeds) **(vii) Leeds City Centre**	£3.7 million	■ junction improvements.
TOTAL COST	£199.1 million	

	Assist economic regeneration	Improve transport efficiency	Reduce pollution and improve environment	Encourage alternatives to private car use	Improve health and road safety	Promote access to public transport	Total score
Leeds Inner Ring Road Stages 6 and 7							
Leeds City Centre Loop Road							
South Leeds Supertram							
East Leeds Quality Bus Initiative							
East Leeds Radial Road							
The 6 transport corridors & the City Centre							

FIGURE 15.7 Matrix for use with question 1

Transport policy in Leeds has the following objectives:

■ to assist economic regeneration
■ to improve the efficiency of the transport system.
■ to reduce transport pollution and improve the environment
■ to encourage people to use alternatives to the private car

■ to improve health and road safety
■ to promote equal opportunities in access to transport.

Figure 15.5 outlines the main transport spending plans in Leeds for the period 1999–2002 while Figure 15.6 shows the location of the main schemes.

STUDENT ACTIVITY 15.1

1 Copy and complete the matrix in Figure 15.7. Fill in each box with a score of 0, 1, 2 or 3 depending on the extent to which you think each of the schemes helps to meet each of the transport planners' objectives. Give a score of 0 if you think a particular scheme does nothing to help achieve a particular objective. A score of 3 means that you think a scheme will be very effective in achieving an objective. You can then calculate a total score for each scheme.

2 The transport planners are asking for a total of £199.1 million from the government for the period 1999–2002. The government rarely funds all of the schemes contained in a TPP. If you were a transport planner in Leeds and the government only agreed to allocate £140 million for 1999–2002 how would you modify your plans? You may want to use your scores in question 1 to help you.

For each of the schemes in the TPP you have four options:

■ complete the scheme as planned
■ abandon the scheme
■ reduce the cost of a scheme by reducing its scale.
■ delay the implementation of the scheme.

You can assume that the funds are divided equally between the three 12 month periods (i.e. 1999–2000, 2000–2001 and 2001–2002). So, for example, in the case of the Supertram you *could* delay starting construction for 12 months. This would save a third of the £139 million. You would then have to try and negotiate an additional £46.3 million of funding from the government for the period 2002–2003.
Write a brief report outlining and justifying your decisions.

16
PLANNING FOR THE FUTURE: URBAN SUSTAINABILITY

Key Ideas

- Cities have a massive impact on the world's environment.
- A sustainable city can be defined as a city which minimises environmental damage and minimises the depletion of natural resources.
- Cities are not currently being managed in a sustainable way. The way in which we organise land use, design buildings and neighbourhoods, organise transport systems, heat and power buildings, and dispose of urban waste are all unsustainable.
- One way of achieving more sustainable cities would be to design cities which are more compact. However, compact cities would have to be very carefully designed if they were to avoid other social and environmental problems.

What is meant by 'urban sustainability'?

Cities have a massive impact on the global environment. Each city 'sucks in' resources including food, energy and raw materials from a large surrounding region, and each city produces an enormous amount of waste which is dumped in the surrounding atmosphere, seas, rivers and land. The resources devoured by a city and the impact of its waste can be referred to as the city's 'ecological footprint'. In the case of the larger and more economically developed cities this footprint covers almost the entire planet. For example, a typical European city will consume resources from almost every continent while its pollution can encircle the globe.

At present cities are organised with little regard for sustainability. For, example most urban buildings are insufficiently insulated and have wasteful heating and lighting systems. This increases pollution levels and depletes natural resources more rapidly. Cities are devouring natural resources and polluting the environment at an increasing rate and this cannot continue without causing long-term and irreparable damage to the planet's natural life-support systems. However, the solution is not to stop living in cities. Cities are not inherently any more damaging to the environment than villages. Resource consumption and pollution are caused by *people* not by cities. For example, if Britain's present population all lived in villages it is unlikely that environmental damage would be reduced. So we need to consider how to make cities more sustainable.

Urban sustainability can be defined as:
- meeting the present needs of urban populations in such a way as to avoid harming the chances of following generations being able to meet their needs, or
- organising cities in such a way as to minimise environmental damage and to minimise the depletion of natural resources.

Figure 16.1 illustrates what is meant by urban sustainability. The sustainable city devours fewer resources and produces less waste, either because resources are used more efficiently or because the bulk of the waste is recycled. In other words, its ecological footprint is reduced. Cities already vary in their degree of sustainability. For example, Copenhagen recycles 55% of its solid waste, compared with 5% in London.

Social and economic sustainability

A wider definition of sustainability includes *economic* and *social* sustainability. Communities and individuals need to have a reliable income, a reasonable quality of life and opportunities to make the most of their abilities and talents. Without these attributes communities will be dissatisfied, insecure and unstable. Even if environmental sustainability were to be achieved a lack of social and economic sustainability would mean that cities were damaging to their populations.

An unsustainable city

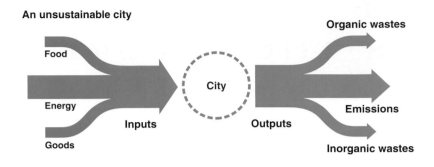

A sustainable city

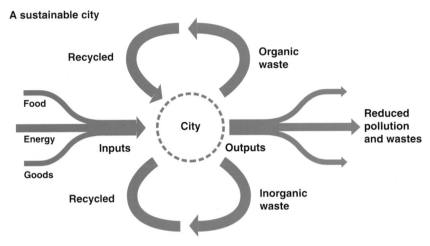

Based on R Rodgers (1997) Cities for a small planet, Faber

FIGURE 16.1 Systems diagrams illustrating the advantages of sustainability within cities

In any case environmental sustainability and social and economic sustainability are interrelated. For example, a heavily polluted city will offer a lower quality of life, but at the same time people living in poverty will not be able to afford or maintain energy efficient homes. Another example is that a poor quality inner city environment encourages migration to the suburbs which in turn increases resource consumption.

So cities which are more sustainable would:

- be less damaging to the global environment
- have a higher quality urban environment
- offer more opportunities and a more fulfilling life for all their citizens.

Compact cities

Urban transport systems are an example of the environmental sustainability of cities. As Chapter 15 explains most cities have transport systems which are very dependent on private cars. Large traffic volumes and congestion produce large quantities of atmospheric pollution and noise pollution. They also deplete our oil reserves and damage human health.

One long-term solution to this problem would be to redesign cities so that they are more compact. This would reduce the distances people had to

travel and more services and facilities would be close to where they live. To create 'compact cities' we would have to use space within the city more intensively by building at higher densities so that larger numbers of people could live in each square kilometre of the city. Decision-makers who favour compact cities argue that we could design high density housing which would provide a pleasant living environment and that it could offer an attractive alternative to low density housing with large gardens. We would also have to reduce the zoning or segregation of land uses so that housing, employment, shopping and leisure were not all spatially separated. Each neighbourhood would have to become 'multi-functional' or have a **mixed use**. Cities could consist of a number of multi-functional 'urban villages', with each village being a mixture of housing, employment, shops and leisure facilities. Figure 16.2 illustrates this idea.

Compact cities, their supporters argue, would offer a number of advantages which would help to create a more environmentally sustainable city:

- a transport system which would be less reliant on private cars
- a greater range of facilities within walking distance of people's homes
- increased pressure to use brownfield sites within the city rather than greenfield sites on the periphery, helping to regenerate inner city areas and helping to conserve countryside
- more efficient use of infrastructure: pipes and cables would have to run for shorter distances to access the same number of users. Higher density buildings would also reduce heat loss from individual buildings
- thriving local shopping centres and local community facilities because more people would live close to each centre. Higher population densities would provide the 'critical mass' needed to sustain a greater number of local events and local services. Public places would become livelier. In other words, compact cities would have greater social sustainability.

Much stricter planning controls would have to be introduced in order to create compact cities. However, a decision to create more compact cities would face opposition. Many people identify high density living with the congested squalor of nineteenth century European cities or with the unpopular high rise estates of the 1960s. During the twentieth century increasing numbers of city dwellers have chosen low density family housing. It could be argued that to prohibit this type of housing in order to create compact cities would be an unacceptable limit on individual choice. Businesses have increasingly chosen large single storey buildings on the edge of cities. These take up more land but they allow firms to operate more efficiently. Such buildings would have to be discouraged if we wanted to create more compact cities. Higher density urban areas may also increase stress and noise levels.

Write a 500 word report outlining the benefits and drawbacks of Camden's car free housing scheme. You should consider social, economic and environmental issues.

For the benefits you could refer to ways in which the Camden scheme:
■ improves environmental sustainability
■ helps London move closer to the situation summarised in the lower diagram in Figure 16.1
■ provides an example of a policy which matches the slogan 'think globally, act locally'
■ supports the development of a more compact city.

For the drawbacks you could consider what problems, if any, this type of higher density car free housing has for an already high density inner city area.

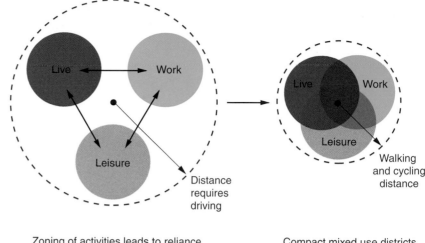

Zoning of activities leads to reliance on the private car

From R Rogers (1997) Cities for a small planet, Faber

Compact mixed use districts reduce travel and allow walking and cycling

FIGURE 16.2 Compact mixed-use city districts could help to create sustainable neighbourhoods

CASE STUDY

Car-free housing, Camden, Inner London

In 1992 an international conference on the global environment took place in Rio de Janeiro. The Rio Conference produced a document called *Agenda 21*. *Agenda 21* was a list of measures intended to address a wide range of global problems which have an impact on quality of life and sustainability. It highlights three main aims:

1 To increase equality of opportunity around the globe.
2 To improve the standard of living and the reliability of incomes for people in poorer countries.
3 To protect and improve the natural environment.

The participants of the Rio Summit realised that to achieve these global aims action would have to be taken at a local level by individuals, groups and local government (summarised by the slogan 'think globally, act locally'). The importance of this was recognised in *Local Agenda 21* which urges government and other organisations to involve local people in building sustainable communities.

The London Borough of Camden has a *Local Agenda 21* action plan and as part of this action plan it has drawn up a *Green Transport Strategy*. One of the policies in this strategy is the promotion of 'car free housing'.

Some parts of the borough suffer from what the local planners call 'on-street parking stress'. This is where inadequate parking space for local residents can lead to problems such as obstruction, double parking and parking on the pavement. In order to control this problem local planners, as in many other urban areas, apply planning controls on new housing which are designed to ensure that all *new* housing has adequate of-street parking. The problem with such controls is that where there is not enough space to provide off-street parking it may reduce the number of new dwellings which can be built or even make a site unusable for housing.

However, Camden has now adapted these controls to fit in with its *Local Agenda 21* action plan. Under certain circumstances the off-street parking standards are waived. In other words, new housing can be designated as 'car free'. This is only allowed where the council controls on-street parking through the use of residents' parking permits. No parking will be provided within the development site and residents moving into the new housing are not allowed to have a residential parking permit. Only residents choosing not to own a car are able to live in such housing.

Such car-free housing offers two advantages:

1 It reduces traffic in the immediate neighbourhood, and as a consequence reduces noise and atmospheric pollution and improves road safety.
2 Land which would otherwise have been used for car parking can now be used for additional housing or open space. Sites which would otherwise have been too small for housing development can now be used.

Both of these advantages favour sustainability. The first reduces environmentally damaging traffic and the second increases housing density and allows a more compact city.

17
GROWING CITIES: URBAN EXPANSION AND ITS CAUSES

Key Ideas

■ Urban growth in the twentieth century has been rapid but uneven over both place and time.

■ The most dramatic urban growth in the late twentieth century has been predominantly located in less economically developed countries (LEDCs).

■ Some less economically developed countries have a long history of urbanisation.

■ In some less economically developed countries one primate city dominates the urban hierarchy. This creates particular problems for these countries.

■ The growth of large urban areas in less economically developed countries occurs through both natural population growth and in-migration.

■ There are many reasons why in-migration to urban areas has occurred in less economically developed countries.

■ Migrants into cities are all individuals but all share aspirations to improve the quality of their lives in some way.

FIGURE 17.1 Cities with a population of over 1 million and their growth rates

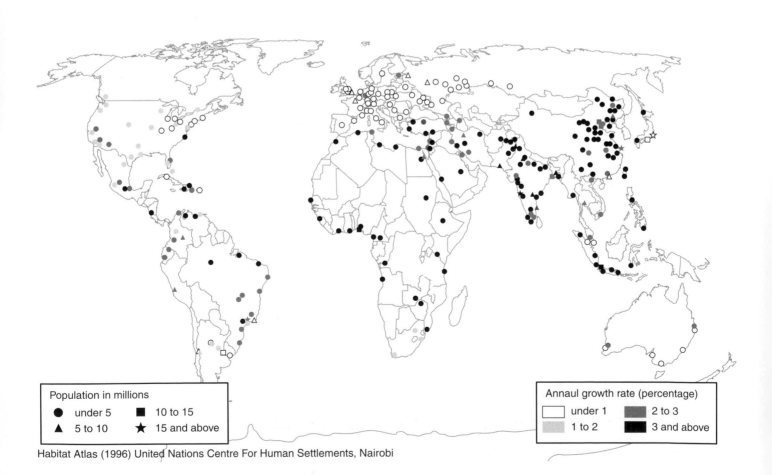

Population in millions
● under 5   ■ 10 to 15
▲ 5 to 10   ★ 15 and above

Annaul growth rate (percentage)
□ under 1   ▨ 2 to 3
▨ 1 to 2   ■ 3 and above

Habitat Atlas (1996) United Nations Centre For Human Settlements, Nairobi

Where are the world's fastest growing cities?

Chapter 1 looked at global urban trends. Figure 1.1 shows that large parts of the world, both LEDCs and more economically developed countries (MEDCs), are now highly urbanised. By the early years of the twenty-first century over half of the world's population will live in urban areas for the first time in human history.

A map showing the annual growth rate of all the worlds cities with a population over 1 million (Figure 17.1) indicates that in the last years of the twentieth century urban growth rates show a clear spatial pattern. The fastest growing urban populations are located predominantly in LEDCs. Less economically developed cities, however, show marked contrasts in their rates of growth. In India for example, Calcutta's population growth at 1.8% in 1995 was significantly lower than the far smaller city of Visakhaptnam's comparative rate of 4.4%.

Industrialisation and colonialism

Urbanisation in LEDCs has occurred primarily as a result of industrialisation. This has taken place at different times in different countries but had occurred in most LEDCs by the late twentieth century. In a large number of LEDCs the beginning of industrialisation was linked to colonialism. Colonial powers, such as Britain and France, created trading and administrative centres. A few of these cities, like Calcutta and Singapore, have gone onto become some of the world's largest and greatest cities. Colonial powers introduced, in a limited way,

technology and a market system but the relationship was primarily an exploitative one. Control of resources, decision-making and profits were all in the hands of the colonial power. It was not until most colonised countries became independent that a true industrial revolution occurred and as a consequence rapid urbanisation did not happen in some LEDCs until the late twentieth century. A model of urbanisation in less economically developed countries (Figure 17.2) describes changes in the rate of urbanisation over time.

The experience of colonialism was not the same for all LEDCs. Some, for example Thailand, were never colonised. Those areas of the world which

FIGURE 17.3 The Central Business District of Jakarta. Indonesia lies at the core of a metropolitan area of 22 million people.

FIGURE 17.2 A model of urban growth rates

Kabul, Afghanistan 6%

Luanda, Angloa 5.2%

Nairobi, Kenya 5.4%
Peshwar, Pakistan 5.1%

Dakar, Senegal 3.9%

most African Cities

Mumbai 3.6%

Bangalore 3%

most Indian Cities

Lima, Peru 2.4%

Kuala Lumpar, Maylaysia 2.2%

Sao Paulo, Brazil 1.6%

Havana, Cuba 0.9%

Urban population growth rate %

Time

Source: Habitat Atlas (1996) United Nations Centre For Human Settlements, Nairobi for current growth rates in all urban areas over 1,000,000 in 1995

were colonised experienced the impact of this process differently and at different times. Most of South America was colonised by the Spanish who had granted independence to countries like Peru (1821) and Colombia (1819) much earlier than the *start* of colonisation in many parts of Africa.

The mega-city in LEDCs

Urbanisation has been at its most dramatic in the late twentieth century in particular LEDCs. Mexico City, Sao Paulo, Jakarta (Figure 17.3) and Bangkok are all examples of 'mega-cities'. The growth of population in such cities has been very rapid in the last half of the twentieth century.

India's largest city, Mumbai, (previously called Bombay, population 18 million in 2000), is an example of a city growing at a rate never before witnessed in human history. In the last 5 years of the twentieth century an additional 2 million people were added to Mumbai's population, an average annual population growth rate of around 3.4 %. This poses a huge challenge for urban decision-makers. Most of this growth in population will live in very poor quality housing, often sited illegally and poorly serviced with basic infrastructure. An example of such an urban environment is Dharavi, a suburb of Mumbai, which has been referred to as Asia's largest slum. It houses nearly 1 million people.

The migrant boom began in the early '50s, drawing impoverished craftsmen from Uttar Pradesh, Bihar, Gujarat, Maharashtra and Tamil Nadu in search of jobs. Perplexed by the influx the state set up the Dharavi Transit Camp, rows of concrete barracks intended as temporary shelters, until their inhabitants found permanent homes. Thirty years later, hardly a single one of those families has moved out despite filthy outdoor toilets, sporadic power supply and the sewage that gushes out of their community taps.

Around the camp, the slum continues to grow and thrive. With nearly one million residents Dharavi is witness to that emerging Indian phenomenon – the growing middle class, which at a robust 70% of the slum's population, has almost doubled since 1990. Dish antennas cling precariously to flimsy rooftops even in poorer areas.
Extract from 'From Dust To Dreams', Farah Baria, Indian Today 15.7.96.

Dharavi, like many such unplanned and unregulated residential areas in LEDCs, is also full of small firms employing tens of thousands of people, making clothes, cigarettes, toys and foodstuffs. Unlike most MEDC cities there is no clear separation of residential, industrial and commercial land uses. This poses a range of environmental hazards for residents of such areas but also brings advantages. By living close to their work people save both time and money.

The growth of million cities

Million cities are those cities that have over a million people living in them. The vast majority of the world's urban population do not live in mega-cities but live in cities of less than 2 million people. In the 1990s it has tended to be these smaller cities that have experienced the fastest rates of population growth.

In India, cities such as Kochi (Cochin) in Kerala and Visakhapatnam in Andhra Pradesh have some of the fastest rates of population growth in India, just under 5% per annum towards the end of the 1990s. Although both of these port cities, with populations of nearly 1,500,000, are not traditionally seen as major urban centres they are seen as highly attractive locations for inward economic investment. They have lower land values than the larger cities of India, and a fraction of the environmental problems that beset cities like Mumbai and Calcutta.

The Dominant City

In some countries the urban hierarchy is dominated by a single city. This tendency is known as **primacy** and occurs when the largest city in the country is many times larger than the second largest. This pattern can occur in both MEDC's (Denmark and Copenhagen), and LEDC's (Uruguay and Montevideo).

The relationship between the size of an urban area and its relative importance within a region or country is an intriguing mathematical aspect of urbanisation. In the 1940s the **rank-size rule** was first suggested as a explanation for this relationship. This rule states that the size of an urban area is inversely proportional to its rank. Using this rule the second largest city should be half the size of the largest city and the third largest city, one-third. This relationship is most easy to identify using logarithmic graph paper, on which a perfect negative relationship would be plotted as a straight

FIGURE 17.4 Rank size rule

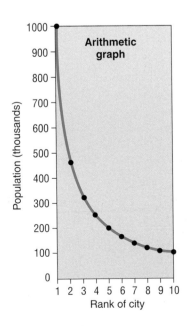

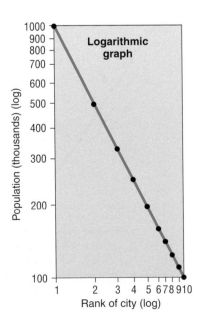

Peru

India

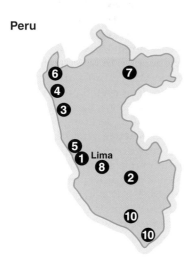

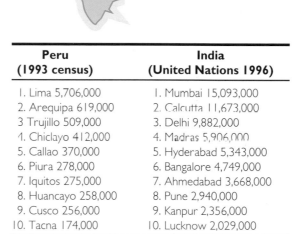

FIGURE 17.5 India and Peru: rank size of ten largest cities

45° line sloping downwards (see Figure 17.4). Primacy is when the largest city is a great deal larger than the second city. A **binary distribution** is when two cities dominate the urban hierarchy, for example in Australia (Melbourne and Sydney).

The rapid growth of urbanisation in LEDCs has reinforced the primacy of many countries. With this comes a number of particular problems. The primate city, nearly always the capital city of a country, dominates the country's economy. It is the location of most of the growth in employment opportunities, trade and wealth. As a consequence the primate city is often the single destination for rural–urban migrants.

The rapid growth of some primate cities in LEDCs creates substantial problems for urban decision-makers in providing housing and infrastructure. Efforts to decentralise economic growth to smaller urban centres in order to reduce congestion and to spread the benefits of economic growth have had limited success.

In China and India where the city hierarchy at a national level does not suggest primacy or conformity to the rank-size rule, major cities within the regional context do show a strong trend towards primacy within regions. An example of this tendency is the Indian state of Karnataka. With a

Peru (1993 census)	India (United Nations 1996)
1. Lima 5,706,000	1. Mumbai 15,093,000
2. Arequipa 619,000	2. Calcutta 11,673,000
3. Trujillo 509,000	3. Delhi 9,882,000
4. Chiclayo 412,000	4. Madras 5,906,000
5. Callao 370,000	5. Hyderabad 5,343,000
6. Piura 278,000	6. Bangalore 4,749,000
7. Iquitos 275,000	7. Ahmedabad 3,668,000
8. Huancayo 258,000	8. Pune 2,940,000
9. Cusco 256,000	9. Kanpur 2,356,000
10. Tacna 174,000	10. Lucknow 2,029,000

FIGURE 17.6 Comparing the rank order of urban areas in Peru and India

---

STUDENT ACTIVITY 17.1

1 Using Figure 17.6 plot the population of the cities against their rank on logarithmic graph paper or standard graph paper for both countries.
2 Draw a line to represent the rank-size rule on each graph. Describe how the urban hierarchies of India and Peru compare with the rank-size rule.
3 What specific problems do you think a primate city such as Lima may cause decision-makers in LEDCs?

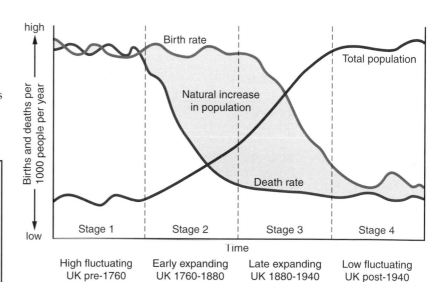

FIGURE 17.7 Demographic transition model

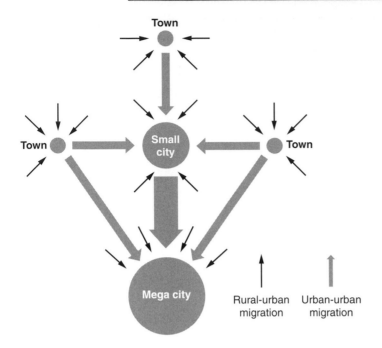

Town

Town   Town

Small
city

Mega city   Rural-urban   Urban-urban
                 migration   migration

FIGURE 17.8 Multi-stage
migration model

Natural population growth in LEDC's can be
analysed using the **Demographic Transition
Model**, (see Figure 17.7). This model is similar to
the model of urbanisation in LEDCs (Figure 17.2) in
that it shows a continuum into which an individual
county can be placed. Some LEDCs are currently
experiencing high levels of overall population
growth (Mozambique 3.4%, Afghanistan 5.6%) that
suggest high birth rates and declining death rates.
Other LEDCs are experiencing a marked decline in
natural population growth rates as a result of
improving economic opportunities, increasing
freedom for women and improvements to welfare
systems. What is notable is that in many LEDC
cities natural population growth rates are normally
lower than in rural areas. However overall the rate
of urban population growth is greater than rural
population growth. This is a result of rural–urban
migration.

Why Migrate To The City?

Migration into the cities of LEDCs has, in the past,
been predominantly a phenomenon of rural to
urban movement. In recent years movement from
small urban areas to larger urban areas, or **inter-
urban migration**, has been increasingly common. In
Bangalore, India, 58% of migrants to the city have
migrated from other urban areas. Often this is a
second stage migration after an initial migration
from a rural area to a local small town or city, (see
Figure 17.8). The rate of increase in the urban
populations of small urban areas has, in the 1990s
been far greater than that of the mega-cities.

Some of this movement into large urban areas is
permanent and some temporary, but the key
motivating factor is normally economic. The city is
seen as a place of opportunity. In LEDC's most
employment growth, improvements in levels of
disposable income, expansion of amenities and

population of 45 million (1991 census), and a land
area of 191,773 square kilometres, Karnatka is larger
than England and Wales. The urban hierarchy of the
State is dominated by the city of Bangalore, which is
seven times the size of the next largest urban area,
Mysore, population 650,000.

Why Has Urbanisation Been So Rapid?

There are two processes that have contributed to the
rapid growth of less economically developed cities;
natural population change and in-migration.
Natural population change is the difference
between deaths and births within an area.
Migration normally has a large additional impact
on the growth of urban populations in LEDCs.

FIGURE 17.9 Health and
Education indicators for
selected countries

INDICATOR COUNTRY	Mortality rate for children under 5 (deaths per 1000 births)	% of children between 12 and 23 months with all vaccinations	Total fertility rate	% of females over 6 years with no education
KENYA (1993)				
Urban	75	81	3.4	13
Rural	96	78	5.8	29
BOLIVIA (1994)				
Urban	104	44	3.8	11
Rural	162	24	6.3	33
BANGLADESH (1993)				
Urban	114	70	2.7	34
Rural	153	57	3.5	50
INDONESIA (1991)				
Urban	84	65	2.6	15
Rural	116	41	3.2	29
SENEGAL (1992)				
Urban	102	65	5.1	51
Rural	184	40	6.7	89

Source: Institute for Resource Development, USA

Push factors	Pull factors
Rural Poverty	Employment opportunities
Sub-division of land to uneconomic size	Higher incomes
Agricultural technology displacing rural labourers	Better health care and education
Lack of public amenities, education, health care etc	Access to urban culture and freedoms
Drought and other natural disasters	Protection from civil and military conflict
Religious, social and political discrimination	Promotion of urban consumer values via media
Unemployment and under-employment	Glamour and excitement
Family conflict	Family contacts
War and civil revolt	Improving transport systems
Government Policy (more state spending in cities)	Government Policy

FIGURE 17.10 Push and pull factors in rural to urban migration

increases in personal freedom have occurred in urban areas.

Knowledge of the opportunities afforded by cities has never been more openly available, even to the most isolated rural communities. Globalisation of telecommunications has meant that knowledge of urban lifestyles and urban opportunities is not only increasingly accessible but also glamourised. The urban consumer culture is the dominant model in the world of advertising, television and radio. These forces are examples of the **pull factors** of rural–urban migration: those considerations which draw migrants towards the city. Two of the most often cited attractions of urban areas for rural migrants are health and education. Figure 17.9 illustrates the difference between urban and rural health statistics in selected countries.

The reality of urban in-migration is that it is an act usually influenced by a range of factors. The potential attractions of urban living must be set against the lived experience of rural life. This

experience is for many a life of poverty, beset by periodic natural disasters. Rural communities often have very little economic and political power to influence and participate in change. **Push factors** are the variety of forces which prompt the consideration of migration into urban areas. Figure 17.10 summarises a range of push and pull factors that may influence rural to urban migration.

STUDENT ACTIVITY 17.2

Read the two case studies of rural to urban migration below.
1 For each case study draw up a list of those factors that prompted migration. Divide these into push and pull factors.
2 Draw a flow diagram which shows the stages in the Ramirez family's search for a home.
3 Repeat the above exercise for Krishna's family.

CASE STUDY

Case Study 1

It was in 1973 when Jose Ramirez, 31, left his wife and three young children at their rented farmstead in Parana State, Brazil, to travel to the city of Sao Paulo to find work. The rains had been poor and the one hectare plot they farmed produced less food every year. There was no extra money to buy fertilisers and pesticides to increase their productivity. Initially Jose lived with a cousin who had moved to the city two years previously. He found temporary work on a night shift at a factory.

When drought destroyed the crops on the farm, Jose's wife and children joined him in Sao Paulo and they were forced to rent a room in an inner-city tenement block. Jose's wife, Ines, found work as a maid which gave them two incomes and with the extra money they were able to get a loan from a money lender to buy a plot of land in an illegal sub-division on the edge of Sao Paulo. The Ramirez family constructed a temporary shack on the land

but after a year floods inundated the site and they were forced to live in a plastic tent for six months. In 1979 Jose lost his job and the private firm which sold drinking water to those in the illegal sub-division from a tanker raised its prices. The Ramirez family could not pay back the loan to the money lender. They were forced to sell the land to pay off the loan and return to a rented room in an inner-city tenement.

In 1981 Jose heard about a squatter invasion of land in the slum of Heliopolis, near to Sao Paulo's main industrial area. The squatters occupied an area that had been set aside as a football pitch in the initial invasion of the area. The family built a temporary shack and began to get involved with local community groups who had been campaigning for improvements to the slum.

It was the election of a new mayor in Sao Paulo in 1983 that led to legal tenure being granted to all residents of Heliopolis and infrastructure improvements were made. By this time both Jose and Ines had found new work, Ines through the skills she learnt in a tailoring school. With other residents the Ramirez family formed a co-operative and applied for a loan from the national housing bank. The co-operative was successful and with the money the Ramirez family were able to build a permanent, one floor structure to replace their wooden shack. This was in 1985, so it had taken the family 12 years to secure a safe, affordable home in Sao Paulo.

CASE STUDY

Case Study 2

Krishna comes from southern Andhra Pradesh, some 300 miles north of Bangalore. This is an arid drought prone area of the Deccan Plateau and for the rural small holders of this area scratching a living from the soil is a lifetime's work. For a Dalit (the lowest caste in Hinduism) like Krishna even farming a small plot of land is beyond his dreams: his family has no land. The extended familiy lived in a collection of one roomed shacks on the edge of the village. Historically his family have made their living as day labourers and as itinerant magicians at religious festivals.

Used to travelling for work Krishana, his three brothers and their families as well as Krishna's parents and grandmother moved to a brick kiln in rural northern Karnataka to work as day labourers. Here they lived in tents but made enough money to feed the whole family. One day a lorry arrived at the brick kiln with some building contractors from Bangalore. They were looking for workers to break stones to make gravel for the new ring road being built around the city. The owner of the brick kiln was given money to release Krishna's family from their work contracts and along with several other extended Dalit families from Andhra Pradesh they were transported to a building site on the northern edge of Bangalore in the back of a lorry.

In Bangalore the family lived in their tents at the road building site and all who could worked. They could not speak the local language, Kannada, but they soon found out that they were earning far less than the local workers. They had no way of complaining so they spent what free time they had looking for better paid building work. Krishna's eldest brother found work on a road building gang in the satellite town of Yelankha but it was 5 kilometres from their present tent site and if they changed jobs they would be thrown off this land.

Eventually a free site in a marsh area at the edge of an existing slum in Yelhanka was found and the family moved with a number of fellow Dalit families. Their current illegally occupied site (see Yelankha New Town Slum, Chapter 19), has no amenities and is prone to flooding. The women, elderly people and children who do not have paid work make toys using papier mache and sticks which they sell at the local markets and on festival days. Although they have now been in this location for nearly two years, using amenities in the neighbouring more established slum areas, Krishna hopes he and his family will one day have enough money to return to his village and buy a house with some land and be able to send their children to school.

18
URBAN STRESS: THE CONSEQUENCES OF RAPID EXPANSION

Key Ideas

■ Urban areas in less economically developed countries are characterised by stark inequalities in the quality of life experienced by residents.

■ These inequalities become even greater as the urban area becomes increasingly incorporated into the global economy.

Demanding Cities

The growth of cities inevitably leads to a growth in the demand for basic services, facilities and opportunities. The demand for housing, water, sanitation, employment and public services such as education is nearly always in excess of the city's capacity to provide them. From an environmental perspective the per capita use of resources is, in most less developed countries, at present higher in urban areas than in rural areas. Urbanisation therefore could be viewed as an increasing drain on a country's environmental capital (i.e. water, land, natural resources).

The principle force behind urbanisation is economic development and this in itself has demands. Economic development demands an increasingly healthy and educated workforce. This workforce needs to be adequately housed and also to have access to the goods and services provided by economic growth. Urbanisation is also demanding of natural resources and the technology needed to turn them into goods and services. Yet it this dynamism and consumption of resources that attracts so many migrants. Cities are where economic growth is visible and tangible for the vast majority of the world's population.

The key issues facing most LEDC cities concern their inability to keep pace with the demands placed on the city's resources. Housing shortages, inadequate amenities, lack of water and unemployment are all examples of this. Competition by citizens for limited opportunities and resources can lead to all types of conflict including social disorganisation, family breakdown, crime, communalism and ethnic violence.

The key problem facing most decision-makers involved in urbanisation in LEDCs is how to address the issue of a mis-match between demand and supply of resources. On another level, the political choices involved in deciding how to bring about development are also highly important. Are urban issues to be tackled by governments, either local or national, using money raised through taxation and borrowing ? Or is the private sector to take a lead, investing capital in those projects which can provide a competitive rate of return? In reality nearly all countries in LEDCs operate a mixed system of resource allocation, both public and private.

Bangalore, the fastest growing city in south Asia?

Bangalore, the regional capital of the Indian state of Karnataka, (see Figure 18.1), is one of India's most dynamic and modern cities. With a population of 5 million in 1995 it has been stated that the city is amongst the most rapidly expanding urban areas in the world. Bangalore has become India's most important centre for information technology, biotechnology, aerospace, machine tools and consumer electronics, all modern industries whose development has fuelled Bangalore's urban expansion.

FIGURE 18.1a Karnataka in India

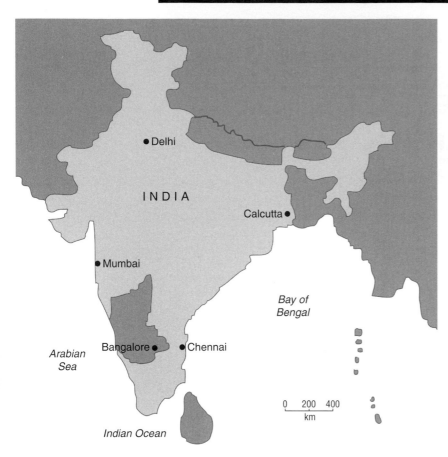

FIGURE 18.1b Bangalore in Karnataka

FIGURE 18.2 Mahatma Ghandi Road in Bangalore's Central Business District

STUDENT ACTIVITY 18.1

Draw a line graph from the data in Figure 18.3 showing the growth of Bangalore's population. Annotate your line graph by adding the statements below to the correct part of the graph.

■ Rapid growth fueled by India's independence creates a large influx of rural migrants into new industrial occupations.
■ The development of a major global information technology industry helps maintain population growth.
■ Steady but low growth rates during the city's occupation by the British.
■ An industrial and commercial boom in the city is created by the growth of modern high technology industries, urban to urban in-migration becomes increasingly important.
■ Estimates for the future suggest a slowing growth rate but high absolute increases in population.

The claim that Bangalore was south Asia's fastest growing city in the 1970s is difficult to substantiate, yet this was a claim made with pride by many in the city who saw population growth as being a clear indicator of economic dynamism. Figure 18.4 shows the growth of Bangalore's population in the twentieth century. Clearly rapid growth of the population has occurred since the 1940s.

In part of the 1970s this was over 10% per year. The most recent population growth statistics from the United Nations suggest that Bangalore is a fast growing city with a growth rate of 3% per year in the late 1990s, increasing its population each year by about 150,000. However even within India some cities, both larger and smaller than Bangalore, are growing more rapidly.

Year	Population	Absolute change	% Change
1901	228000		
1911	280000	52000	22.80%
1921	311000	31000	11.00%
1931	396000	85000	27.30%
1941	510000	114000	28.70%
1951	991000	481000	94.30%
1961	1207000	216000	21.70%
1971	1664000	457000	37.80%
1981	2913000	1249000	75.00%
1991	4086000	1173000	40.20%
2001	5800000	1714000	41.90%
2011	7000000	1200000	20.60%

FIGURE 18.3 (opposite) Population Growth Bangalore 1901–2011

Whatever the arguments about relative rates of urban growth, Bangalore is a major urban area under increasing stress. Figure 18.5 illustrates the size and nature of the challenges facing modern Bangalore.

The Growth of Bangalore

Bangalore has had a proud and diverse history between its founding in 1527 and the arrival of the British in 1791. Yet it was the British who, in setting up their largest military garrison in southern India, were the major influence on the development of Bangalore into a major city. The British were attracted by the city's pleasant climate, a result of being located on a 1000 metre plateau. This was later to prove an attraction for many academic and high technology establishments which located in the city.

The city, was throughout the nineteenth and first half of the twentieth century, essentially two cities next to each other:

■ The original city of Bangalore – a densely populated area with fortifications, a palace and numerous temples.
■ The British city, called the **cantonment** – a military garrison town with barracks, parade grounds, churches and bungalow accommodation for the senior political and military administrators. Between the two centres lay the 'civil lines', an area set aside for the traders and Indian support staff of the British army. The extensive Cubbon Park, a horse racing course and numerous lakes were also located in this area. The Indian and British districts of Bangalore were highly segregated.

It was not until India gained independence in 1947 that the administration of Bangalore became unified. A huge parliament building for the State of Karnataka, called the Vidhana Soudha was constructed in Cubbon Park. At this time, the decision by the Indian central government to concentrate certain industries and educational and research centers in Bangalore provided the impetus for the city to grow rapidly. In the 1980s Bangalore became the location for the first major foreign high technology investment in India (Texas Instruments of the USA).

The presence of numerous research institutions in the city created a pool of experienced, well qualified and, in global terms, inexpensive computer technologists. This attracted nearly every major information technology firm in the world many of whom still have some part of their operations in the city. By the late 1990s Bangalore confidently asserted itself to be the high technology capital of south Asia. It also claimed that it was the greenest and most pleasant city in India to live. By 2011 it is estimated that the population of Bangalore will reach 7 million.

Common problems of urban stress in LEDC cities

The issues of urban stress experienced in Bangalore are common in most LEDC cities. A study of any major city in an LEDC will indicate similar problems to those found in Bangalore. An indication of some of these problems in other cities around the world is shown in Figure 18.5.

FIGURE 18.4 Problems facing major cities in LEDC's

Bangkok, Thailand

Rapid urban and economic growth in Bangkok in the 1990s has produced a massive increase in traffic on the roads. Over 1000 people a year die in traffic accidents in Bangkok even though the average rush hour speed of traffic in the central part of the city is less than 10 miles an hour as a result of congestion.

Beijing, China

The city of Beijing has one of the lowest levels of private car ownership of a major city in the world. Yet the city has not escaped high levels of air pollution, particularly suspended particles and sulphur dioxide. The pollution is due to the dependence of the city's poor on coal as the major source of heating during Beijing's extremely cold winters. The inexpensive coal used has a very high sulphur content and the smoke given off hangs over the city like a dense fog during wind-less days.

Kinshasa, Zaire

About half of Kinshasa's population are not served by a piped water network. High income areas have a continuous supply of piped water. The rest of the city relies on water from wells or rivers. There is a flourishing business in water sales in those areas of the city which lack any method of supply, mainly the city's most recent slums.

Kingston, Jamaica

Only 18% of the population of Kingston are connected to the dilapidated sewage system which dates from colonial times and only covers the central part of the city. Nearly half of the population have to use pit latrines which cause serious contamination of ground water supplies. One in 12 residents of the city have no access to any toilet facilities.

Energy demand far outstrips the authority's ability to provide electricity. Wealthy citizens rely on back-up diesel generators for electricity. Poorer citizens often have to make illegal connections to electricity supplies in order to have even the most basic of facilities such as a light bulb.

Housing shortages are most acute for the city's poor. Recent migrants from the country often build makeshift shacks on land at the edge of the city or on the building sites where they work in order to get a foothold.

Water supply and sewage disposal are particularly difficult problems to address. Residents in some areas have no regular water connections. The poor often travel to other areas which are connected. Wealthier people often buy water from tankers which deliver supplies to their homes. Sewage disposal is at worst non-existent and at best overburdened.

FIGURE 18.5 Major challenges facing Bangalore in the twenty-first century

Demand for housing by the urban middle class has created growth in the number of residential tower blocks. These new buildings are sometimes constructed with poor health and safety standards and built prior to a connection with an already overburdened urban infrastructure. Water and electricity connections can be problematic and the sewage connections are sometimes non-existent.

STUDENT ACTIVITY 18.2

1 Research on Bangalore has been made easier with the development of the World Wide Web. Bangalore is well served by web sites giving all sorts of information about the city. Explore some of these web sites and use the information you find to help you write a concise but detailed introduction to the city.
2 Draw a time line indicating the major events in the development of Bangalore.
3 Choose another city in an LEDC. Using the World-Wide Web, newspapers on CD-ROM, books and magazine sources research and write a brief presentation about the development and current problems of your chosen city.

Traffic on Bangalore's roads has grown far quicker than the road system can develop to accommodate it. Pollution, congestion and traffic accidents have become common place for many of Bangalore's citizens.

19
CITIES OF EXTREMES: INEQUALITY IN THE CITY

Key Ideas

- Urban areas in less economically developed countries are characterised by stark inequalities in the quality of life experienced by residents.

- These inequalities become even greater as the urban area becomes increasingly incorporated into the global economy.

From penthouse to slum

Urbanisation in LEDCs has often been studied with a particular focus on the extremely poor quality of life experienced by the residents of slum housing. Figure 19.1 shows that, in fact, the proportion of urban residents who live in such housing is highly variable. National definitions of slum housing may also vary considerably.

Figure 19.1 indicates that the majority of residents in cities of the less developed world live in housing which is planned and regulated by local government. This housing is located in neighbourhoods with highly variable qualities of life. Residential environments can vary from penthouse apartments for the rich to legally recognised slum areas with basic amenities.

Inequality in Bangalore

Bangalore is one of the most economically successful cities in India. In the past 30 years it has attracted both a major influx of industries and migrants looking for work. An important aspect of this development has been the growth of an urban middle class employed increasingly in service industries, information technology and high technology manufacturing. This group make up 40% of the city's population. Bangalore has also become home for an urban elite who work in the trans-national companies (TNCs) that have located part of their operations in the city.

However, a large number of people are excluded from the benefits of this economic development. Nearly a million people, representing 20% of the population live in slums.

	Dar Es Salem, Tanzania	Istanbul, Turkey	Karachi, Pakistan	Kingston, Jamaica	Rio de Janeiro	Bogota, Colombia	Manila, Philippines
% slums as a total of all housing	51	51	44	33	16	8	6

FIGURE 19.1 The prevalence of slum housing in selected cities of less economically developed countries

CASE STUDY

Measuring Residential Inequality in Bangalore

The material for this case study was collected from fieldwork, the 1991 Indian census and the Bangalore Development Authority.

- Figure 19.2 shows the location of six residential districts within Bangalore.

- Figure 19.3 is a set of data giving general information about each area, some from the 1991census.
- Figure 19.4 is a table of results of a fieldwork exercise in which the quality of life of each area was assessed using a range of criteria.
- Figure 19.5 outlines the criteria used in the quality of life fieldwork exercise.

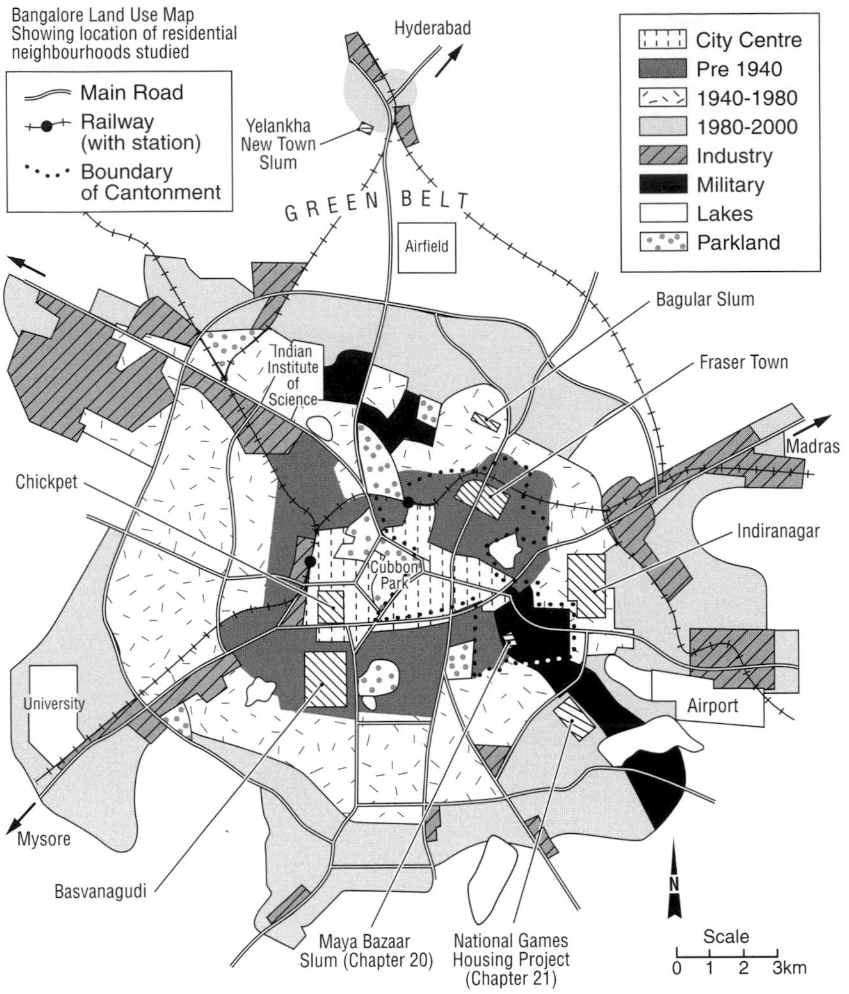

Bangalore Land Use Map
Showing location of residential
neighbourhoods studied

::::	City Centre
▨	Pre 1940
▨	1940-1980
▨	1980-2000
▨	Industry
■	Military
□	Lakes
░	Parkland

STUDENT ACTIVITY 19.1

Study the map, data, photographs and the short descriptions of each area.

1 Draw an annotated sketch map showing the locations of each area within Bangalore. Include in your annotation a brief description of each area.

2 Devise a bi-polar table to evaluate each area based upon the information and photographs. Figure 19.6 is an example of a bi-polar table and two criteria. Think of at least another six criteria with which to evaluate each area.

3 How do your bi-polar results compare to the results of the quality of life index?

4 Study the criteria used in the quality of life index. Do you think that they are appropriate criteria to use? How do you think you would go about collecting the data needed to complete this fieldwork exercise?

5 Write down five more public amenities that could have been used in this exercise.

6 How might you change the weighting given to the criteria in order to make the quality of life index more reflective of residents interests? Would you for instance give water supply and road infrastructure an identical weighting ?

7 Draw a scatter graph plotting quality of life score against distance from the city centre. Is it possible to identify any patterns?

8 Design a set of criteria you could use for a quality of life index to be used in a British city. Remember to think about how you would get the information to complete it.

FIGURE 19.2 Bangalore's six residential districts

FIGURE 19.3 Residential difference six areas of Bangalore

	Chickpet	Basavanagudi	Fraser Town	Bagular Slum	Indiranagar	Yelankha New Town Slum
Age of settlement	300 years	100 years	85 years	40 years	20 years	I year
Distance from centre[1]	2.2km	4km	3.5km	5km	5km	15km
% literacy	78	81	73	47	n/a	10
% pop' SC/ST[2]	0.2	4	23	65	n/a	100
Density: people/hectare	802	233	307	1200	149	n/a

[1]Centre of Bangalore Vidhana Soudha, (Karnataka State Parliament Building), Cubbon Park. This is located between traditional Bangalore City and the British colonial cantonment and is a compromise location for a two centred city.
[2]SC/ST (Scheduled Castes/Scheduled Tribes) is useful measure of poverty because these sections of Indian society are often rural in origin, poorly educated and most discriminated against in society.

FIGURE 19.4 Quality of life index for residential areas in Bangalore

	Chickpet	Basavanagudi	Fraser Town	Bagular Slum	Indiranagar	Yelankha New Town Slum
Water Supply	+3	+3	+3	+1	+4	0
Electricity Supply	+2	+2	+2	+1	+3	0
Communications 1	+2	+2	+2	+1	+3	0
Communications 2	+1	+1	+2	+1	+2	+1
Built Environment	+2	+3	+3	+1	+4	0
Built Environment	+3	+4	+4	+1	+4	0
Public Amenities	+6	+8	+10	+4	+10	+2
Total Score	17	23	26	10	30	3

1 Water supply
   +4 virtually all households have a personal water supply 24 hours a day
   +3 virtually all households have a personal water supply at some time in the day
   +2 over half of households dependent on public water supply
   +1 virtually all households dependent on public water supply
    0 no water supply in the area.
2 Electricity supply
   +3 virtually all households have a legal electricity supply which is continuous
   +2 over half of households have a legal electricity supply which is intermittent
   +1 majority of households have access to illegal electricity supplies
    0 no electricity
3 Communications 1
   +3 over one half of households with satellite and Internet connections
   +2 public and private telephones installed
   +1 public telephones only
    0 no telephones
4 Communications 2
   +2 most residents have access to private transport
   +1 access to affordable public transport
    0 poor access to public transport
5 Built Environment
   +4 all roads paved and well maintained, clear pavements, tree lined
   +3 75% of roads paved and tree lined
   +2 paved roads poorly maintained and crowded
   +1 unpaved road layout
    0 haphazard, unplanned, unpaved layout
6 Built Environment 2
   +4 fully sewered sanitation connecting majority of households
   +3 partial sewage system connecting most households
   +2 open sewers or malfunctioning sewers for most households
   +1 few public toilets for overall population
    0 no public toilets available in immediate area
7 Public Amenities
   +2 for all public amenities in list below (+10 maximum score)
■ daily police patrol (security)
■ public hospital within 30 minutes travelling time (health)
■ tenants or residents association (empowerment)
■ public/welfare organisation primary school within residential area (education)
■ public greenspace within or adjacent to residential area (recreation)

FIGURE 19.5 Criteria used in quality of life index

FIGURE 19.6 Bi-polar table and two criteria

	+1	+2	+1	0	−1	−2	−3	
Well maintained								Poorly maintained
Quiet								Noisy

Descriptions of six residential areas in Bangalore

Chickpet

This is the oldest residential district in Bangalore. Along with the neighbouring districts of Balepet and Cottonpet, Chickpet is on the site of the original fort built in 1537 by Kempegowda I the founder of Bangalore. This area, located next to the main city market and Tipu Sultan's Palace, was the core of the original city of Bangalore. The area is the most densely populated in the city and is characterised by a mixture of old and new buildings containing businesses of all types and residential accommodation. Open urinals, overflowing bins and narrow congested streets are typical here.

FIGURE 19.7 Chickpet: crowded markets dominate the narrow main roads

FIGURE 19.8 Chickpet: new apartments jostle for space in this long established area

The sewerage system is overloaded and in a state of chronic disrepair. Many residents have been unable to use their toilets and have to use those of relatives who live in neighbouring areas. However commerce is booming in the area with shops of all kinds, warehouses, medical facilities and small scale manufacturing all crammed together in streets barely wide enough for a single car to pass. Land prices are high because of the area's central locality.

Basavanagudi

When in the late 1890s bubonic plague broke out in the densely populated old city, a number of residential extensions where built on what was then the edge of the city of Bangalore. These include Malleswaram to the north, Chamarajet to the west and Basavanagudi to the south. Basavanagudi, built in 1901–1905, was full of spacious residences in extensive grounds, laid out in a series of tree-lined avenues radiating from a central square. Water supply and sewage were adequately provided for and few commercial activities took place. The area was initially dominated by high caste Brahmins who held the majority of jobs in government and education. A preponderance of ornate Hindu temples in the area indicates this community's influence on the area.

By the 1970s demand for land in Bangalore was so intense that most of the old houses had new apartments built in their grounds. Shops, hotels and cottage industries started to spill into the area having been pushed out of the neighbouring city centre due to lack of space. The roads are now congested with traffic passing through the area from the suburbs to the city centre. Many of the old original Brahmin families have relocated to new residential areas towards the edge of the city. However the area still contains popular schools, restaurants and temples.

FIGURE 19.9 Basavanagudi: nearly 100 years old the original villas retain their grandeur

FIGURE 19.10 Basavanagudi: trees line well laid out roads providing welcome shade

Fraser Town

Although the British established a cantonment (military and political base), in Bangalore in 1809 it was not until the 1860s that development in this area to the east of the old city began in earnest. A large area of green space, Cubbon Park, separated the British residential cantonment and its military

FIGURE 19.11 Fraser Town: old and new together on one plot

facilities from the Indian town. Around the cantonment area, a planned civil area grew, centred around Russell Market. This was where the native administrative staff of the British Army lived and where the businesses serving the military were based.

Fraser Town was a residential district of the cantonment area and spacious bungalows set in gardens were the dominant type of house. Many examples of these colonial bungalows remain but demand for land has seen a proliferation of apartment blocks, often built in the spacious gardens that once separated the bungalows. These apartments, although targeted at the upper-middle class, are putting a serious strain upon the existing water and sewerage infrastructure which dates from the late nineteenth century. Water rationing is now common and pollution of watercourses and the neighboring Ulsoor Lake are serious environmental problems, as are the slums which have grown on the edge of the area to house the construction workers of the new apartment blocks.

Bagular Slum

Established in 1962, at that time this slum area would have been at the periphery of the city, but urban growth now places it well within the city. The slum is recognised as legal by the city authorities and a number of improvements have been made both to the infrastructure and housing in recent years. With a population of 6000 crammed into 900 houses stretched along a strip of land bordered by a cemetery, railway and two main

roads, Bagular Slum is typical of hundreds of similar areas scattered throughout the city.

Most residents are Tamils, in-migrants from rural areas of the neighbouring State of Tamil Nadu. They belong to the lowest Hindu caste groups or are Christians. The homes, the majority of which were built by the residents, are normally one or two roomed constructions with either a thatch or tile roof. All water comes from 12 street taps, although it is an intermittent service. Toilet facilities comprise a number of community built concrete blocks and a corporation run bathroom and shower complex. Electricity, from either illegal or legal connections, is only found in 25% of homes although the slum has a network of functioning street lamps. Prostitution, illegal drug use, alcoholism and violence are all features of this slum. The average monthly household income in this area is approximately £35. Rental of land can be as low as £1 a month. Food normally accounts for 70% of household income.

FIGURE 19.12 Fraser Town: new houses await completion

FIGURE 19.14 Bagular Slum: houses cling to the edge of an open sewer

FIGURE 19.15 Indiranagar: architect-designed houses line well-maintained roads

FIGURE 19.13 Bagular Slum: satellite dishes bring the world into the slum but still people queue for water

Indiranagar

Indiranagar is considered by many to be Bangalore's most select residential area. Laid out in the 1970s, the large plots were soon filled with individual architect designed houses. Uncluttered pavements edge tree-lined, well maintained roads in a grid pattern. No slums fill public spaces and the local shopping streets include pizza takeaways, designer clothes shops and expensive restaurants. All households have access to private transport. Situated close to the airport, about halfway between the International Technology Park and the city centre, Indiranagar is a popular location for Bangalore's growing population of trans-national company executives.

FIGURE 19.16 Indiranagar: Bangalore's super rich enjoy all the trappings of the modern world

FIGURE 19.18 Yelankha New Town Slum: a simple brick built hut with a palm roof is the next step up from a tent

Indiranagar is not without problems. Electricity supply fails almost daily, but all homes have petrol run generators to cover these times. Cows still wander the roads grazing on the lush grass verges and traffic is on the increase. A common complaint is that Bangalore's best schools are situated too far from the area, resulting in a lengthy car journey in the morning rush hour.

Yelankha New Town Slum

Ten kilometres beyond the northern boundary of the Bangalore City Corporation, The Bangalore Regional Development Authority has developed the satellite town of Yelankha on the main national highway north. This is an attempt to absorb some of the pressure of urban growth on the city. The residential plots and the factory units that have been built here since the start of development in 1989 have also attracted the most recent migrants to the Bangalore area. Unable to find accommodation or land in an already crowded city, land prone to flooding at the edge of Yelankha is the only option for new migrants from the countryside.

About a hundred Telegu migrants (from the state of Andhra Pradesh) live in makeshift tents and a few very basic brick and thatch huts on vacant land adjacent to a more established slum. They are some of the poorest of Bangalore's residents. They have no access to water supply or sanitation within their own residential area and they have to travel into other areas where they are met with hostility as they are competing for already scarce resources.

FIGURE 19.17 Yelankha New Town Slum: Krishna and his extended family

They do not speak the local language of Kannada and all are illiterate. Their children have no access to a school. Work is available on road building projects in the local area. The residents do not see their migration as permanent: they have been in this location less than a year but expect to move on in the near future. They are constantly looking for a better site as their current location floods in the monsoon and their slum is unrecognized by the local authority and so they have no legal protection from eviction.

Differences in Income and lifestyle in Bangalore

All urban areas support a wide range of incomes and lifestyles. Bangalore is no exception. The following activity examines income inequality within Bangalore and how such inequality may be linked to residential quality of life.

Profiles

Mohan Desai

Age 24. Police Constable: £43/month. Spends salary on food and movies. Eats out daily. Does not go on holiday. Travels by bus. Educated to secondary school standard in Kannada, the local language. Reads Kannada newspapers and watches cable television. Ambition to be promoted to sergeant and earn £70/month.

Dr Ajanta Chandra

Age 38. Consultant hospital doctor: £215/month. Spends salary paying back loans, buying clothes and supporting her two children. Eats out every week. Likes to watch British comedies on cable TV but prefers going out to visit friends. Educated at Bangalore University and in the USA where she spent 5 years as a junior hospital doctor. Reads *Femina* and *Cosmopolitan*. Drives a Ford Escort. Carries a pager. Ambition to become a senior consultant and earn £350/month basic salary.

Krishna

Age 29. Building site labourer: £1.50/day as a casual worker. Spends money on food for family, never eats out, walks from home to building site. Does not read or watch television and has never attended school at any level. Ambition to return to village in Andhra Pradesh with enough money saved to buy a house and send his children to school.

Vinay Reddy

Age 35. Director foreign owned telecom company: £350,000/year. Spends money on clothes, children's education and entertainment. Eats regularly at the top restaurants in Bangalore. Educated at Universities in USA and Britain and has also worked in both countries in the past. Watches CNN and Discovery Channel and reads *India Today*, *Business Today* and *Readers Digest*. Favourite holiday locations are Australia and the Kovalam Beach Resort in Kerala. Drives a top of the range Mercedes car, owns a lap top computer, mobile phone and pager.

Ayesha Moorjani

Age 36. Account manager, advertising company: £145/month. Spends salary on food and clothes. Lives with his wife, a school teacher, and their two children in an extended family home with his parents and one grandparent. Goes on holiday once a year to Kodaikanal, a fashionable hill resort south of Bangalore. Educated to BA standard at Trivandurum University, Kerala. Watches ZeeTV and reads movie magazines. Rides a Suzuki motorcycle to work.

Chandamma

Age 42. Domestic help: £28/month plus 3 meals a day. Spends money on household. Does not eat out. Commutes by bus. Does not go on holiday. Educated at primary school for two years before dropping out. Watches Kannada movies on TV which she bought second hand from her employer. Spends time with her four children. Does not read.

Some other monthly salaries in Bangalore in May 1998 are:

- MTV veejay: £1100
- Software engineer, international company: £500
- Bank Manager: £385
- Japanese–English Interpreter: £242
- Chef in 5-star hotel: £170
- School teacher: £115
- Bus driver: £65
- Secretary: £57
- Petrol station cashier: £21.

STUDENT ACTIVITY 19.2

1 Six profiles of citizens of Bangalore are provided. These contain details of employment, income and lifestyle. Study the profiles and write down which individual you believe is likely to live in which residential area. All salaries given are monthly and the values are calculated using an exchange rate of 70 rupees to the pound. All case studies are based upon real individuals although names have been changed. The sources are fieldwork and an article in *Bangalore* magazine (May 1998) entitled 'Bangalore Salaries' (http://www.bangaloremag.com).

2 Share your assessment with your fellow students. Do you agree? Also consider these issues:

- What factors most informed your decisions?
- How does the way in which citizens in Bangalore spend their leisure time compare to citizens in a MEDC city?
- How do wage differentials compare to wage differentials in Britain?
- How are salaries linked to the transport that citizens use in Bangalore?
- How is educational attainment linked to employment opportunities?

20
SLUMS AND SQUATTER SETTLEMENTS: HOUSING THE URBAN POOR

Key Ideas

■ A slum is a low income residential area often lacking even the most basic infrastructure.
■ Slums are clear evidence of the intense inequality that exists in less economically developed cities.

■ It is possible to observe a pattern to the location of slums in less economically developed cities.
■ Residents of slum locations are often involved in action to improve their quality of life.

What is a slum?

There is a great deal of debate as to whether 'slum' is an appropriate word to use to describe the poorest quality urban housing. Some commentators consider it a derogatory expression and prefer to use terms they feel are more appropriate such as 'squatter settlements', 'informal housing', 'unregulated housing', 'shanty towns' or 'spontaneous settlements'. Some countries have their own terms for slum housing such as 'favela' in Brazil, 'gecekondus' in Turkey and 'pueblos jovenes' in Peru. In India local names are used, (such as bustees in Calcutta) but officially the term 'slum' is used to describe the housing of the poorest communities.

Whatever label is given to the housing of the urban poor, the image remains the same across the world. A slum is a housing area devoid of the most basic amenities which are taken for granted in more affluent neighbourhoods and countries. Unplanned and uncontrolled, slums mainly exist outside the regulated structure of the city.

Slums are often associated with :
■ a lack of basic sanitation
■ inadequate supplies of clean water
■ high incidences of disease, infant mortality, mental and physical disabilities
■ poor access to basic health care provision
■ illiteracy and limited access to education
■ crime and social disorder
■ overcrowding in poorly constructed housing made from low quality materials
■ no security of tenure
■ limited public participation in decision-making
■ locations on low value land often associated with major environmental hazards such as flooding, landslides and pollution.

FIGURE 20.1 City of the Dead, Cairo, Egypt. This slum area has developed in a graveyard close to the city walls

Why do slums exist?

Economic development led by industrialisation has been a feature of the recent history of most LEDCs. As a result, most of the world's population now works in urban-based manufacturing and service industries. In the 1950s most of the world's population was employed in agriculture. Although the world's economy has grown many times, population growth and unequal development have led to a growing number of people living in poverty in urban areas.

In cities throughout the world the rich and poor are spatially segregated into separate neighbourhoods. The formation of slum areas is an inevitable consequence of inequality. Most LEDCs have no welfare system, and planning and regulation of urban development can be haphazard. Slums are often spontaneous developments built by residents simply because they cannot afford the alternatives. Such slum areas in LEDCs differ from poor residential areas in MEDC cities. They have no access to basic urban infrastructure (roads, water, sanitation and electricity) or urban services (education, health and maintenance).

Where are slums located in urban areas?

Studies of slum housing in Asia, Latin America and Africa have shown some generalised locational features.

■ Slums are located in areas of low land value.
■ If possible they are located to minimise the cost and time of travel to work for slum dwellers.
■ They are often in locations prone to environmental hazards such as noise, air pollution, poor drainage, flooding, landslides and water pollution.
■ They are located in areas where the inhabitants are less likely to be evicted by land owners. Examples of such areas are government land, civic authority land and land adjacent to transport networks.
■ They are located away from areas of high income housing and high order commercial activities.
■ Many slums are found in locations on the periphery of the urban area.

FIGURE 20.2 Slum locations in Bangalore and 1 km zones around the dual city centres

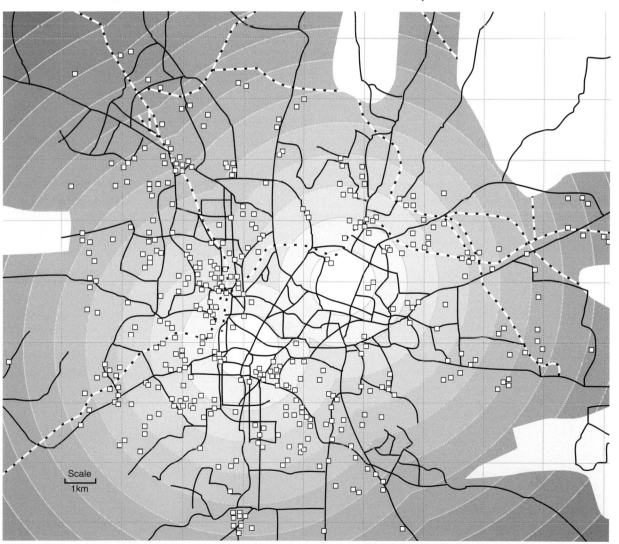

Scale
1 km

CASE STUDY

Slum location in Bangalore

To test whether the general observations of slum locations have any validity in Bangalore, Dr M. J. de Wit of the University of Amsterdam carried out a research project in 1992. Using computer geographical information systems and remote sensing techniques, 411 slum areas were identified and plotted on an outline map of Bangalore (see Figure 20.2). Researchers examined whether there was any observable spatial pattern of slum locations.

Note that Bangalore is considered to have two city centres. One is based around City Market, close to the original fort in the old town, and one is based around Russell Market, the main commercial area of the Cantonment area. Dual centres are typical of cities which developed under colonialism.

A statistical technique called the chi squared test was used. This test shows whether there is a relationship between two set of variables when the data for those variables is grouped together in categories. The variables in this case are distance from city centre and number of slums. The chi squared test assesses whether the observed pattern of slum locations in Bangalore is similar or different from the expected pattern.

The first stage, therefore, is to define the null hypothesis: if there is no observable pattern between distance from the city centre and slum location we would expect an even distribution of slums throughout the city. Then we define the alternative hypothesis: distance from the city centre influences the number of slum locations observed.

Next we calculate the expected frequencies assuming an even spread of slum locations across the city. To see how this was done refer to the table below (see Figure 20.3).

To calculate chi squared (X^2) for each zone the following formula is used:

$$X^2 = \Sigma \ \frac{(O-E)^2}{E}$$

where O = observed sites
E = expected sites
Σ = sum of

STUDENT ACTIVITY 20.1

1 Make a copy of the table shown in Figure 20.3 and complete it by calculating the final value for chi squared.
2 Once you have calculated the final value of chi squared, you must calculate the degrees of freedom. This tells you whether the number you have calculated for chi squared allows you to reject or accept the null hypothesis.
In this example the degrees of freedom is: (the number of rows−1) × (the number of columns −1) = or 17 × 1 =17.
3 Using a set of statistical tables look up the critical values for chi squared for 17 degrees of freedom. This is normally shown for two measures of probability (or levels of significance). 95% means that there is a 1 in 20 chance of your result occurring by chance. It is best to use the 99% level of significance as there is only a 1 in 100 probability of the result occurring by chance.
4 The calculated value of chi squared must be the same or greater than the value given in the table in order to reject the null hypothesis. If you reject the null hypothesis you also accept the altenative hypothesis that there *is* a relationship between slum locations and distance from the city centre.
5 Draw a simple bar graph to plot the number of slums in 1 km zones from the city centre using the data shown in Figure 20.3. Label both axes appropriately and write a short commentary underneath describing the pattern of slum distribution you observe.
6 Look back at the map evidence in previous chapters and consider the historical development of Bangalore's urban morphology and then attempt to explain why this pattern might have occurred.

FIGURE 20.3 Observed and expected values for number of slum locations in Bangalore

Distance From Centre	% Cover of Total Urban Area	Expected Sites	Observed Sites	Chi-squared
1km	1.6%	6.4	15	11.6
2km	4.3%	17.5	50	60.4
3km	5.5%	22.5	99	
4km	6.7%	27.6	69	
5km	8.1%	33.2	64	
6km	9.4%	38.7	48	
7km	10.1%	41.5	40	
8km	10.1%	41.5	14	
9km	10.4%	42.9	7	
10km	10.2%	42.1	1	
11km	8.9%	36.6	3	
12km	6.8%	28.1	1	
13km	4.8%	19.7	0	
14km	1.7%	7.1	0	
15km	0.4%	1.5	0	
16km	0.5%	1.9	0	
17km	0.5%	1.9	0	
18km	0.0%	0.1	0	
Totals	**100%**	**411**	**411**	

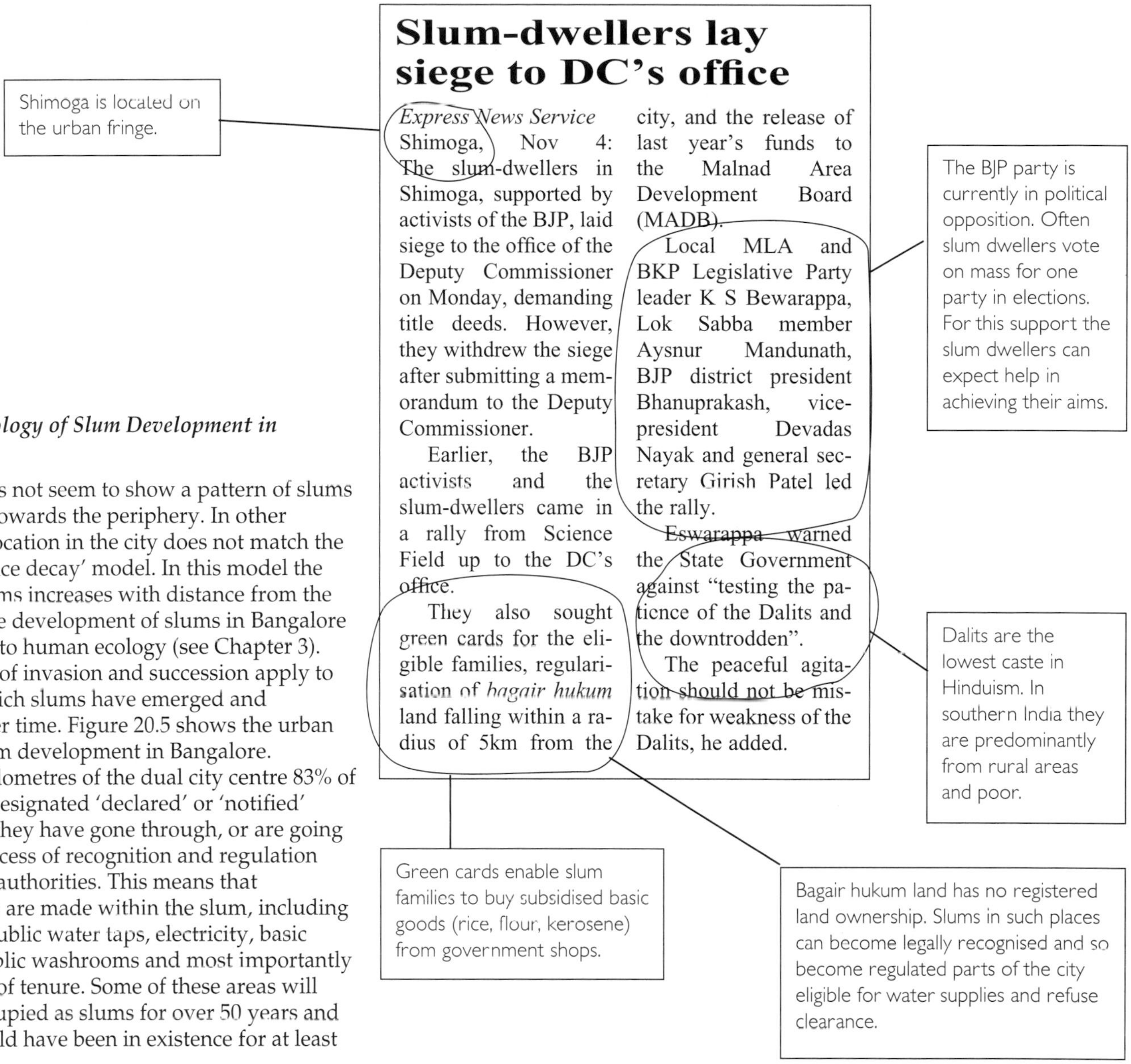

Slum-dwellers lay siege to DC's office

Shimoga is located on the urban fringe.

Express News Service
Shimoga, Nov 4: The slum-dwellers in Shimoga, supported by activists of the BJP, laid siege to the office of the Deputy Commissioner on Monday, demanding title deeds. However, they withdrew the siege after submitting a memorandum to the Deputy Commissioner.

Earlier, the BJP activists and the slum-dwellers came in a rally from Science Field up to the DC's office.

They also sought green cards for the eligible families, regularisation of *bagair hukum* land falling within a radius of 5km from the city, and the release of last year's funds to the Malnad Area Development Board (MADB).

Local MLA and BKP Legislative Party leader K S Bewarappa, Lok Sabba member Aysnur Mandunath, BJP district president Bhanuprakash, vice-president Devadas Nayak and general secretary Girish Patel led the rally.

Eswarappa warned the State Government against "testing the patience of the Dalits and the downtrodden".

The peaceful agitation should not be mistake for weakness of the Dalits, he added.

The BJP party is currently in political opposition. Often slum dwellers vote on mass for one party in elections. For this support the slum dwellers can expect help in achieving their aims.

Dalits are the lowest caste in Hinduism. In southern India they are predominantly from rural areas and poor.

Green cards enable slum families to buy subsidised basic goods (rice, flour, kerosene) from government shops.

Bagair hukum land has no registered land ownership. Slums in such places can become legally recognised and so become regulated parts of the city eligible for water supplies and refuse clearance.

The Urban Ecology of Slum Development in Bangalore

Bangalore does not seem to show a pattern of slums concentrated towards the periphery. In other words, slum location in the city does not match the 'inverse distance decay' model. In this model the number of slums increases with distance from the city centre. The development of slums in Bangalore can be related to human ecology (see Chapter 3). The processes of invasion and succession apply to the way in which slums have emerged and developed over time. Figure 20.5 shows the urban ecology of slum development in Bangalore.

Within 3 kilometres of the dual city centre 83% of all slums are designated 'declared' or 'notified' meaning that they have gone through, or are going through, a process of recognition and regulation with the local authorities. This means that improvements are made within the slum, including provision of public water taps, electricity, basic sanitation, public washrooms and most importantly of all security of tenure. Some of these areas will have been occupied as slums for over 50 years and nearly all would have been in existence for at least 20 years.

Over time citizens of these slum areas have used community organisations and the political process to gain improvements to their area. This process of democratic accountability through the ballot box has played an important role in change. This type of approach is clearly identifiable in Figure 20.4. However, India's post-colonial history as a strong and active democracy is not shared by all countries in the developing world.

Further out from the city centre, from 6 kilometres outwards, nearly half of all slums are unrecognised, indicating that they are much more recent, less secure, and less likely to have basic infrastructure. Slum areas have developed along side each successive planned extension to the city. The poor rural migrants who initially occupied these slums were often attracted by the labouring work available during the construction of the planned residential developments.

The most recent poor migrants to the city have a number of choices for accommodation. Some

through family and kinship ties, will be able to find accommodation in existing slums which will lead to even higher population densities. Others will occupy temporary structures on, or near, their place of work, such as building sites (see Figure 18.4). This is tolerated because of their current employment. Some will occupy sites which had previously remained undeveloped for environmental reasons such as periodic flooding or proximity to pollution. The locations of these sites will get progressively further and further from the city centre. It is estimated that some 60,000 people sleep on pavements in Bangalore. Many of these are children who have been neglected, abandoned or orphaned.

FIGURE 20.4 Analysing The News. The BJP political party organizes slum dwellers to campaign for improvements in their quality of life. A mutually beneficial relationship? From *The Indian Express* (Bangalore Edition) (4.11.98)

FIGURE 20.5 The urban ecology of slum locations in Bangalore

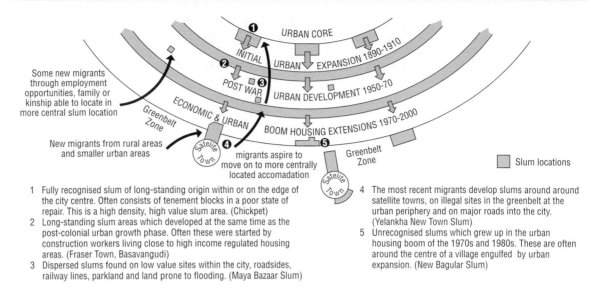

1   Fully recognised slum of long-standing origin within or on the edge of the city centre. Often consists of tenement blocks in a poor state of repair. This is a high density, high value slum area. (Chickpet)
2   Long-standing slum areas which developed at the same time as the post-colonial urban growth phase. Often these were started by construction workers living close to high income regulated housing areas. (Fraser Town, Basavangudi)
3   Dispersed slums found on low value sites within the city, roadsides, railway lines, parkland and land prone to flooding. (Maya Bazaar Slum)
4   The most recent migrants develop slums around around satellite towns, on illegal sites in the greenbelt at the urban periphery and on major roads into the city. (Yelankha New Town Slum)
5   Unrecognised slums which grew up in the urban housing boom of the 1970s and 1980s. These are often around the centre of a village engulfed by urban expansion. (New Bagular Slum)

Community Development and Empowerment

CASE STUDY

FIGURE 20.6 Maya Bazaar Slum

FIGURE 20.7 The inauguration of the women's food co-op in Maya Bazaar

Maya Bazaar Slum, Austin Town, Bangalore.

Maya Bazaar Slum, located 3 kilometres south-east of the city centre, began its existence in the 1950s when migrant workers from nearby Housur province, in the State of Tamil Nadu, began to arrive in Bangalore. They were drawn by employment opportunities and the relative prosperity of the city. Initially, the object of migration was to earn enough money to return home to their villages but for most this would remain an unfulfiled objective. Many of the original migrant families are now landlords within the slum. They rent out properties to more recent migrants. Rents are approximately £3.50 a month for a one room hut.

Improvements to Maya Bazzar slum have been a long time coming. They have been closely linked to the success or failure of the political party that the majority of slum inhabitants tends to vote for. This is known as a 'vote bank' in Indian politics. Furthermore, the slum, housing some 3,700 individuals, is occupied by some of the most marginalised people in Indian society: 89% are Scheduled Castes (low caste Hindus's and tribals) , 80% of households (average size 5) survive on an income of less than £25 a month and illiteracy is high (50% on average but significantly higher for women). Many of the men are employed as construction workers, hotel workers, and electrical or plumbing assistants. Female domestics can earn about £6 a month for a 4 hour working day while young girls can earn £15 a month for a 10 hour day in clothing sweat shops.

The slum occupies land originally belonging to the military but was recognised in 1995 by the Bangalore Slum Clearance Board which is now in the process of acquiring the land for the dwellers.

This will give the residents security of tenure. Infrastructure improvements have also been made. Granite blocks have been provided to cover the dirt lanes, street lamps installed, drinking water supplied through street taps, communal toilet blocks built and rudimentary storm sewers constructed. Most citizens of Maya Bazaar have access to a government ration card (green card) which allows them to buy subsidised basic foods and cheap kerosene for fuel, but the quality of these products is often poor.

Women in Maya Bazaar have recently been inspired by the AINA Trust, a voluntary group set up to aid the empowerment (raising the skills and confidence) of women in Bangalore's slums. A group of 50 woman in the slum have now set up a micro-credit union into which each member pays 100 rupees (£1.30) a month. Each woman plays a role at monthly meetings in deciding how loans are distributed. Defaulting on loans in such organisations is rare because of the members' commitment. Loans for home improvements, small businesses and marriages are offered to the micro-credit union members. This has reduced the burden of expensive debt incurred by taking loans from the money lenders who slum dwellers normally use because banks will not offer them loans.

Encouraged by the success of this scheme AINA is now organising a food purchasing co-operative which will enable the slum dwellers to buy good quality basic food in bulk and at a greatly reduced price. The money required to start up the food co-operative and to expand the micro-credit union to families who cannot afford the current full monthly contribution is estimated to be just £2000. This is £4 for every family member linked to the co-operative. Of equal importance to this self-help, welfare safety net that the women of the slum are building is the increase in self-confidence that they have experienced. They have gained the confidence to organise, to lobby authorities, to hold meetings and to confront deep-rooted gender stereotypes. This is providing them with more power to change things for the better.

CASE STUDY

Heliopolis favela in Sao Paulo, Brazil

The growth of favelas in Sao Paulo began in earnest in the 1970s. This was mainly as a result of rural–urban migration, fueled by a growth in employment opportunities created by industrialisation. Much of the land occupied by the incoming migrants was public land on what was then the periphery of the city. By 1994 almost 70% of housing in the metropolitan region of Sao Paulo had been constructed without regulation and the proportion of the urban population living in housing for which they had no security of tenure was nearly 8%, or about 800,000 citizens.

Heliopolis favela was accidentally created in 1972 when the city administration relocated a few favela dwellers (favelados) to a site 8 kilometres from the city centre. This was owned by the Institute of Administration and Social Welfare (IAPOS). The slum dwellers were moved from land needed by the city authorities for road building. The site at Heliopolis is close to a major industrial area and was soon invaded by individuals and groups (grileiros), who subdivided the land and then sold it on to new migrants for profit.

Throughout the 1970s the grileiros exercised an illegal influence over the lives of the favela dwellers, using violence and extortion to uphold their illegal authority. This led to the formation of numerous residents' associations which campaigned for protection and a better infrastructure, particularly for a water supply and electricity. It was the conflict between favelados and grileiros which, in 1983, led IAPOS to attempt to reclaim ownership of the land. From this moment, the key area of political activity for the favelados was the regulation of the site. Using the media to generate interest in their plight, the faveledos finally persuaded the city authorities to acquire the area and provide basic amenities.

The provision of basic amenities, the restriction on further expansion of the area and security of tenure suddenly made land in Heliopolis far more valuable. A growing market in house sales developed along with further unauthorised occupation of land. At this time the population of Heliopolis was 20,000. The city authorities began a project in 1987 to construct apartment blocks for lower/middle-income households on the site. However, under pressure from Heliopolis's poorer residents, further provision was made for self-build housing with basic amenities, the favoured solution of the urban poor. The government even provided some of the materials for construction.

With security of tenure most favela dwellers began improvements on their homes and a market in housing was created. As a result, the socio-economic profile of the favela changed rapidly, with new residents moving to the area who had higher incomes and who wanted to move from less secure sites. An informal economy of shops, bars and small businesses also started to grow.

By the late 1990s Heliopolis had a population of over 50,000 and had become a fully integrated, regulated low to middle income housing area. It was no longer situated on the periphery of the urban area as the expansion of the city had pushed the periphery back a further 10 kilometres. The evolution from an illegally occupied slum to a poor but legally regulated residential neighbourhood was complete.

FIGURE 20.8 Comparing slum areas

	Maya Bazaar Slum Bangalore, India	Heliopolis Favela, Sao Paulo, Brazil
Initial development of slum area		
Involvement in political process		
Changes in urban infrastructure		
Assessment of quality of life improvement		

Adapted from: Maria Ruth Amaral de Sampaio (1994) 'Community Organization, Housing Improvements and Income Generation; A Case Study of Favelas in Sao Paulo, Brazil', in Habitat International *18: 4, London.*

FIGURE 20.9 Planned and unplanned housing jostle for space in the rapidly expanding favelas of Brazilian cities

STUDENT ACTIVITY 20.2

Make a full size copy of the table in Figure 20.8. Read the two cases studies on slum development. Complete the table with your observations under each heading.

FIGURE 21.4 Source 'India Today'

Bangalore

Real Estate Rules

A housing project is gobbling up a big swath of open space

BANGALORE's spiralling real-estate priceline has driven land speculators almost berserk. Urban planning, already shortsighted and confused, has become even more chaotic. As if this were not enough, the new Karnataka Government is doing its mite to add to the chaos: by breaking and bending urban planning rules, a National Housing Games (NHG) complex is coming up on 57 acres of prime land that was, till recently, meant to be a park.

The National Games, scheduled for January next year in Bangalore, served as the perfect excuse for the government to sanction an elite housing-complex project at Koramangala, in the heart of the city. The 2,800 flats in the complex will house 5,000 athletes and games officials for just 11 days, after which half the flat will house government officials and the rest will be sold to the public at a profit. The £52 million complex has been termed a "special project" to give government procedures the go-by.

Even as construction is on at full swing to meet an impossible deadline, six Bangalore-based citizen's groups are fighting a legal battle against the NHG complex. Led by the Citizens' Voluntary initiative for the City (civic), the groups have filed a public-interest petition in the high court, seeking an immediate stay and scrapping of the project.

The petitioners contend that the housing complex will lead to the destruction of a fragile ecosystem, consisting of wetlands which support a large number of bird species. But more important, the land was meant to be one of the few open spaces in a city already choking on its own development. Overnight, the Government allowed the Bangalore Development Authority to change the land use from "park and open space" to "residential". Says S. Majunath of CIVIC: "The sudden change effected in land use is dubious. On a project of such a scale, the government should have sought public opinion.

In 1984 the Government conceptualised a Comprehensive Development Plan (CDP) to check the city's haphazard growth. The CDP for the city (area 1.279 sq km) comprised a 830 sq km green belt and specified that 15 per cent of the land had to be earmarked for "parks and open spaces". When the CDP came up for review last year, however, the authorities were forced to take note of the fact that rampant and unauthorised development in the city's outskirts had caused the green belt – the city's lung – to shrink. Accordingly, the revised CDP reduced the green belt or the agricultural zone by 110 sq km. To push through the complex, the new Government made a summary change in the revised CDP to exclude 57 acres of Koramangala land from the "parks and open spaces" category.

In doing so, instead of protecting Bangalore's rapidly disappearing open spaces, activists complain that the Government is only hastening the city's destruction. With growth continuing in such a chaotic fashion, the country's boom city of the '80s could well be on its way to going bust.

Saritha Rai

> NGOs contend that the complex will destroy the eco-system of a city choking on its development.

Planning for Growth

The growth of road traffic in LEDCs has in the 1990's been greater than population growth in many countries particulary in Asia and South America. This may be interpreted as a reasonable indicator of increasing economic prosperity in such countries, yet this trend comes at a price. Increased congestion, air pollution, noise and danger. The Red Cross's *World Disaster Report 1998* illustrates the rapid growth of road accidents in LEDC's, where 350,000 people are killed and over 10 million injured a year. It is estimated that by 2020 road accidents will be the biggest cause of premature death in the world, overtaking HIV, tuberculosis and even malaria.

Bangkok, the primate capital city of Thailand, has gained international notoriety for the worst traffic congestion in the world. The average rush hour speed is between 8 and 12 kilometres per hour.

Even though 90% of journeys are still made by public transport, car ownership grew by a staggering 150% between 1986 and 1993. It is estimated that the average citizen spends five hours a day in traffic and that the cost to the economy in lost productivity is $US 400 million per annum. One in six residents suffer from some kind of respiratory ailment associated with air pollution and over 1000 people are killed and 12,000 injured every year. In order to address this transport crisis the city has three major public transport systems under construction or proposed. These include an elevated light rail system along major trunk roads, a combined elevated road and train system on expressways leading into the city and a city wide subway system.

Progress on these projects has been slow since the decline in the Thai economy in 1997 but at the same time growth in car ownership has also slowed.

FIGURE 21.5

Dear Consultant,
Enclosed are a number of sources of information about the current transport situation in Bangalore. We are
currently preparing a bid for funds from the World Bank's Mega-City Transport Infrastructure Fund. This
fund is a source of capital for cities in less developed countries wishing to improve their transport infrastructure. The funds are available as a 50% grant if matching funds can be found from either national, state
or city authorities in the home country.

The World Bank is keen to receive applications which:
■ improve the economic competitiveness of the city
■ contribute towards a sustainable urban future for the city
■ improve access to transport within the city for as many citizens as possible
■ reduce air pollution and associated ill health.

The national government in New Delhi have offered the Bangalore Development Authority a grant of £10
million towards funding, but all other sources of capital will have to be raised through local taxation.
Currently Bangalore metropolitan area raises £10 million a year through transport taxation and this is available for one or a number of transport infrastructure projects.

We have five major transport infrastructure projects we would like to pursue, the details of which are included. In submitting our bid we must be aware that we are competing with many other cities around the
world for limited funds. It is important, therefore, that we address the four key criteria upon which allocation of the funds will be based.

I should also point out that, although additional funds may be raised through taxation, this would be unpopular. A 50% increase in transport taxation is possible, and this may be acceptable to the electorate if they
can be convinced that it is a worthwhile sacrifice. Most transport taxation revenue currently comes from lorries and other commercial vehicles and some of this money is needed for existing general maintenance. A
final consideration is that taxation revenues are collected every year and large scale infrastructure projects
can take many years to complete. We have included in our project brief an estimate of the time the project
will take.

The requirements of your consultancy are to:
1   Write a brief summary of the schemes focusing on whether each one meets the criteria laid down by the
World Bank. We would prefer this to be in the form of a matrix on a single side of paper so it can be quickly
appraised by members of the planning committee.
2   Make a case for a project or set of projects that you feel offer the greatest benefits to the city given the
World Bank's criteria and the available financing. Outline the cost implications and explain fully why you
have not adopted other available schemes.
3   Find a case study from either the more developed or less developed world in which the type of transport
scheme or schemes you have proposed, or something similar, has been adopted. Write a brief summary of
this transport solution to help the planning committee make an informed choice.

Yours sincerely
Bhanu Ramaswamy
Director
Bangalore Development Authority

Project outlines

1   Extension of Bangalore Urban Bus System
Total Cost   £21.8 million (18 months)

This proposal involves buying 1400 new buses, the construction of 10 new depots, 2 workshops and 35 new local bus stations. The new buses would improve passenger comfort – the current service is overcrowded and dilapidated. A modernised fleet would produce lower exhaust emissions and this could be improved still further if the new fleet was gas powered rather than petrol or diesel powered. Purchasing a gas powered fleet would involve an additional cost of £2 million. It has also been proposed that dedicated bus lanes be created on the city's main arterial roads to allow much quicker connections between the main bus station and the key suburban bus stations. However the Bangalore bus operators, BTS, currently operates at a loss and has none of its own capital to purchase new equipment.

2.   Arterial Road Improvements
Total Cost   £9.5 million (2 years)

The key element of this project is the improvement of the main arterial roads into the city centre in order to accommodate higher traffic flows. This scheme will involve the construction of elevated expressways on four main arterial roads into the city (see map) with improvements to other roads and junctions. All the technology required for this project is available in Bangalore although the local government will have to pay all the cost. It is hoped that this project will ease traffic congestion in the city centre and improve accessibility between the city centre and the urban fringe.

3.   Construction of Outer Ring Road
£13.1 million (3 years)

Bangalore is a key junction in the national highway system with most road traffic from north India to south India passing through the city. This has resulted in a very high number of lorries passing right though the city centre. It is hoped that an outer ring road will substantially alleviate this problem. Furthermore, an outer ring road will connect up many of the expanding developments located on Bangalore's urban fringe, including technology parks, the airport, manufacturing plants

FIGURE 21.6a Main bus station

and new high to middle income housing. A start has already been made on construction of the outer ring road and this project will complete the dual carriageway around Bangalore and will involve the construction of junctions with key arterial roads. In order to reduce the cost to the government a toll road could be proposed. A private consortium might be attracted to contribute 50% of the cost with a 25 year concession to collect tolls.

FIGURE 21.6b A recently completed section of the outer ring road

4.   Elevated Rapid Transit System
£200 million (4 years)

This project is phase one of a much larger £840 million elevated rapid transit system along six routes. It will be an electric powered, air-conditioned, light rail system, elevated above the streets with connections to street level via escalators. Such a system would allow for the maximum use of existing roads by vehicle traffic. The project would be funded by the government in partnership with a private consortium under a deal in which the private developers lease land from the government, construct the system and are given a 50 year concessions to run the system in order to recover their capital. Interest in this scheme has been shown by a consortium of Indian building companies and European manufacturers of light rail rolling stock. This first phase of construction would involve building a 23 kilometre section from Jayanagar, (a large middle income housing extension to the south of the city centre) via the central bus station to Yeshwantpur (the major industrial area in the north-west; see map).

FIGURE 21.6c Constructing a flyover on a crowded arterial road

5. New International Airport
Total Cost   £25 million (2 years)

FIGURE 21.7 Extract from Bangalore Development Authority Comprehensive Development Plan

'The present developed area of Bangalore is around 300 square kilometres. Absence of natural barriers has encouraged the restless sprawl of the city in all directions. Scattered allocation of work centres and lack of work–home relationship has resulted in omni-directional traffic along inherited radial routes. The phenomenal increase in population, the unabated significant outward sprawl of the city and the high concentration of economic activities have contributed to a sudden spurt in the number of motor vehicles.

The steep increase in ownership of private cars and two wheelers due to inadequacy of mass transportation system has created problems of congestion, accidents, parking, energy wastage and pollution.'

Bangalore has seen a rapid increase in air traffic in recent years, although there are limits on future expansion. Currently only a few international flights from Singapore and the Gulf States land at Bangalore. Flights to Europe and North America have to go via Mumbai, Madras or Singapore. The demand for direct flights to Bangalore has increased in the 1990s as more European and American information technology companies have located operations in the city. The key restraint is that the runway is not long enough to accommodate long-haul jets such as Boeing 747s. A new airport is proposed 30 kilometres to the north of Bangalore, connected to the city via an expressway link. It is proposed that a private developer acts as a partner in the development in exchange for the concession to run the airport for 25 years. A private developer has already shown interest and is prepared to pay 50% towards initial capital costs.

FIGURE 21.8 Extract CIVIC Bangalore 1996

'The number of motor vehicles registered in Bangalore is increasing by 25,000 a month of which 74% are two wheelers, 13% cars and less than 1% buses. However 60% of the 4 million trips made everyday in Bangalore are made by bus. Half of all households in the city rely on public transport having no access to a motorised vehicle. It estimated that by 2011 even with the introduction of some form of rapid transit system, public buses will carry nearly 4 million passengers a day. The number of buses per 100,000 of population is 31, in Delhi this figure is 47. To meet demand it is necessary to add 1,400 new buses to the current number of 1,900. The Bangalore Transport Service who run the buses operate at a loss even though they receive a significant subsidy from the government.'

FIGURE 21.11 Proposed transport infrastructure in Bangalore

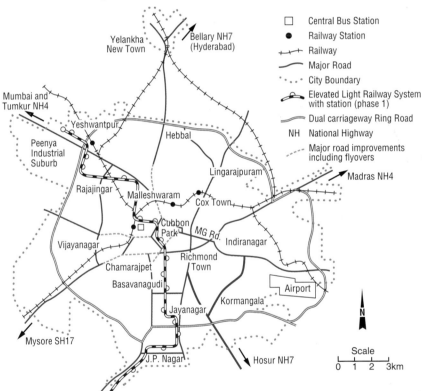

Travel Mode	Fare (1994) pence/km
Public Bus	0.2p
Elevated Rapid Transit System	1.1p
Private Two Wheeler	2p
Auto Rickshaw	5p
Private Car	10p

FIGURE 21.9 Comparative estimates of fare cost by different modes of transport in Bangalore (1994)

FIGURE 21.10 Vehicles registered and accidents in Bangalore

Year	Number of vehicles registered	Accidents	Number injured	Number killed
1983	236,045	4539	3724	388
1984	277,650	4931	3966	423
1985	319,422	4805	3892	419
1986	373,776	5161	4398	397
1987	434,122	5597	4567	419
1988	460,875	5985	4926	504
1989	524,261	6441	5531	512
1990	601,059	6729	5677	562
1991	665,221	7042	5671	550
1992	684,497	7377	6371	575
1993 (Up to Dec)	697,335			

22
GLOBALISING CITIES: THE IMPACT OF ECONOMIC CHANGE

Key Ideas

■ Increasingly cities in less economically developed countries are being integrated into a globalised economy.

■ Globalisation has had both positive and negative impacts on less economically developed cities.

■ Firms have been attracted to many less economically developed cities by lower labour costs. Many cities have highly educated and skilled workforces who can be employed at rates substantially lower than in more economically developed countries.

■ Less economically developed countries which are rapidly urbanising offer expanding markets for firms.

■ Urban culture is increasingly internationalised. Many brand names have become completely international in their availability.

■ In order to attract inward investment from abroad many less economically developed countries reduce restrictions on business operations such as health and safety legislation or planning controls. They also offer subsidies or tax incentives.

■ Increasingly the decisions that affect economic activities in less economically developed cities are being made by people and firms based in the more economically developed countries.

What is Globalisation?

Production of goods and services has become increasingly footloose. Firms are increasingly able to locate anywhere in the world. This has been made possible by advances in transport and communications. The declining importance of national boundaries in the decisions of firms is referred to as **globalisation**. However, globalisation involves not just the production of goods and services, but also consumption. Many well-known brand names are available globally and identical products are demanded throughout the world.

One example of globalisation is the growing importance of transnational corporations (TNCs), firms which have operations in a number of different countries. The largest of these corporations, General Motors based in the USA, was valued in 1998 at £147 billion, a figure that far exceeds the Gross National Product of many LEDCs. The decision-making of TNCs is predominantly based in MEDCs, with the cities of New York, London and Tokyo having the largest number of TNC headquarters (see Chapter 2).

FIGURE 22.1 The Petronas Twin Towers, the world's tallest building dominates the skyline of Kuala Lumpur, Malaysia

Geographers increasingly refer to the global economy as being a **core/periphery** economy. The core of the global economy is where most of the decisions about economic activities are made. The core includes the major cities of MEDCs and a few key cities in LEDCs. The periphery includes those areas where there is little influence over economic activity. This includes most rural areas in both LEDCs and MEDCs, most urban areas in LEDCs and some MEDC cities experiencing severe deindustrialisation.

The extent to which globalisation has exerted an influence on cities in LEDCs varies. Some cities, such as Jakarta, Kuala Lumpar (see figure 22.1) Sao Paulo and Lagos are well integrated into the global economy. They house regional headquarters of TNCs, and produce goods and services which are exported around the world. They are also centres of government and administration for large numbers of the world's population. Other cities attract little global inward investment and have economies which are predominantly focused on the rural region surrounding the city.

Bangalore: A globalised city?

Bangalore's recent rapid population growth is a product of its economic development in the last twenty years of the twentieth century. Sometimes referred to as 'Silicon Plateau', Bangalore is often cited as the most globalised city in south Asia. In November 1998 the US magazine *Newsweek* described Bangalore as one of the top ten 'Hottest Tech Cities' in the world (see figure 22.2). The list of high technology TNCs which have operations in Bangalore is comprehensive and includes Texas Instruments, Compaq, Apple, Siemens Nixdorf, Acer, Hewlett Packard and Philips as well as Indian high technology leaders, BPL, IBM Tata and Infosys. Many of these companies have web sites with information on their Bangalore operations.

Bangalore is also a centre for aeronautics, machine tools, engineering, watch making, brewing and silk production. In 1999 Volvo and Toyota will be constructing vehicle assembly plants in the Bangalore region. The economic growth of the city, particularly in high technology sectors, has been aided by a large number of research institutions located within the city including the Indian Institute of Science, Indian Space Research Organisation, National Aerospace Laboratory and the Indian Centre for Advanced Computing.

FIVE-HUNDRED-YEAR-OLD BANGALORE has been a trading center for silk and sandalwood, as well as a retreat for Hindu kings and British colonialists. Situated on a cool plateau above the hot Indian plain, it was a serene place full of tree-lined streets, red-tiled bungalows, hundreds of temples and no history of the sectarian strife endemic to India.

The next 500 years in this city may be slightly more hectic. Since local entrepreneurs and the American giant Texas Instruments discovered Bangalore in the early 1980s, the city has boomed. It's now home to 250 high-tech companies, including homegrown multinational software and networking giants Infosys and Wipro, and another hundred software firms on the outskirts of town. Glass-and-steel skyscrapers are being built, while cybercafés multiply. At the BAIT – the Beer Drinkers Association of Information Technology-Club, engineers and executives brainstorm over brews and golf. But amid all the modern bustle, much of Bangalore's old-fashioned way of life remains unchanged. A typical scene: outside the glittering new Prestige Opal building, home to units of Citibank and Hughes Aircraft, a man sells guavas from a rickety wooden puschart. "The cyber-culture coexists peacefully with the traditional Indian culture," says V. Narasimhan, an architect who has designed several of the new tech headquarters. "You find many high-tech professionals visiting temples, instead of pubs, after they finish work."

But there is a darker side to Bangalore's boom. Since 1981, the city's population has more than doubled, from 2.4 million to 5 million, while the number

Bangalore, India

No. of high-tech firms: 250
Anchor companies: Texas Instruments, Infosys
Top dog: N. R. Narayana Murthy, chairman and CEO of Infosys
Local research center: Indian Institute of Science
Hot gathering spots: Black Cadillac Pub, exclusive country clubs
Status toy: A home theater system
Median home price: $50,000

of vehicles has gown even faster, from fewer than 200,000 cars and scooters to 1.6 million. Unregulated expansion has clogged the narrow roads and fouled the cool upland air, while doing little to alleviate poverty. The government is starting to take action. It is pushing unleaded gas and building overhead highways to handle traffic. And some companies are trying to spread the benefits of technology. Infosys gives used computers to schools and brings children into its offices to train them. Whatever Bangalore's problems, it is closely watched by the rest of India. For the many would-be Silicon Plateaus around the country, ancient Bangalore is the model for the next millennium.

Sudip Mazumdar

FIGURE 22.2 Source: Newsweek, November 1998

The recent success of Bangalore in attracting a large number of high technology TNCs has its roots in a number of government decisions made post-independence in the 1950s. Government owned firms producing aircraft, telephones, electronics and machine tools were all located in Bangalore. This was partly due to the pleasant climate enjoyed by the city which made it attractive to technologists and academics. To house the employees of these large operations industrial townships (HAL, BEL, HMT and ITI) were built on the edge of the city. The emergence of a highly educated workforce, a concentration of government research establishments and a city which was well laid out and maintained all combined to make Bangalore a highly attractive location for TNCs wishing to take advantage of the growing Indian economy.

Texas Instruments were the first major high technology TNC to move to Bangalore in 1982. 15 years later nearly all the major high technology companies either have operations in Bangalore or recruit staff from the huge pool of computer software and hardware engineering staff in the city. Other cities in India have looked at this rapid growth of high technology industry in Bangalore. They are now are in direct competition with Bangalore for this globally mobile investment, offering incentives such as tax free status, subsidised power and infrastructure and exemption from employment law and health and safety legislation. Hyderabad, the State capital of neighboring Andhra Pradesh, has succeeded in attracting major investment from Microsoft, while Calcutta, and Trivandurm, the State capital of Kerala, (see Figure 22.4) have also had success in attracting significant inward investment in high technology infrastructure and employment.

From a consumption point of view, Bangalore has many of the trappings of the developed world including nightclubs, bars, theatres, hundreds of cinemas, international class sports facilities and an impressive array of 5 star hotels. Global brands are widely available for those that can afford them.

The Dual Economy Of The Global LEDC City

One of the key attractions of Bangalore for TNCs is the relatively cheap pool of highly educated, English-speaking technologists available to employ. Salaries for comparable staff in MEDCs would be much higher. Yet the real value of salaries in Bangalore is high because living costs are significantly lower than in MEDCs.

One of the outcomes of globalisation in Bangalore has been the creation of a dual urban economy. Approximately 30–40% of the population enjoy unprecedented levels of economic well-being, The lifestyles and aspirations of this part of Bangalore's society are reflected in the monthly magazine, *Bangalore* (available at www.bangaloremag.com).

FIGURE 22.3 The International Tech Park, Bangalore, a major urban fringe high technology science park

FIGURE 22.4 Cover of an advertising brochure for Technopark Campus, Trivandrum, Kerala State, India

The majority of Bangalore's citizens, however, enjoy little if any of the benefits of globalisation. Their lives remain rooted in poor environments, uncertainty and poverty.

There are links between these dual elements of the Bangalore economy. Employment opportunities for in-migrants have been created in the building boom in apartment housing. Increased economic activity within the city has created a growth in informal occupations, from taxi driver to street shoe shiner. Evidence from research in slum housing areas in Bangalore has shown that many of the televisions within the slums are hand-me-downs to domestic staff from middle-class families who were upgrading their televisions. The aspirations of lower income groups are being increasingly shaped by the images and information carried by an increasingly globalised media. MTV and other satellite channels are watched by all sections of Bangalore society.

Not everybody in Bangalore is happy with the arrival of TNCs and global culture. Protests from local farmers and nationalist groups have led to attacks on Kentucky Fried Chicken and Pizza Hut restaurants in the city (see Figure 22.5).

The dual economy of LEDC's is starkly visible in cities such as Sao Paulo, Jakarta and Cairo, where modern sky-scrapers dominate a city centre surrounded by sprawling areas of slum housing.

FIGURE 22.5 From: The
Times (Travel), 7/11/98
(PART OF)

It was 10am and customers were tucking in to Colonel Sanders' Bargain Bucket Breakfast Burgers in the gleaming new Kentucky Fried Chicken in Bangalore, when ten burly farmers walked in, prised the ice-cream freezer up from the floor, and hurled it through the plate-glass front window.

As customers and staff looked on in astonishment, hundreds of rustics dressed in Gandhian homespun poured through the breech into Colonel Sanders' Indian flagship and began hurling furniture around. Others used chairs to shatter the strip-lights and air-conditioning units.

Heavily built village wrestlers ripped the fans from the ceiling and the tables from the floor, while a couple of cowherds attacked the Pepsi machines and chip-friers. The cash till was smashed and the contents sprayed with tomato ketchup. Buckets full of Finger-Lickin' Chicken Nugget Combo Meals were scattered over the road and trampled in to the dust by some elderly village patriarchs who had taken up station outside.

Wading though the sticky quagmire of Pepsi, batter and shattered glass, the farmers announced that they were marking the anniversary of the assassination of the Mahatma by launching a "second freedom struggle" against "the invasion of India by multinationals". Then they shouted a few slogans denouncing the "non-veg poison" served by the Colonel and praising the virtues of "good *masala dosas*", before vanishing into the crowds outside.

It was not the first time the Karnataka State Farmers' Association had taken a somewhat assertive stand against what they perceived as an invasion of foreign companies intent on wrecking Hindu culture. Nor were the farmers the only protesters.

On October 1 1996, the All-Karnataka Youth Council decided to celebrate Mahatma Gandhi's birthday by ransacking the newly opened Bangalore Pizza Hut: The Youth Council lobbies for businesses in Karnataka to operate in the local Kannada language, and the attack was a protest against Pizza Hut's refusal to translate its logo in to the local script.

Normally these sorts of Hindu Luddites might be dismissed as just another example of India's incurable eccentricity, a modern manifestation of the Mahatma Gandhi syndrome. Yet the fact that the protests took place in Bangalore made India-watchers sit up. For although since 1947 India has had an understandable fondness for protectionist isolationism, the one place you would *not* expect to find any such introversion was Bangalore, which has long prided itself on being the most cosmopolitan city in India.

Once a favourite retirement destination for blimpish ex-servicemen and elderly tea-planters, it has recently reinvented itself as "India's Silicon Valley", South Asia's flagship town for software and high technology.

The place still basks with satisfaction in Bill Gates's much-quoted (though possibly apocryphal) remark that "After the Chinese, the south Indians are the smartest people in the world," which the intelligentsia of Bangalore understood to be specifically referring to them.

Since Western software companies started arriving in the city ten years ago – attracting in the process a wave of highly skilled expatriate Indian soft-ware engineers to return home to work for them – the Bangalore streetscape has altered beyond recognition. The city now has the only supermarket in the subcontinent, and a shopping mall modelled, so proud Bangaloreans will tell, on one in Los Angeles.

"These are luxuries unknown even in go-ahead Bombay," said one student who offered to show me what he claimed was "India's first all-glass elevator".

"Actually," he said, "Bangalore is our model town. It is number one place for comfort in India."

One aspect of this is the dazzling variety of pubs on offer, most of them bizarrely themed: some are dressed up as pseudo-Wild West saloons, others as wannabe NASA space stations. There is a Baskin-Robbins, a Wimpey, and of course the Pizza Huts and Kentucky Fried Chicken parlours, which despite the attacks are both in great demand.

Source: William Dalrymple "The Age of Kali"
(1998) Harper Collins

STUDENT ACTIVITY 22.1

Increasingly, cities across the world are competing with each other to attract inward investment and employment opportunities. This involves a great deal of promotion on a world stage, advertising the advantages of your city over other locations. This exercise is a research based task: you take on the role of an advertising executive with a brief to market a city to TNCs looking for investment locations. You may either use Bangalore as your city or choose any other LEDC city you can access information or data on.

The brief
1 Design an A4 page advert for the city you are promoting to be placed in a US business magazine. You will need to think about the features which will attract future inward investment from US companies.
2 Storyboard a 30 second TV advert promoting inward investment into your chosen city for a satellite business channel.
3 Make a list of the potential short-comings of your chosen city for inward investors so you can brief your sales staff to answer criticisms.

23
SURVIVING THE FUTURE: SUSTAINABLE APPROACHES TO CITY MANAGEMENT

Key Ideas

■ With less economically developed countries becoming increasingly urbanised the need for sustainable urban development becomes more important.

■ Urban sustainability in less developed countries is often considered to be in conflict with other objectives such as economic growth.

■ There are numerous examples of less economically developed cities engaging in planning and development which embraces urban sustainability. These examples are at a variety of scales.

Sustainable Development in LEDCs

Sustainable development is an apparently self-evident concept. Surely everybody wants to sustain and improve the environment and the quality of life on the planet in a way which does not harm future generations? In MEDC countries urban planners are accepting that they must embrace the concept of sustainability even if they are unsure what it means in practice (see Chapter 16).

However LEDC countries are often faced with far starker choices about development. Limited resources, capital and technology have often meant that economic growth is pursued without much consideration for environmental consequences. A key element of sustainability is the belief that

reducing inequality is essential if development is not to reduce the quality of life for future generations.

The rapid growth of cities in LEDCs has led to a range of environmental problems, (see Figure 23.2) and an increasing concentration of poverty and inequality, (see Figure 23.3). Attempts to address these issues with an urban sustainability perspective have started in many LEDCs. The United Nations is promoting the adoption of Local Agenda 21: Planning for Sustainable Urban Development. By 1999 three pilot cities in LEDCs had been selected: Nakuru in Kenya, Essaouria in Morocco and Vinh City in Vietnam. Details of this project are available at the United Nations Habitat website.

FIGURE 23.1 Cartoon depicting the problems of urbanisation in Bangalore

FIGURE 23.2 Fortune
Magazine Dec 1996

"There is a seamy underbelly to the stupendous economic expansion that has brought so much prosperity to Asia. With every up-tick in industrial production has come a surge in smoke and hazardous waste, with every point in GDP growth has come an almost precisely predictable increase in garbage.

Now an increasingly affluent, well-educated middle class is starting to realise that deadly pollution is a high price to pay for the ability to buy Toyotas and Big Macs. In burgeoning democracies across the region, they are raising their voices and prodding their leaders to focus on quality of life and not just growth. "Living here is like living in hell by American standards", says mechanical engineering professor Jeff Chiang as he looks out over Taiwan's smoky landscape studded with refinery smokestacks and riddled with oil black streams.

The potential of this market is obvious – just look at the sulfurous black skies over the steel towns of China, look at the contaminated soil around Korean petrochemical plants, look, if you dare, at the sewage of Calcutta. The Asian Development Bank says that $80 billion to $100 billion of investment would be required in the next five years just to lay the foundation in Asia for an acceptable water infrastructure, the regions most serious problem. Asia already buys $5.7 billion of air pollution equipment a year, and the World Bank figures that the regions plans to double electric power capacity between 1993 and 2002 will create the need for another $50 billion or so in scrubbers, electrostatic precipitators and the like. Billions of dollars more need to be spent treating and cleaning up the regions sewage and industrial waste"

Source: 'Asia Stinks' by Susan Moffat in Fortune magazine 9/12/96

FIGURE 23.3 The *Guardian*
December 11th 1998

Rural poor are overtaken by desperate urban underclass

John Vidal

Forget images of starving children in a barren drought-baked country-side. The stark new face of global hunger, says the United Nations, is to be seen in rapidly growing African and Asian cities where up to 1,000 million people now face severe malnutrition and food shortages.

A new UN Food and Agriculture Organisation report paints a bleak prospect for the poorest urban dwellers in developing countries. Infrastructure in these burgeoning, chaotic cities is unable to keep pace with the demand for food. People are being forced to spend up to 80 per cent of their income on what they eat, while paid work is scarce or non-existent.

According to World Bank figures, the number of poor people in cities has more than doubled globally in 10 years and should reach a billion by the end of next year. The urban poor now outnumber the rural poor in many countries, a trend that is expected to grow as the world becomes more urbanised.

Cities are exploding worldwide, says the report. Asian cities are growing by 3 per cent a year and African ones by approximately 4 per cent.

Burgeoning cities are unable to keep pace with demand for food

People are exchanging rural poverty and lack of opportunity for appalling city conditions and dismal living standards, says the report.

The implications for food security, says Rachel Nugent, one of the FAO economists who wrote the report, are alarming. "The poor are growing in number every day. They often have neither access to nor the money to buy food."

The price of food has risen as cities have grown, and urban food prices have risen more than the cost of living and more than incomes, says the report. One study showed that consumers in cities spend, on average, 30 per cent more on food than rural consumers do, but get fewer calories.

Physical conditions also pose problems for the poorest, who lack transport but have to go long distances to markets; and their food is often contaminated because of crowded conditions.

Food supplies, says the report, do not always reach the consumer. "Up to 30 per cent of all food has been lost by the time it reaches the market, which adds to prices and further marginalises the poorest."

As cities grow, they require bigger and more developed transport and distribution to get goods to consumers. But in many cases there is little public money available for roads, vehicles and market places, and the private sector is less interested in feeding the poorest.

Many cities have been unable to cope with the extra demands of their new inhabitants. A city of 10 million people may need to import at least 6,000 tonnes of food every day: this requires much co-ordination between producers, transporters, markets and retailers. City administrators and the private sector find themselves struggling to cope.

What is needed, says the report, is more investment in infrastructure and more encouragement by the authorities to allow people to grow food in cities. In China, up to 20 per cent of the food needs of cities is met by urban farming. Havana provides almost 5 per cent of Cuba's food.

"The poor are being ignored," says Dr Nugent. "The situation could get worse. It's pretty scary."

Curitiba – Sustainable City of the Future?

Curitiba, the capital city of the Brazilian State of Parana has often been cited as a model for other LEDC cities to follow when pursuing policies which are considered to be sustainable. In many ways Curitiba is typical of LEDC cities. Population growth has been extremely rapid, from 300,000 in 1950 to 2.1 million in 1990. This growth is largely a result of rural to urban migration, encouraged by the industrialisation of Curitiba. The long standing mayor of the city, architect Jamie Lerner, introduced a range of policies which promoted urban sustainability. This was so successful that, in 1992 after 12 years in power, he enjoyed a 92% approval rating with city residents.

The heart of Curibita's urban sustainability is a master plan which intervened directly in urban development and aimed to improve the quality of life for all citizens. The key points of the plan are:

■ A commitment to involve citizens in decision-making at all levels, but with a particular emphasis on the local neighbourhood. Low cost, low technology solutions are encouraged.
■ An emphasis on high quality, affordable, public transport in preference to private transport. Buses have their own dedicated road lanes which enable them to travel at the speed of a subway system but at one-eightieth of the cost. The city centre has also been extensively pedestrianised.
■ The development of extensive urban green space. 17 new parks have been laid out in recent years. Cycle lanes have been created, 1.5 million trees have been planted and areas prone to flooding have been turned into wetland habitats rather than developed.
■ Recycling of all forms of waste is given a high priority. Citizens living in the many slum areas that still exist in the city can exchange their waste for free bus tickets or even food. The city currently recycles two-thirds of all its waste.
■ The development of environmental education for all citizens through an innovative University of the Environment.
■ The urban poor are involved in development projects. Street children are paid to maintain parks and clean streets and recent migrants sort recycled rubbish. Shops and industries are encouraged to adopt orphaned children and provide a small wage, food and education in exchange for light maintenance and gardening chores.

Problems still exist in Curitiba. Migrants are still attracted by the high quality of life, slums still proliferate and the city consumes an increasing amount of resources as its population grows. Yet the solutions with which Curitiba addresses these are a model to large cities in LEDCs and MEDCs across the world.

A Vision of Sustainability in Shanghai

In 1991 the British architect Richard Rogers was invited to put forward a design for a major development in Shanghai, China, one of the largest cities in the world with a population of 13 million at the time of the commission. Rogers is an advocate of **sustainable compact cities**, cities which are designed to reduce the consumption of energy by placing residential, commercial and entertainment districts in close proximity to each other, (see Chapter 16). His design for a new district of the city incorporating these concepts was located in the Lu Zia Sui district. This district, close to the existing city centre, is on a site similar to London's Isle of Dogs where Canary Wharf was built. It was to be a multi-functional development served by an extensive public transport system.

Rogers's plan was created around a circular park and emphasised pedestrian streets, cycle paths and public open space based around markets. Six large compact neighbourhoods each of 80,000 residents were to radiate from the central park. A key objective was to reduce energy consumption by up to 50% from that of a conventional city. Recycling of both organic and inorganic waste was planned to reduce the impact the city made on its surrounding area. The project, however, was turned down by the Shanghai city authorities who opted for a market-driven development dominated by the car and office developments including China's largest skyscraper. In this case the need for rapid economic growth outweighed the desire to create a sustainable city. Much of the commercial office space remains unlet due to the down turn in the Asian Economy in the late 1990s.

FIGURE 23.4 Lawyers protesting in Cubbon Park about the development of buildings in this, the largest park in central Bangalore

Urban Sustainability in Bangalore

The rapid urban growth experienced by Bangalore in the last 30 years of the twentieth century has led to a wide range of environmental and social problems. Development has been encouraged with an emphasis on economic growth rather than long term urban sustainability. As Figure 23.1 indicated dissatisfaction at the deteriorating quality of Bangalore's urban environment is common amongst its citizens. The loss of green space and many of Bangalore's tanks or lakes, the rapid increase in road traffic and associated pollution, water and sewage systems that can barely cope with demand and increasing inequality between the rich and the poor have all contributed to the threat to the quality of life in the city from the lack of sustainability.

Like many LEDC cities Bangalore is developing greater environmental awareness and, in many ways, already practices aspects of a sustainability agenda. Recycling in Bangalore is far more advanced than in many MEDC cities although the incentives for this are as much economic as environmental, (see Figure 23.5). Across the developing world recycling has become an economic opportunity which the poorest and most marginalised in urban society have exploited for economic gain.

Campaigns by middle-class Bangalorian citizens to preserve the fast diminishing urban green space of the city have become a major political issues. Cubbon Park, the central green lung of the city is being increasingly lost to developments. Environmental groups, such as CIVIC, have organised local citizens to challenge this (Figure 23.4).The city is yet to develop an Local Agenda 21 plan. Economic development remains a key priority. In order to attract TNCs in the high technology field they are offered exemption from the State's anti-pollution legislation.

23.5 The urban waste economy of Bangalore

In Bangalore some 50,000 people make a living through recycling, some 2% of the workforce. This includes some 25,000 waste pickers who are mainly women and children, 4,000 itinerant waste buyers of newspapers, plastics, glass, metals, clothes and other materials and up to 50 wholesalers in wastes. From this a number of enterprises using recycled materials have developed including two glass and four paper recycling units as well as eight aluminium recyclers.

It is estimated that street pickers retrieve 15% of wastes put out in street bins amounting to some 300 tons a day. Along with other recyclers in total it is estimated that some half a million tons of inorganic waste are recovered and recycled every year in Bangalore.

Organic waste is collected and recycled in different projects across the city. Some 100 tons of market waste a day is composted and some 210 tons of cow dung is collected from city roads each day and turned into fuel for low income residents in Bangalore's slums. It has even been estimated that up to 5% of all waste is reconsumed by the cities stray dogs, cows and pigs. Some local citizen's groups have been experimenting with community composting with the resultant material being used to encourage urban horticulture to reduce dependence on rural areas for food although this is not widespread at present. For many migrants from rural areas urban agriculture, the rearing of goats, cows and pigs in urban environments and community composting are low cost ways of improving diet and earning additional income with skills they have familiarity with. It is very common for urban slums to contain a very high density of livestock who consume a large proportion of the organic waste generated locally.

STUDENT ACTIVITY 23.1

At the start of the twenty-first century, the majority of the world's population is living in urban areas and the majority of that in LEDC cities. The issue of urban sustainability in LEDC cities is of growing importance.

The cities discussed in this chapter provide a few examples of the type of material that is available to students researching this important issue.

The aim of urban sustainability is to ensure the best possible quality of life for all global citizens, both rural and urban, now and in the future. Is this achievable? What evidence is there to suggest that this concept is being addressed in LEDC cities? Research and write an essay addressing either of the questions below. Your essay should not exceed 2000 words.
1 'Only economic growth can reduce inequality in LEDC cities'. Does this position conflict with the principles of sustainable urban development?
2 'Sustainable urban development in LEDCs is the responsibility of everyone from national governments and city planners to individual citizens in their communities'. Using examples from across the world discuss the progress that has been made so far on this central aim of the 1992 Rio Earth Summit.

24
A SUMMARY MODEL FOR BANGALORE

Key Ideas

- The cities of less economically developed countries share some common features but also exhibit variety in both their urban morphology and development.
- There have been numerous attempts to create urban models of less economically developed cities although it is not possible to explain all such cities through one single model.
- Models of less economically developed cities often only apply to a particular region or type of city.
- Urban models of less economically developed cities can help planners address the problems of urbanisation.

FIGURE 24.1 A model of Latin American cities

Models of LEDC cities

There have been a variety of attempts by geographers to create urban models for different types of cities in LEDCs. There are models of Latin American cities, Islamic cities, African cities, colonial cities and Indian cities. Many of these models are evolving and changing over time as more research is carried out. All of these models are based upon specific research located in particular types of cities, therefore it is not possible to create one single model for an LEDC city.

The purpose of modelling urban morphology is to help describe and understand the processes which have created cities. They also inform debate into how urban areas may change in the future. An example of such a model is shown in Figure 24.1. This model has been constructed after studying cities in Latin America . The common features of rapidly growing Latin American cities are central business districts dominated by skyscrapers with high status housing in close proximity. Recent slum developments (squatter settlements) ring most of the city's periphery and are also located along arterial roads where industry is often found. There are some similarities in form to Burgess's concentric ring model and Hoyt's sector model (see Chapter 3). The model which can be most usefully applied to Bangalore is a four stage model which attempts to explain the development of Indian cities over time.

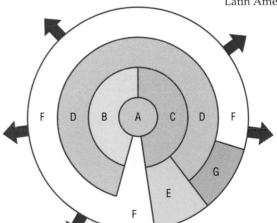

A: **Central Business District** - often dominated by high rise buildings.
B: **Slums and Tenements**- old run down housing. Very overcrowd and often sub-divided between a number of families - more than one family may share a room. Few amenities.
C: **High Status Housing** - high-rise expensive modern apartment blocks. Blocks may even have their own security guards.
D: **Poor to Medium quality Housing** - some of this zone will consist of *consolidated squatter settlements*.
E: **Outer Suburban High Status Housing** - this zone may be similar to zone C or it may consist of low density housing (i.e. large houses with large gardens).
F: **Squatter Settlements** - also known as *informal housing, spontaneous settlements* or *shanty towns*. Most of this zone is on the city's periphery but squatter settlements are also found closer to the central business district where land is available (e.g. steep slopes, alongside railway lines, close to polluting factories, rubbish dumps and land liable to flooding).
G **Low Cost Housing in Government Funded Improvement Schemes** - includes 'site and service schemes' and 'core housing'.

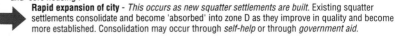
Rapid expansion of city - *This occurs as new squatter settlements are built.* Existing squatter settlements consolidate and become 'absorbed' into zone D as they improve in quality and become more established. Consolidation may occur through *self-help* or through *government aid*.

FIGURE 24.2 A model of
Indian cities

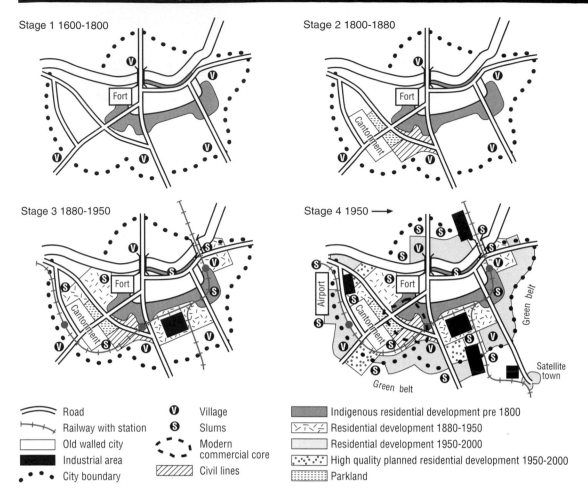

Stage 1 1600-1800

Stage 2 1800-1880

Stage 3 1880-1950

Stage 4 1950 ⟶

⟪⟫ Road	🅥 Village	▨ Indigenous residential development pre 1800
⊢⊣ Railway with station	🅢 Slums	⊻⊤⊻ Residential development 1880-1950
☐ Old walled city	⊙ Modern commercial core	▥ Residential development 1950-2000
■ Industrial area		⋯ High quality planned residential development 1950-2000
•‥• City boundary	▨ Civil lines	▤ Parkland

FIGURE 24.3 A summary
model for Bangalore

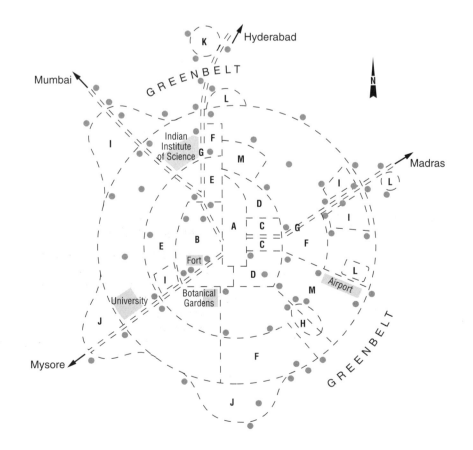

FIGURE 24.4 An outline map for Bangalore

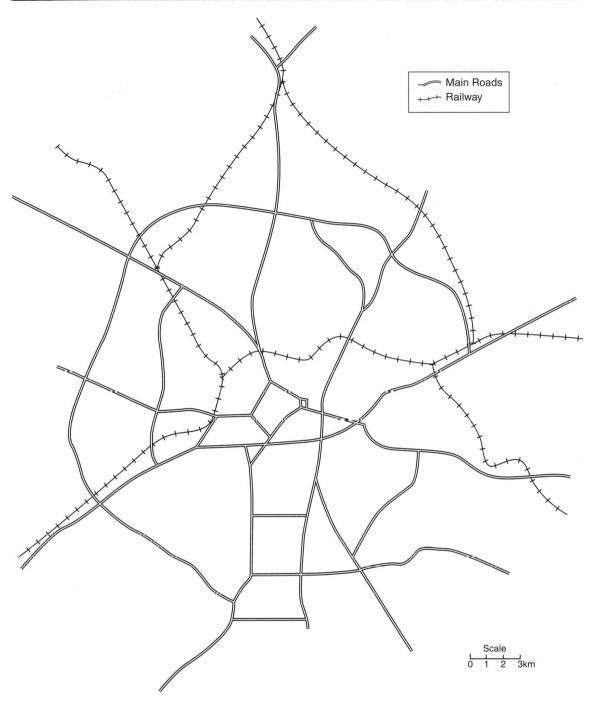

Main Roads
Railway

Scale
0   1   2   3km

In this model, (Figure 24.2), the various stages in the historical development of cities within the Indian sub-continent are outlined. It does assume that a colonial cantonment developed in the nineteenth century and that such cities are located either on coastal or river sites. This may not be the case in all Indian cities. Bangalore can be evaluated by comparing the land use map shown in Figure 24.3 with stage 4 of the Indian city model in Figure 24.2.

STUDENT ACTIVITY 24.1

Trace a copy of the outline map of Bangalore (Figure 24.4). Use the information from the summary model of Bangalore and the information and maps in the preceding chapters to annotate your outline map showing urban growth and environmental problems in the city.

FIGURE 24.5 Table for
urban model of
Bangalore

		Relevant chapters
A	Cubbon park, (laid out in 1849). Horse racing course and Maharaja's Palace gardens. Now under threat from development proposals to infill sections of the park with new housing and commercial developments.	Chapter 23
B	The core of the original Indian city of Bangalore founded in the sixteenth century. This area is a highly congested mix of commercial, industrial and residential uses. Roads are narrow and the sewage system is close to collapse. The area is still the main centre of Bangalore for most residents, with markets, the central bus station and railway station located here.	Chapter 19 (Chickpet)
C	This area was previously known as civil lines, the area where the Indian employees of the British army lived and worked in the nineteenth century. Today it is the modern hub of Bangalore's globalised economy with office blocks housing banks and firms both Indian and international. Indoor shopping malls, cyber cafes, expensive restaurants and pubs are intermixed with some high quality residential apartment blocks and a few remaining colonial villas.	Chapter 22
D	The cantonment area. This was the residential area of the British during colonial times. The well laid out streets of bungalows with extensive gardens have now been extensively infilled by new apartment blocks with infrastructure struggling to cope with the new demand. Some well established slums exist within this area.	Chapter 19 (Fraser Town)
E	Turn of the century residential layouts built to relive pressure on the highly congested old city. A mixture of villas in their own grounds in a well laid out structure incorporating small parks, temples and wide tree-lined roads. These areas have in recent years seen much redevelopment with the commercial activities of the central area spreading into them and new apartment blocks being constructed.	Chapter 19 (Basavanagudi)
F	Low density, high income residential areas are located away from industrial areas but with good transport links into the city. These areas contain out of town shopping areas, well maintained infrastructure and good schools.	Chapter 19 (Indiranagar)
G	Traffic congestion in the city is rapidly increasing. Traffic corridors are being upgraded with dual carriage-ways, fly-overs and a new public transport system.	Chapter 21
H	National Games Housing Project, Kormangala. A huge scheme to construct new middle income housing as a result of investment linked to the location of a major sporting event. The National Games housing project was partly sited on military land and open space.	Chapter 21
I	Industrial areas of varying age. Industry is always in close proximity to main transport corridors. Often major industries have housing projects incorporated for the workforce and their families.	Chapter 22
J	Middle and upper income residential layouts at the edge of the city currently being developed. Surrounded by slums housing construction workers.	
K	Satellite town built to relieve population pressure on the city. A planned mixture of housing and industry which is now fringed by some of Bangalore areas most recent slums.	Chapter 19 (Yelankha Slum)
L	Fringe city developments linked to Bangalore's high technology sector including science parks, research campuses and integrated edge of town residential, retail and commercial development. These are located close to the newly built outer ring road to aid access.	Chapter 22
M	A legacy from colonial cantonment is the large amount of land occupied by the military in Bangalore. These contain barracks, training grounds and often slum areas due to military land being difficult to get evicted from.	
●	Slum locations. Slums are located all over Bangalore but certain patterns do exist. Some long standing slums exist in the central core of the city but they are far more common in close proximity to main transport routes, industrial areas and the periphery of the city.	Chapter 20

25
MEDC CITIES AND LEDC CITIES COMPARED

Although the trends and processes affecting cities throughout the world show considerable variation from city to city, it is possible to make some very generalised observations about the similarities and differences between LEDC and MEDC cities:

FIGURE 25.1

	MEDC cities	LEDC Cities
Population trends	Slow growth or decline in the percentage of the total population of each country living in cities. Individual cities are either experiencing a low rate of population growth or population decline.	Continuing rapid in-migration combined with rapid natural population growth mean that many cities continue to have a high growth rate. However, there has been a recent decline in the growth rates of the mega-cities.
Urban hierarchies	Hierarchies can be identified at a national and international level. The World Cities at the top of the global hierarchy are located in the MEDCs.	Hierarchies can be identified in LEDCs. Some LEDCs contain a primate city which dominates the national economy.
Population movements within cities	The dominant movements are outwards, i.e. suburbanisation, urban sprawl (including the creation of edge cities) and counterurbanisation. In some cases extensive sprawl has created large urban regions.	Urban sprawl is an important process in most cities. This is partly a result of new unplanned or informal housing, but in some cities it is also a consequence of suburbanisation with the construction of planned formal housing and industry. Extensive urbanised regions are also forming around some of the larger cities
Urban morphology	The quality of life generally improves with distance from the city centre although there are considerable variations in this pattern. For example, deprived social housing estates can be found on the periphery of the city while affluent gentrified areas can be found in the inner city.	No consistent morphology can be identified since there are large differences in their historical development. However, there is a tendency for high income districts to be located in the inner city and low income areas to occur more frequently towards the periphery.
Urban inequality	Cities contain considerable inequality and social segregation. Some neighbourhoods have populations which suffer from multiple deprivation and are excluded from employment, education and housing opportunities.	Inequality is more extreme than in MEDCs. There is considerable social segregation. In some cities globalisation and rapid economic development are deepening these inequalities. Many neighbourhoods have populations which are excluded from employment, education and housing opportunities.
Housing	Virtually all residents live in planned, regulated and formal housing provided with basic amenities. There are large variations in the quality of this housing.	Many residents live in informal self-built housing lacking basic amenities although there are considerable variations in the percentage of the city's population living in such housing. Some housing is of a very high quality.
Employment and the location of economic activity	Many cities have suffered from deindustrialisation since the 1970s causing higher long-term unemployment. Tertiary employment has increased. There is intense competition between cities to attract scarce inward investment. Globalisation is intensifying this competition. Economic activity, including retailing, has increasingly located in the suburbs or on the periphery of cities causing abandonment and dereliction of inner city industrial sites.	Industrialisation is a key feature of LEDC cities. This creates new employment opportunities which attract in-migrants to the city. Increasingly transnational corporations are locating in the larger cities so that they are in a position to exploit the growing markets in LEDCs. Firms are increasingly locating on the periphery of cities.

Urban policies	Current urban policies are focused on: ■ reducing deprivation in the inner city and in the social housing estates ■ attracting inward investment and finding a new economic role for cities following a period of deindustrialisation ■ controlling urban sprawl ■ dealing with the consequences of changes in retailing and tackling the threat to the future of city centres ■ improving transport infrastructure.	Current urban policies are focused on: ■ providing basic amenities for all residents ■ providing the infrastructure necessary for economic development (e.g. reliable electricity supplies) ■ creating new employment opportunities by promoting economic growth ■ controlling rapid population growth and the resulting urban sprawl ■ providing the infrastructure to meet the massive growth in demand for transport ■ developing systems to manage urban areas more effectively.
Urban sustainability	Decision-makers are having to consider ways of increasing urban sustainablity.	Cities are increasingly unsustainable as a result of population growth and economic development. However, many small-scale projects and some large-scale projects aimed at improving sustainability are in operation.

INDEX

Addressism 35
African Americans 36–7
Agenda 21 19, 89, 125
agglomeration 6
agglomeration economies 75

Ballymun 39
Bangalore 96, 97–100, 101–7, 110–13, 116–20, 122–4, 128, 130–2
Bangkok 100, 117
Barnsbury 55
Battersea 55
Beijing 100
bi-polar evaluation 15, 103
Birmingham 19
black Americans 36, 37
black Caribbean 38
Bluewater shopping centre 65, 66
Bradford 19
Bristol 21
brown field development 61
Burgess 9, 19, 129
bus lanes 83
busways 83

California School 12, 59
Camden 89
car-free housing 89
cars, congestion 82, 100, 117
    cost of 81, 117
    impact on land use 56, 57, 58, 81–2
    ownership 81, 100
    restricting use of 82–6
Castlefield, Manchester 45, 46
central business district 66–9
Central Manchester Development
    Corporation 45
central place 4
centrally planned economies 30
centrifugal movement 18, 19–20, 21
chi squared 110
Chicago 10
city centres 66–9
City Challenge 42
classical urban models 9–11, 52
colonialism 91
Coleman, Alice 48
collectivism 31
Commonwealth Games 44
communism 30
communist cities 30–3
communist urban planning 30
commuter villages 18, 21

commuting 53
compact cities 88–9
competition, between cities 7
competition, for land 9
Comprehensive Redevelopment Areas 41, 42
concentric model 9–10, 12
congestion pricing 83
Conservative government 43
conurbation 6
core city 58
counterurbanisation 3, 18–19 21, 61
crime 36, 40, 48, 60
cultural industries 74
Cultural Industries Quarter, Sheffield 73–5
culture 76–9
Curitiba 127

decentralisation 19
decision-makers 16
deconcentration 19
defensible space 48
deindustrialisation 41, 70–1, 73, 74
deprivation 24, 25, 35, 36, 39–40
derelict land 41
Detroit 59–60
dinkies 53
drug abuse 40
Drumchapel 39–40
Dublin 39

eastern Europe 30–3
Eastlands, Manchester 44
ecological footprint 87
ecology, human 9, 111
edge cities 58–9
enterprise zones 42, 43
enveloping 42
ethnic minorities 26, 36–8
ethnicity 26

family life-cycle model 20
filtering 18, 19–20 21
footloose industry 7
Fordism 71, 72
functions 4–5, 6

gated suburbs 59
gentrification 20, 21, 52–5
ghettos 36–8
Glasgow 8, 39–40, 77–80
globalisation 7, 121–4
Grands Ensembles 36

green belt 21, 60–3
green field development 61

Harris (and Ullman) 10
hierarchy 5–6, 93
high rise housing 39, 45, 48
high-tech industry 71–2, 122–3
hinterland 4
Housing Action Areas 41, 42
Hoyt 10, 129
hypermarkets 65–6
hypersegregation 36

ideology 41
index of dissimilarity 37–8
indicators, statistical 25
Industrial Revolution 19
industrialisation 19, 91
inequality 23–6, 101–7, 123
inner city 34–5, 52
inner city decline 20, 21, 35
inner city policy (British) 41–6
invasion 10

Kingston, Jamaica 100
Kinshasa 100

land use 9
Latin Quarter, Paris 54
league tables of cities 7
Leeds 48, 84–6
leisure 76–7
Les Minguettes, Lyon 36
leverage 49
London 6, 38, 43, 55, 89
London Docklands Development
    Corporation 43, 53
Los Angeles 57, 59, 82
Lyon 36

malls 65–6
Manchester 44–6
Mann's model 11
manufacturing industry 70–2
Marais 54
market, for land 31
marketing, of cities 78–9
Maya Bazaar Slum, Bangalore 112–3
mega-cities 2–3, 92
migration, rural-urban 1, 95–6
    inter-urban 94
million cities 2, 92
mixed-use neighbourhoods 88–9

models, Bangalore summary 130–2
  demographic transition 93–4
  classical 9–11
  communist city 30
  Indian city 130
  Latin American city 129
  retail change 65
  urban 9–12
  Urban change 12, 17
  urbanisation 91
  western European city 11
mortality ratio 29
multiple nuclei model 10
Mumbai 92

New Deal for Communities 42, 47
New York, 6, 25, 54
Newcastle-upon-Tyne 26–9
Newman, Oscar 48

office location 64
out-of-town shopping centres 65–6

Paris 6, 54
partnership 47, 49
peripheral housing estates 39–40, 42
pollution 87, 88, 100, 126
population processes 18–21
post-Fordist 71, 72
post-industrial society 70
post-war consensus 41
poverty 23–5, 126
Prague 31–3
primacy 92–3
private sector 16
privatisation 31
property-led regeneration 43
public sector 16
public transport, decline 81
  promotion 82–3, 84–6

quality of life 7–8, 24, 25, 101–7
quaternary industry 72–3

racism 36–7
rank-size rule 92–3
recycling 128
redevelopment 41
refurbishment 41
regeneration 41, 43, 44–6, 47–51
Regional Development Agencies 42
reimaging 77–80
rent gap 52
retailing, changes 64–6
reurbanisation 20, 52, 61
Rio de Janerio 115
Rio Summit 89
Rogers, Richard 127

Salford Quays 44
San Francisco 59, 60
Sao Paulo 95–6, 113
Sarcelles 36
secondary industry 70–2
sector model 10, 12
segregation, ethnic 36–8
  social 10, 25, 31, 57, 58
Shanghai 127
Sheffield 12–17, 49–51, 73–5
shopping, changes 64–6
Single Regeneration Budget 42, 47, 49–51
slums, definition 108
  in LEDC cities 109, 113–4
  in Bangalore 110–3
  clearance 41, 42
social cohesion 26
social exclusion 36
social housing, definition 34
  estate decline 35, 39–40
  in France 36
Solihull 61–3
Southampton 67–9
sphere of influence 4
spillover 37
sport 76–7, 117
sprawl 12, 18, 56–63

controlling 60–1
  in U.S. 57–60
standard of living 25, 107
suburbanisation 18–9, 20, 21, 56–63
  in U.S. 57–60
  of offices 66
succession 10
sustainability 87–9, 125–8

TECs 49
tertiary industry 72–3
Thatcher, Margaret 43
Tokyo 6
tourism 76–7
tower blocks 39, 42, 45, 48
traffic management 82–6, 118–120
Trafford Centre 44, 46
Trafford Park Development Corporation 44
trans-national companies 121–2
twenty-four hour cities 67

UDCs 42, 43, 44
Ullman 10
underclass 36
unemployment 29, 31
United Nations 125, 126
urban areas, definition 3
urban development corporations 42, 43, 44
urban models (see models)
urban region 19
urban renaissance 61
urbanisation 1–2, 19, 91, 94
urban-rural fringe 56
urban-rural shift 73

water supply 100
West Midlands conurbation 61–3
white flight 37
World Bank 118
world cities 6

yuppies 53